THE HOLOCAUST AND *NOSTRA AETATE*
TOWARD A GREATER UNDERSTANDING

National Catholic Center for Holocaust Education, Seton Hill University

The National Catholic Center for Holocaust Education (NCCHE) was established on the campus of Seton Hill University in 1987. Seton Hill initiated this national Catholic movement toward Holocaust Studies in response to the urging of Pope John Paul II to recognize the significance of the *Shoah*, the Holocaust, and to "promote the necessary historical and religious studies on this event which concerns the whole of humanity today." The NCCHE has as its primary purpose the dissemination of scholarship on the root causes of antisemitism, its relation to the Holocaust, and the implications of both from the Catholic perspective for today's world. Toward this end, the Center is committed to equipping scholars, especially those at Catholic institutions, to enter into serious discussion on the causes of antisemitism and the Holocaust; shaping appropriate curricular responses at Catholic institutions and other educational sites; sustaining Seton Hill's Catholic Institute for Holocaust Studies in Israel through a cooperative program with Yad Vashem, the Isaac Jacob Institute for Religious Law, and the Hebrew University; encouraging scholarship and research through conferences, publications, workshops for educators, and similar activities; sponsoring local events on the Holocaust and related topics in the university and the community; and enhancing Catholic-Jewish relations.

THE HOLOCAUST AND *NOSTRA AETATE*

TOWARD A GREATER UNDERSTANDING

Carol Rittner, R.S.M.
Editor

Tara Ronda
Managing Editor

THE HOLOCAUST AND *NOSTRA AETATE*
TOWARD A GREATER UNDERSTANDING

Editor, Carol Rittner, R.S.M.
Managing Editor, Tara Ronda

Published in the United States by
Seton Hill University
National Catholic Center for Holocaust Education
1 Seton Hill Drive
Greensburg, Pennsylvania 15601-1599
724-830-1033
ncche@setonhill.edu
http://ncche.setonhill.edu

Copyright ©2017 Seton Hill University
All rights reserved. No part of this book may be reproduced, stored in a retrieval system, or transmitted, in any form or by any means, electronic, mechanical, photocopying, recording, or otherwise, without the written permission of the publisher.

ISBN 978-0-9830571-2-3

Funding from The Ethel LeFrak Holocaust Education Conference Endowment made possible both The Ethel LeFrak Holocaust Education Conference and publication of The Ethel LeFrak Holocaust Education Conference Proceedings.

The papers contained in this publication express the opinions of the individual authors and do not necessarily represent the views of the National Catholic Center for Holocaust Education or Seton Hill University.

Cover: Adapted from the Poster *Save Human Lives*, New York, 1944
Image Courtesy of The Arthur Szyk Society. Used with Permission.

Design and artwork by Glen Powell Graphic Design
Printed by Laurel Valley Graphics, Inc., Latrobe, Pennsylvania 15650

The Holocaust and *Nostra Aetate*

is dedicated

to

Sister Gemma Del Duca, S.C.,

and

Sister Mary Noël Kernan, S.C.,

Co-Founders and Co-Directors Emerita,

National Catholic Center for Holocaust Education, Seton Hill University

in

Grateful Recognition

for all that they have done over many years

to educate

Catholics about Jews and Judaism

and about

the Holocaust.

Table of Contents

Part 1: Introduction   1
   Carol Rittner, R.S.M.

Teaching for the Future: *Nostra Aetate* and the Holocaust   9
   Elena G. Procario-Foley

Part 2: The Holocaust

The Holocaust by Bullets   29
   Patrick Desbois

Wartime Rape: Understanding Women's Experiences During the Holocaust   43
   Alysa Landry

The New Normal – A Street Boy   51
   George D. Schwab

Injustice Illuminated: The Holocaust Art of Arthur Szyk   67
   Irvin Ungar

When Theology and Racism Mix: Catholicism, Antisemitism, and National Socialism   80
   Kevin P. Spicer, C.S.C.

Part 3: *Nostra Aetate*

The Unfinished Reforms of *Nostra Aetate*: Five Areas for Further Consideration   101
   Dennis McManus

Nostra Aetate and the Failures of Ethics   119
   John K. Roth

Fifty Years of Catholic-Jewish Relations: The Continuing Challenges   141
   John T. Pawlikowski, O.S.M.

Teaching, Preaching, and Witnessing: Three Women Who Made a Difference   153
   Carol Rittner, R.S.M.

Whither Christian-Jewish Relations in the 21st Century?   168
   Steven Leonard Jacobs

Dare We Hope?   180
   Mary C. Boys, S.N.J.M.

Part 4: Beyond the Holocaust & *Nostra Aetate*

The Authority of Those Who Suffer   193
   Mary Jo Leddy

Reconciliation: A Commitment to Unsettling Empathy   205
   Björn Krondorfer

Part 5: Afterwords

Ethel LeFrak   221
   Gemma Del Duca, S.C.

Acknowledgments   224
   Editors

Index   227

1946. New York. Ink and Blood, *Frontispiece by Arthur Szyk*
Image Courtesy of The Arthur Szyk Society

PART I: INTRODUCTION

Introduction

Carol Rittner, R.S.M.

Editor, **The Holocaust and *Nostra Aetate*: Toward a Greater Understanding**; *Distinguished Professor of Holocaust & Genocide Studies Emerita and Dr. Marsha Raticoff Grossman Professor of Holocaust Studies Emerita, Stockton University, Galloway, NJ*

According to Rabbi Jonathan Sacks, the well-known British scholar and religious leader, "It took the Holocaust to bring about *Nostra Aetate*."[1] Point taken. For nearly two millennia, the persistent Christian "belief" that Jews were responsible for the death of Jesus fed and kept alive anti-Jewish prejudice and hatred among Christians and in society generally. The Nazis used racist antisemitism bolstered by theological anti-Judaism to justify the "legal" discrimination and persecution of the Jews of Germany in the 1930s, the arrest and deportation of Jews from throughout German-occupied Europe to concentration and death camps in the 1940s, and the use of modern industrial methods to murder Jews in the very heart of Christian Europe between 1939 and 1945. How else can one explain the existence of places like Auschwitz and Birkenau, Chelmno and Treblinka, Sobibor and Mauthausen in *Christian* Europe during World War II and the Holocaust (*Shoah*)? Why didn't more Christians help Jews in Europe during the Nazi era, World War II, and the Holocaust?

The traditions of theological anti-Judaism and social antisemitism played a major role in isolating Jews from their neighbors both before and during these years. Only with the defeat of Nazi Germany in May 1945 were the Nazi concentration and death camps finally closed down, even if the underlying ideologies that helped sustain them continued to linger in the Christian churches and civil society long after the end of World War II and the Holocaust (1945).

For centuries the Christian Churches – Catholic, Protestant, and Orthodox alike – more or less held the following religious and theological concepts:

- The Jews did not recognize or accept Jesus as the Messiah.
- Because they did not, God punished the Jewish people for their rejection and killing of Jesus, the Son of God, Messiah and Savior of all people. (This is the so-called "deicide" charge).
- As a result of this deicide charge, the Jews have forsaken all rights to God's promises in the Jewish Old Covenant.
- The Jewish Old Covenant is completely replaced by the Christian New Covenant (this is the concept known as "supercessionism").
- Like sinful Cain, God condemned the Jews to wander the earth as vagabonds without a homeland.
- But God also sustained the Jews' dispersed existence to remind Christians of the divine blessings of the New Covenant.
- Jews can share in this New Covenant only if they convert to Christianity and accept Jesus as the Christ (Messiah) of God.

This is the theological and religious context one should keep in mind when learning and teaching about the Holocaust and about *Nostra Aetate* (1965).

The Holocaust

What was the Holocaust? In her book *War and Genocide: A Concise History of the Holocaust*, Doris Bergen writes, "The Holocaust was an event of global proportions with worldwide repercussions." It "happened step by step," was "intertwined with World War II," and needs to be "understood in the context of that conflict." Bergen says very clearly that "Jews were the primary targets of Nazi destruction, but their fates were linked with those of other victim groups: people with disabilities, Roma and Sinti, Polish elites, Soviet prisoners of war, and homosexual men."[2] Not all victims of the Nazis were Jews, but all Jews were victims, and that is what we need to keep in mind, particularly when teaching about the Holocaust.

The Holocaust and Nostra Aetate: Toward a Greater Understanding, the volume you are holding in your hands, focuses on the Holocaust, on Nazi Germany's effort to annihilate the Jews of Europe. It also focuses on Jews and Judaism and on *Nostra Aetate*, the 1965 document issued by the Roman Catholic Church at the end of Vatican II. Most of the essays give attention in one way or another to this important document, to its impact and shortcomings, and to the Roman Catholic Church's efforts to rethink and make real in its teaching and preaching a renewed approach to Jews and Judaism after the Holocaust.

Vatican II and *Nostra Aetate*

The 1965 Vatican document *Nostra Aetate* ("In Our Time") emerged out of the Holocaust and out of Vatican II, an impressive event held in St. Peter's Basilica in Rome between October 1962 and December 1965. Vatican II was a worldwide ecumenical council convened by Pope John XXIII (Angelo Cardinal Roncalli, 1881-1963). It was intended to renew and refresh the teachings of the Roman Catholic Church. Over a four-year period, some 2,400 Roman Catholic bishops, archbishops, and cardinals from every corner of the world and representing an enormous range of opinions met 168 times; heard some 2,200 speeches; submitted over 4,000 written interventions; consulted with 460 officially designated experts; discussed and debated questions ranging from liturgy to nuclear warfare, from education to mass communications; and in the end adopted 16 documents that would have an enormous impact on the Catholic Church, its millions upon millions of adherents, and other religions and peoples as well.[3]

Nostra Aetate, the shortest of Vatican II's 16 documents, is five paragraphs long – 41 sentences in all. Paragraph 4, which is about the Church's religious relationship with the Jewish people, is the longest section in the document. It transformed Catholic-Jewish relationships and precipitated a revolution in Catholic teaching on the Jews and Judaism. As John K. Roth writes, *Nostra Aetate* was

> [A] turning-point document in Christian-Jewish relations. ... [It] did not explicitly mention the Holocaust, but [*Nostra Aetate*] did reject key elements of what the French Jewish historian Jules Isaac called the Church's "teaching of contempt" toward Jews and Judaism. Insisting that "the Jews should not be presented as rejected or accursed by God," *Nostra Aetate* decried "hatred, persecutions, displays of anti-Semitism, directed against Jews at any time and by anyone." In addition, it rejected a pernicious deicide charge by proclaiming that the crucifixion of Jesus Christ "cannot be charged against all the Jews, without distinction, then alive, nor against the Jews of today." Furthermore, emphasizing the Jewish origins of Christianity, *Nostra Aetate* affirmed that "God holds the Jews most dear."[4]

Rarely has so short a text had such far-reaching effects. *Nostra Aetate* is not a perfect document, but what document is? Some of its imperfections are identified in various essays in this volume (see, for example, the essays by John K. Roth and Mary Boys), but in 1965, when the bishops, archbishops, and cardinals of the Roman Catholic Church overwhelmingly approved it, *Nostra Aetate* was considered a revolutionary document. Rabbi David Rosen, the American Jewish Committee's International Director of Interreligious Affairs, says that *Nostra Aetate* "took us from a situation where the Jewish people were seen as cursed and rejected by God, and even in league with the devil, to a situation now where popes say it is impossible to be a true Christian and be an anti-Semite, and that the covenant between God and the Jewish people is an eternal covenant, never broken."[5]

Learning and Teaching about the Holocaust
Nostra Aetate does not mention the Holocaust, but it has impacted – or *should* impact – what teachers learn and teach about the Holocaust. What do I mean? Among other things, I mean the following: learning and teaching about the Holocaust is not easy. It can be particularly difficult for a teacher who takes seriously her/his Christian faith tradition. Why? Because learning about the Holocaust requires one to look at the dark side of history, to examine what one philosopher referred to as "the slaughter bench of history," and to explore the underside of Christian theology, those concepts and ideas in Christian teaching and preaching that over the centuries demeaned Jews and contributed to blaming Jews for the death of Jesus (the deicide charge).

It is not easy for serious, well-meaning, committed Christians to engage in such study or to admit that *Christian* theological concepts and religious practices have helped over the centuries to reinforce human blindness, hate, and violence against Jews, even helping to prepare the seed-ground for the Holocaust. Nevertheless, such study is something one must do if she/he wants to try to understand the role of the Christian Churches – Catholic, Protestant, and Orthodox – in Europe before, during, and even after the Holocaust.

For more than 1,500 years, the leaders of Christian Churches, as well as ordinary Christians, with few exceptions, disparaged Jews and Judaism in their teaching and preaching. This "teaching of contempt" toward Jews and Judaism was not something just done by Church leaders, however. *Good* Christians – monarchs and ordinary people alike – reinforced this "teaching of contempt" by pushing Jews out of cities, towns, and villages; condemning them to the margins of society in *Christian* Europe; excluding them from guilds, universities, and professions; even excluding them from what today we refer to as the "universe of moral obligation," that is, the circle in which people honor reciprocal obligations to protect each other.[6]

Many Christians, including teachers, are often unaware of this history – that is, until they begin studying the Holocaust and all that helped make it possible during the Nazi era and World War II. As Doris Bergen said, the Holocaust happened "step by step" and many of those steps were taken throughout more than 1,500 years of Christian preaching and "teaching of contempt" for Jews and Judaism in Europe and beyond.

Years ago, Father Edward Flannery (1912-1998), a well-known Catholic priest and scholar committed to improving Catholic-Jewish relations, commented that the pages of history Jews have committed to memory are the very pages of history

Christians have torn out of their history books.[7] If we Christians engage in studying the Holocaust, we are forced to confront those torn-out pages of history and hopefully do what we can to repair and improve our understanding of and relationships with Jews and Judaism. Surely this should be one important outcome of learning and teaching about the Holocaust.

Into the Future

Nostra Aetate set in motion a process of learning in the Roman Catholic Church – and subsequently in the other Christian churches, as well. Like all good theology, *Nostra Aetate* did not aim to provide answers to every question that human endeavor throws up. Rather, I think it has tried to inspire a more informed and humane approach to Jews and Judaism – and also to how we teach about the Holocaust.

In the more than 50 years since Vatican II, several Roman Catholic Church documents have taken the initial promptings of *Nostra Aetate* forward. For example, "Guidelines and Suggestions for Implementing the Conciliar Declaration *Nostra Aetate* (n. 4)" (1974); "Notes on the Correct Way to Present Jews and Judaism in Preaching and Catechesis in the Roman Catholic Church" (1985); "We Remember: A Reflection on the *Shoah*" (1998), and most recently, "'The Gifts and the Calling of God are Irrevocable' (Rom 11:29): A Reflection on the Theological Questions Pertaining to Catholic-Jewish Relations on the Occasion of the 50th Anniversary of *Nostra Aetate* (No. 4)" (2015). These are but a few of the documents issued by the Vatican over the past five decades since the end of Vatican II that can help to inform our learning and teaching about the Holocaust and about Jews and Judaism.[8] Like *Nostra Aetate* itself, none of these documents is perfect, but they exemplify, I think, a genuine effort on the part of the Roman Catholic Church to admit failings and improve relationships with living Jews and Judaism, and to learn how more humbly to reveal the human face of God in our conflicted and fractured world.

The Holocaust and* Nostra Aetate*: Toward a Greater Understanding is a modest effort, the published proceedings of a conference of Christian and Jewish scholars and teachers gathered together at Seton Hill University in a spirit of collaboration and dialogue about the Holocaust and *Nostra Aetate*. This book "does not aim to provide answers to every question that human endeavor throws up" about the Holocaust and *Nostra Aetate*. Its purpose is to inspire more informed teaching and learning about the Holocaust and about *Nostra Aetate* in our schools, colleges, and universities, as well as in our seminaries, synagogues, and churches.

Questions for Discussion

1. Is it valid to say that *Nostra Aetate* contributes to learning and teaching about the Holocaust? If so, how? If not, why not? Be specific in your response.

2. What other documents issued by Christian churches – Roman Catholic, Protestant, and/or Orthodox – also have addressed post-Holocaust Christian-Jewish relations? How do they contribute to learning and teaching about the Holocaust? If they do not, what is missing from the documents that could help them address Christian-Jewish relations more effectively?

3. Are there any post-Holocaust documents issued by Jewish groups – organizations or groups of scholars – that are intended to contribute to improving relationships between Jews and Christians? How do they contribute to learning and teaching about the Holocaust? If they do not contribute to such learning and teaching, what is missing from those documents that could help them do so?

Further Reading

Flannery, Edward H. *The Anguish of the Jews: Twenty-Three Centuries of Antisemitism* (2nd ed.) (New York: Stimulus/Paulist Press, 2004).

Rittner, Carol (Ed.). *Teaching about the Holocaust and Genocide* (Galloway, NJ: Stockton University, 2016).

---------*Holocaust Education: Challenges for the Future* (Greensburg, PA: Seton Hill University, 2014).

Rittner, Carol, Stephen Smith, and Irena Steinfeldt (Eds.). *The Holocaust and the Christian World* (2nd ed.) (New York: Stimulus/Paulist Press, forthcoming 2017).

Roth, John K., and Elizabeth Maxwell (Eds.). *Remembering for the Future: The Holocaust in an Age of Genocide/Volume II: Ethics and Religion* (New York: Palgrave, 2001).

Film and Video Resources

Archbishop [Wilton] Gregory on Nostra Aetate (7 mins). Produced by Archdiocese of Atlanta. Available at https://www.youtube.com/watch?v=hLk3KJUYdu0.

European Antisemitism from its Origins to the Holocaust (13:44 mins). Produced by the U.S. Holocaust Memorial Museum. Available at https://www.ushmm.org/confrontantisemitism/european-antisemitism-from-its-origins-to-the-holocaust.

"It didn't begin with the Nazis": Antisemitism (3 mins). Produced by Facing History and Ourselves. Available at https://www.facinghistory.org/resource-library/video/it-didn-t-begin-nazis-antisemitism.

PC Experts: 50th Anniversary of Nostra Aetate (4:34 mins). Produced by Providence College. Available at https://www.youtube.com/watch?v=RKxRJ3bUeBw.

The Uniqueness of Nazi Antisemitism (3 mins). Produced by Yad Vashem. Available at http://www.yadvashem.org/yv/en/holocaust/insights/video/nazi_antisemitism.asp.

Notes

1. Jonathan Sacks, "Nostra Aetate Fifty Years On"; see http://www.rabbisacks.org/nostra-aetate-fifty-years-on/.
2. Doris L. Bergen, *War & Genocide: A Concise History of the Holocaust* (3rd ed.) (New York: Rowman & Littlefield, 2016), p. 1.
3. See further, John W. O'Malley, *What Happened at Vatican II?* (Cambridge, MA: Belknap Press, 2010).
4. John K. Roth, *The Failures of Ethics: Confronting the Holocaust, Genocide, & Other Mass Atrocities* (Oxford, UK: Oxford University Press, 2015), p. 118.
5. Quoted in Sylvia Poggioli, "'Nostra Aetate' Opened Up Catholic, Jewish Relations 50 Years Ago"; see http://www.npr.org/2015/11/01/453448972/nostra-aetate-opened-up-catholic-jewish-relations-50-years-ago.
6. Richard L. Rubenstein and John K. Roth, *Approaches to Auschwitz: The Holocaust and Its Legacy* (Rev. ed.) (Louisville, KY: Westminster John Knox Press, 2003), p. 248.
7. Edward H. Flannery, *The Anguish of the Jews: Twenty-Three Centuries of Antisemitism* (2nd ed.) (New York: Paulist Press, 2004), p. 1.
8. See further, http://www.vatican.va/roman_curia/pontifical_councils/chrstuni/sub-index/index_relations-jews.htm

1944. New York. To Be Shot as Dangerous Enemies of the Third Reich
Image Courtesy of The Arthur Szyk Society

Teaching for the Future: *Nostra Aetate* and the Holocaust

Elena G. Procario-Foley

Associate Professor, Religious Studies and Brother John G. Driscoll Professor of Jewish-Catholic Studies, Iona College, New Rochelle, NY

Those who dare to engage in prognostication about the future may be subject to the Hosean caution that those who sow the wind reap the whirlwind (Hosea 8:7). The 2015 golden jubilee of the Declaration on the Relation of the Church to Non-Christian Religions: *Nostra Aetate* (hereafter, *NA*) has proven rich in papers, symposia, and new statements to celebrate the document.[1] It seems, therefore, safe to opine that Catholic dialogue with other religions, and with Judaism especially, is bright with possibility. The future of any relationship, of course, depends on the foundation upon which it is built. Since The Ethel LeFrak Holocaust Education Conference is a conference that always attends to pedagogical issues as well as to new research, this essay will offer for consideration some of what I do in the undergraduate classroom. Our work with students remains crucial to any constructive future relationship between Christians and Jews committed to their religious identities, and it is a necessary and fundamental labor that will help us prevent the repetition of past mistakes.

Many conferences dedicated to the golden jubilee of the Second Vatican Council reflect on the revolutionary impact of *NA*, and particularly of *NA*, no. 4, which is the focus of this essay. Anniversaries provide occasions for recommitment to vows, ideals, and goals yet outstanding. We see the impact of *NA* performed when we witness high-profile, official interreligious dialogues and rituals, such as the September 25, 2015, multi-religious prayer service conducted at the September 11, 2001 National Memorial and Museum, which has given us the enduring image of Pope Francis sitting between a rabbi and an imam. At scholarly conferences, academics probe difficult questions in dialogue together, and the impact of *NA* 50 years later is understood and taken for granted by such scholars. But there is a gap in our transmission of the very document whose jubilee was commemorated throughout 2015. The gap is evident at every level of education: young people have not received the *NA* "memo." Of course there are exceptions, but in general we have not done a good job in spreading the fact and the implications of *NA* for Christian life. A condition for continuing positive progress in Jewish-Christian relations is to pay attention to the foundation of the new relationship: education and dialogue. The revolution of *NA* cannot be taken for granted and each new generation of students needs to be taught its insights. We must explore with today's students why it was necessary to promulgate such a document and explain its importance for Jews and Christians. I will describe the intersection of *NA* and Holocaust education as I have experienced it with my college students.

Who Are Today's College Students?

Who are today's college students? What do they know about the relationship between Christianity and other religions? Is *NA* old news to them, or is it instead very new and surprising news for them? How do they think about their own religious identity in relationship to other religious forms?

I think it is extraordinarily complicated and difficult to sort out and attempt to generalize American college students' attitudes toward religion. Many factors are in play, including but not limited to previous religious education, level of affiliation with a religious tradition, and variations among ethnic groups and their approaches to religion. Pew Research Center reports are well-known, sparking concerns about the rise of the "nones" and telling us that a little over one-third of people ages 33 and under do not affiliate with a religious identity.[2] The February 2010 Pew report "Religion Among the Millennials" is also instructive and pertinent to thinking about *NA*. It is worthwhile to quote at length:

> Young people who are affiliated with a religion are more inclined than their elders to believe their own religion is the one true path to eternal life (though in all age groups, more people say many religions can lead to eternal life than say theirs is the one true faith). Nearly three-in-ten religiously affiliated adults under age 30 (29%) say their own religion is the one true faith leading to eternal life, higher than the 23% of religiously affiliated people ages 30 and older who say the same. This pattern is evident among all three Protestant groups but not among Catholics.

Interestingly, while more young Americans than older Americans view their faith as the single path to salvation, young adults are also more open to multiple ways of interpreting their religion.[3]

What do we do with such information, telling us as it does that a third of our affiliated students can think in terms of the truth of only one religion, while 70% of religiously affiliated students have more openness to diverse interpretations of their religion? In truth, I would have to say that it captures fairly well the very mixed composition of most of my classes, though I do not know what to do with the fact that it says that the pattern does not hold for Catholics. In that particular report there was no other commentary on that statement, so it is unclear if the percentages were higher or lower for Catholics. Given, moreover, the wealth of Protestant statements since *An Address to the Churches: The Ten Points of Seelisberg*,[4] I would not rush to assume that the reason the pattern does not hold for Catholics is because of any salutary effects of *NA*.

I teach in a suburb of New York City and students there swim in the sea of religious diversity. Their daily commerce with people of other faiths provides a rudimentary tolerance toward people of other religious traditions, but it does not necessarily prompt self-reflection on how one's own religious commitment is related to another person's religious commitment. In a classroom, we can begin to approach the difficulties of sorting out college-age students' attitudes towards lived religious diversity as a datum of their contemporary experience from a substantive pluralist attitude as part of one's religious self-identity.

Last year I received a call from a Catholic student at a Catholic university whose introductory theology class had read David Bentley Hart's 2003 article "Christ and Nothing."[5] The student was upset and he told me that the article and the professor's presentation had the effect of insulting all the non-Christian students. Moreover, many of the Christian students were angry and embarrassed in front of their non-Christian friends, and the non-Christian students felt dismissed by both the professor and the author. They thought the article and the professor were rejecting the value of all other religions. This particular Catholic student had the sense that Catholicism was not so dismissive and he was searching for a language so he could speak with his professor. We talked about *NA* and I directed him to the famous line from no. 2: "The Catholic church rejects nothing that is true and holy in these religions." I offered him the basics of the traditional schema of exclusivist, inclusivist, and pluralist approaches to religion so that he had a quick way to organize his thoughts in order to meet with his professor. Was his sensitivity to that particular day in class due to the Church's success in teaching *NA* or his sociological status as a millennial? I suspect that it is a combination of these and other factors, but I wonder how representative he may be. Also, were his classmates simply upset because they felt that the professor had committed an offense against good manners? In other words, in a generation and society characterized by a basic fact of religious diversity, did the students think the professor was not politically correct? Or did the students have a deeper sense that the integrity of each religion represented in the room was trespassed by a triumphalistic and universally supersessionist presentation by the professor and/or Bentley Hart? Did the students have an incipient multi-textured pluralist sensibility? Why could the Catholic students in the class not draw on Vatican II and *NA* to question their professor during his lecture? There was a disconnect between their lived experience of religious diversity and their ability to articulate a theological rationale for their rejection of what they perceived to be their professor's exclusivist position. The revolution of the religious leaders and the academics had not yet reached them.

In my own classes, I teach a lot of students in required core classes, a good number of students who are the first in their families to attend college, and an increasing number of students from Mexico, Central, and South America. Some are from Catholic schools, most identify with some form of Christianity, the Muslim student population is growing, we have students from mixed Jewish and Christian families, and there is a scattering of other students. How do they approach the significant change in attitude in the Catholic Church sparked by *NA*? The student who called me and his classmates seems to represent the 70% mentioned in the Pew survey – students who could perceive multiple interpretations of their religion – while my classes tend to represent roughly the 30% of religious affiliated students who think in religiously exclusivist terms. It seems that our first-generation immigrant Catholics or other Christians are less comfortable thinking about religion and religious dialogue outside of their ethnic and more traditionally devotional contexts. This tends to be true, as well, of many of our Muslim students, at least those in my experience. On the other hand, it is difficult to generalize attitudes of Jewish students since they usually do not disclose their religious identity until after the class is concluded.

When my students are confronted, therefore, with Vatican II statements such as, "Those who, through no fault of their own, do not know the Gospel of Christ or his Church, but who nevertheless seek God with a sincere heart, and moved by grace, try in their actions to do [God's] will as they know it through the dictates of their conscience – these too may achieve eternal salvation" (*Lumen Gentium*, no. 16), or "the right to religious freedom is based on the very dignity of the human person as known through the revealed word of God and by reason itself" (*Dignitatis Humanae*, no. 2), they are genuinely surprised to discover that these statements are from the Roman Catholic Church. There is always a number of very shocked and animated responses: "No, it's not!" "Is it really?" "It can't be." "I was always taught that only Catholics could be saved." "Why weren't we taught this?" "This is great! I didn't know this was possible." The student who voiced the last comment was genuinely happy, expressing almost a relief that such views existed in Catholicism. While none of the quotes was from *NA*, the reaction still indicates what a surprise the Vatican II turn toward dialogue and away from an exclusivist attitude of "no salvation outside the Church" is for these students. The reactions I cite do not mean, however, that all of my students were pleased with this new posture in the church.

A great number of my students remain exclusivist in their understanding of Catholic teaching about other religions and Christian denominations – they are quite simply parochial. What happened to the great *NA* revolution? This parochialism functions on two levels: Catholics either hold the position themselves when confronted with the question, or they just assume it is the hard and hardened position of their Church, whether or not they agree with the position. Further, non-Catholic students make the same assumption. My students are definitely parochial in their assumptions about what they think they understand of Catholic attitudes toward other religions, even as they are generally comfortable in a *de facto* religiously diverse daily social existence.

Teaching *Nostra Aetate* and the Holocaust

We must challenge our students' assumptions and parochialism with the teaching of *NA* (as well as with the Protestant, Catholic, and Jewish documentary history from Seelisberg through to the present).[6] I teach *NA* regularly in three different courses: an introductory course called "Religion in the Contemporary World," "Theological Renewals" (an introduction to Vatican II), and "Memory and Reconciliation: The Churches and the Holocaust." As I have indicated, in my classroom the fundamental student assumption at the beginning of a course is the idea that Catholicism is not open to dialogue with or the ideas of other religions. The assumptions preclude, in general, any idea of dialogue as being central to the identity of the Church and its contemporary position toward other religions.

The introductory course allows for an initial overview of *NA*; we read the document at the beginning of the course for its basic positions. I ask students to imagine why such a document would be necessary. They have to consider the question, "What does the existence of the document imply about Catholic positions toward other religions prior to the Second Vatican Council?" We then discuss why such a document was needed and if it coheres in any way with the social movements of the time. Studying *NA* at the beginning of an introductory survey course in religion provides students with an opportunity to think in preliminary ways about how relationships to other religions may affect their self-understanding of their own religious traditions. Students often experience this opportunity as a welcome freedom to explore the boundaries of the parochialism of their thinking that our discussions and reading of *NA* have revealed to them. On occasion, I discover that the notion of Catholics-in-dialogue is perceived as a possible threat (to Catholic identity) or hegemonic move (dialogue is a cloaked path to proselytizing). One experience of the latter is illustrated by the negative reactions of Pentecostal Christians who made it clear, primarily in their written work (and a few remarks and looks in class that I was not supposed to have caught and which indicated my lack of credibility for them), that Pentecostal Christianity was the only path to salvation. I suspect that their discomfort stemmed from the challenge of learning about a more nuanced Catholic position of which they were unaware.

In the Vatican II class, we analyze *NA* more deeply and it is read in a section of the course called "Christ, Religious Freedom, and Religious Pluralism." In this section, *NA* is read along with the Declaration on Religious Liberty (DH)[7] and the Decree on Ecumenism (UR).[8] In this course, the three documents are grouped together to foster some introductory Christological thinking. I provide some of the history of the development of each text and the controversies surrounding that development. In this course, *NA* functions with the other two documents to prompt students' thinking about the variety of religious relationships raised in those documents. We discuss the exclusivist, inclusivist, and pluralist models, and students debate how they might classify *NA* within this basic typology. The goal of this section of the course is for students to recognize the important achievement of these documents in advancing a Catholic Christological understanding that promotes human dignity and thus fosters respect for religious freedom and dialogue. Students also need to identify the lines of theological coherence with *Lumen Gentium* (Dogmatic Constitution on the Church),[9] *Gaudium et Spes* (Pastoral Constitution on the Church in the Modern World),[10] and *Sacrosanctum Concilium* (Constitution on the Sacred Liturgy).[11] At the end of this section, can they express how *NA* represents the fundamental stance for constructive engagement with the world that the Council in its constitutions demanded? What does such engagement mean for their own religious self-understanding and identity? Does *NA* challenge them to articulate a new stance toward other religions? For many students, answering these questions first requires some explicit self-reflection about their own attitudes toward other religions, attitudes they somehow appropriated and perhaps did not realize they held.

The course "Memory and Reconciliation: The Churches and the Holocaust," however, provides a lab for teaching *NA* in depth. It immediately confronts students with questions about the relationship between Judaism and Christianity, the role of dialogue between the two religions, and the Church's relationship to other religions. The course is conducted during the spring semester and it includes seven days of study at the Center for Dialogue and Prayer in Oświęcim, Poland, across from the site of Auschwitz I. I construct the course out of the very tenets of *NA*.

Students take an anonymous survey at the beginning of the first class session and their task is to identify the religion of Jesus of Nazareth at his birth, death, and resurrection. Many students are surprised to learn that Jesus was Jewish. Though more and more students know that Jesus was born into a Jewish family, most assume he was a Christian throughout the rest of his life. The course, then, begins within this context of disorientation. Many Christian students (Catholic, Protestant, Orthodox) are simply stunned to learn that there is any appreciable connection between Judaism and Christianity or that they must understand and appreciate a certain amount of Judaism in order to understand Christianity. It is a surprising revelation for students that though Judaism can exist without Christianity, Christianity cannot exist without Judaism.

The first introduction to *NA* in this course is similar to that described above. Students are asked to imagine why such a document would have been necessary. Along with the initial confrontation with the Jewishness of Jesus, the first reading of *NA* prompts students to begin to examine their assumptions. Though the focus is on *NA*, no. 4, in this course, attention must be paid to *NA*, no. 1, before getting into the details of no. 4. Even if it is a very rudimentary discussion with students, it is important in a first discussion of the document to identify its epistemology. *NA*, no. 1, proceeds on the classically Catholic foundation that truth is one, with the concomitant metaphysical posture that all people are oriented toward God. Students can put the rest of the document into context against these premises and then debate them. But they do so aware that they first have to understand the document on its own terms, based on its own distinctive Catholic premises. Such clarity is important for the intellectual and moral honesty required in a course studying the Holocaust through the prism of Jewish-Christian relations.

NA provides the foundation and framework for students to study the relationship between Judaism and Christianity and to consider that relationship against the shadow of the *Shoah*. Space constraints allow me to describe only the following three components of the course: two different historical contexts, an introduction to the Holocaust through a focus on Auschwitz, and a concluding section on the teaching of respect which returns to *NA* and puts it in relation to other documents.

Historical Contexts

Students need fundamental historical context in order to understand the transformative power of *NA*. For a document that is at least one score and ten years older than its young readers and written in the unfamiliar language of Vatican documents, it is necessary after the initial discussion of the document to become familiar with some basic history, without which *NA* cannot be adequately understood. I focus, on the one hand, on the perspectives of Vatican I and Vatican II and, on the other hand, on the classical Christian "Teaching of Contempt" for Jews and Judaism.

Two Vatican Councils and the Decades before NA

Some discussion of Vatican II (and therefore Vatican I) in general is necessary. Following John O'Malley, some basic presentation of "the long nineteenth century" is helpful to provide a contrast for students with the social, political, and historical context of Vatican II.[12] Similarly, O'Malley argues for paying attention to the change in rhetoric between the councils. Examples of the rhetoric of pre-Vatican II Conciliar pronouncements – perhaps using examples of anathemas leveled against so-called non-believers – help to paint a broad-strokes picture for students. Students who hold a basic exclusivist position with or without accurate knowledge of the history and theology of the Catholic Church on this issue and those who reject the position but assume that it accurately represents the current positon of the Church all live in a society that is culturally and religiously plural. They sit next to each other in our classrooms. The shift that *NA* represents is not fully appreciated, therefore, without historical contrast. The risk, of course, is caricaturing either historical periods or their respective theological positions. The first surprise of *NA* for my "parochials" at finding out that the Catholic Church does not reject the religious reality of others out of hand can yield, at a second glance (and stemming from the empirical fact of living amid religious plurality), to a "so what-ness?" when they encounter the mild statements about dialogue in *NA*. But, as the discussion deepens and they awaken to their assumptions and their assumptions about Church teaching, historical context helps them begin to do two things: (1) construct a basic understanding of the Church's relationship to other religions in the twenty-first century, and (2) plumb deeply the theological relationship between Jews and Christians before and after Vatican II.

Depending on the conditions and restrictions of the particular semester, the brief contrast of the two councils is well-complemented by an equally brief introduction to the theological work preceding *NA* that historian John Connelly presents in *From Enemy to Brother: The Revolution in Catholic Teaching on the Jews, 1933–1965*.[13] One of the things that his work does is demonstrate the tenacity of the teaching of contempt even among the very people who worked tirelessly, and at great risk to themselves, against racial antisemitism. Though making a distinction between racial antisemitism and theological anti-Judaism is controversial, teaching the controversy is important when teaching *NA* and the Holocaust. Connelly's work is instructive within this context because his chronicling of the theological journeys of the people he dubs "border-crossers," pioneering thinkers and activists like Karl Thieme, John Oesterreicher, Dietrich von Hildebrand, Annie Kraus, Gertrude Luckner, and Irene Harand (to name but a few and who were converts in one way or another), demonstrates three important realities: (1) just how difficult the road to relinquishing the theology of contempt at Vatican II was, because even for converts to Catholicism, anti-Jewish attitudes could be deeply held; (2) that the effort of the Second Vatican Council to produce *NA* was successful in part because of the relationships and efforts that date from before the beginning of World War II; and (3) that the very nature of the converts as border-crossers provided an urgency to the arguments surrounding the development of *NA* since they understood from personal experience the origins of Christianity in Judaism, the real dangers of antisemitism, and the incoherence of a Christian faith that deplored the very Judaism of Jesus. Connelly sees in their efforts a "struggle among theologians extending from the 1930s to the 1960s about how to revise centuries of teaching" of contempt.[14]

In teaching undergraduates, Connelly's research – to which I have not done justice in any way – is important to give students an insight into how deeply the promulgation of *NA* mattered for many people. *NA* was not simply the response to an "Aha!" or, more appropriately, an "Oh, no!" moment for the Church when confronting the devastation of the *Shoah*. Connelly's work demonstrates that the "fraternal dialogues" that *NA* recommends as a path toward mutual understanding and respect were lived out long before *NA* by people who were trying to understand their own personal religious identities, even as they fought racial antisemitism. Their work is a necessary context for understanding *NA*, and students need to understand the importance of such relationships, forged across religious boundaries during the Nazi era, for articulating the theological and moral insights that constituted *NA*.

Teaching of Contempt

When teaching *NA* and the Holocaust through the lens of Jewish-Christian relations, the historical context needs to reach back to the beginning of the relationship between Judaism and Christianity. The course needs to turn to the first centuries of Christianity and learn what Jules Isaac meant by his phrase "the teaching of contempt." The first step, though, is to address the Jewishness of Jesus. One particularly innocent freshman wrote in her course blog that questioning the religion of Jesus at the beginning of the course just "blew her mind" and she asked, "Isn't it hard enough to study the Holocaust? Now this!" It is a surprise to many students, as noted above, that Jesus practiced the Judaism of the first century throughout his life or that when studying the *Shoah* we benefit from understanding the relationship between Christianity and Judaism.

Some introduction, therefore, to Second Temple Judaism is in order. Certain basics need to be introduced that fill the gap for students represented by their shock at the Jewish origins of Christianity. These elements include but are not limited to a brief chronology of the First and Second Temple periods to place Jesus and his practice of religion in historical context; the lens of covenant as an important, but not exclusive, expression of the Jewish relationship to the divine; the variety of Jewish practice at the time of Jesus – including that there was diversity concerning messianic expectation and diversity around the idea of resurrection; and, finally, the relationship between *Tanakh* and the Christian Bible. For the significance of *NA* within the study of the Holocaust to become pedagogically effective, foundational elements of the relationship between Judaism and Christianity must be explored. These elements introduce students to Judaism on its own terms (admittedly in big, broad strokes) and to Judaism as a source of Christian self-understanding. In learning about the Jewish roots of Christianity, Christian students learn about their own tradition. The comparison of the two canons is always instructive, for instance, and that discussion can lead to a first example of the teaching of contempt in Marcion's attempt to eliminate the shared texts from the Christian canon.

Having established some fundamentals about Judaism and the origins of Christianity, the false and blasphemous tenets of the classical teaching of contempt, of Christian anti-Judaism, must be presented. One might summarize the teaching of contempt as follows: "Jews are a stubbornly messiah-rejecting, Christ-killing, deicide people who brought the blood curse down on themselves and deserve all manner of dispossession and calumny that they suffer." The depth of the importance of *NA* cannot be conveyed unless students understand the complete reversal that *NA* represents in the face of the *adversus iudaeos* tradition.[15] Some courses could be organized to spend a good deal of time on lengthy texts of contempt from the New Testament to Chrysostom, Augustine, Luther, and, sadly, many others. Instead of focusing on complete texts, however, I present a series of brief representative texts as illustrations of the different elements of the teaching of contempt (for example, the idea of the Jewish people as demonic, as dismissed from revelation, or as dispersed from the land). If possible, I use images as well. As just one example, in order to talk about the deicide accusation, I might use Eusebius' statement, "Since their deicide, the Jews have been blinded" and Chrysostom's "They have denied the Father, crucified the son. Henceforth their synagogue is the house of demons and idolatry." The texts are then amplified by showing the picture from the Nazi children's book *The Poison Mushroom* of two Aryan children looking up at the cross as their mother teaches them, "When you see a cross, remember the gruesome murder of the Jews on Golgotha."

This part of the course is particularly disconcerting and paradoxical for most Christian students who maintain any level of religious practice. Without necessarily knowing the term deicide, some students consciously hold this traditional position. Other students have not consciously thought about the question, "Who killed Jesus?" but when asked, they somehow always seem to answer, "The Jews, right?" When faced with a litany of anti-Jewish Christian texts and ecclesiastical laws, Christian students confront several challenges:

1. They have to sort out their theological assumptions. One such assumption is the stereotypical, "My religion Christianity teaches love; it can't teach this contempt."
2. They begin to realize that their religion has historically taught things that fly in the face of their easygoing daily relationships with people and

friends whom they know to adhere to other religions. They begin to understand that they must question what their tradition has taught about relationships to other religions, especially Judaism.

3. They realize that they might actually hold some positions (e.g., "the Jews killed Jesus") or think that they are required to hold certain positions, which now makes them uncomfortable at best in the context of a course studying the Holocaust.

To do all of this within the context of studying the *Shoah* throws the paradox of their parochialism as described above into sharp relief. To be sure, I use "parochial" as an adjective guardedly and to suggest that most students have not taken the time to reflect on their religious assumptions. As the Pew survey suggested, young students practicing a religion are both more prone to thinking their religion is the only way to salvation and to being open to multiple interpretations of their religion. It is quite difficult for them to reconcile the stereotype of the Christian love teaching with the *adversus iudaeos* tradition and to become conscious of the fact that on some level they held to some basic part of that tradition while also being accepting of religious difference in day-to-day life.

With even a rudimentary knowledge of the contempt tradition and Christianity's relationship to Second Temple Judaism, students begin to think about the relationship between Judaism and Christianity in complex ways. They begin to sort out the historical question of "Who killed Jesus?" from the theological question of "Why did Jesus have to die?" They understand that conflating the questions into a single statement, "Jesus died because of the Jews," has had severe consequences for Jewish well-being. By addressing complexity within the relationship and recognizing the slow and complicated separation of Christianity from Judaism as separate religions, Christian students make a significant step forward toward a more powerful and purified understanding of their own religion. This understanding deepens when Christian students are eventually able to look at the New Testament passion narratives with different eyes. Suddenly familiar stories become uncomfortable for them when they realize the deadly effect these stories told in the wrong key have had over the centuries.[16] Their parochialism is challenged: many Christian students learn that what they thought was an important tenet of belief – that the Jews killed Jesus – is rather a shameful shadow on the cross. I have given but the single example of the deicide charge, the central theological plank in the teaching of contempt, to demonstrate the importance for students studying the Holocaust of learning the teaching of contempt. It changes their entire approach to studying the *Shoah*.

Once students have a grasp of the basic theological and historical contours of the teaching of contempt, I pose an open-ended question concerning the question of the relationship of Christian anti-Judaism to the *Shoah*. Is there any connection? It becomes a meta-question to the course, something for the students to ponder and to which they can return during the course. The question remains open and part of the interpretative context within which students think about perpetrators, collaborators, and bystanders. We discuss the maxim that Christian anti-Judaism is a necessary but not sufficient cause of the *Shoah*. Students need to come to terms with their own understanding of the effect of the teaching of contempt, its relation to the *Shoah*, and its relation to how Christians might understand or misunderstand contemporary Judaism. These questions and their responses to them provide students with another lens for understanding both *NA* and the Holocaust.

Studying the *Shoah* at Auschwitz

I recognize that most classes about the Holocaust cannot study abroad. Nonetheless, when teaching the Holocaust from the perspective of Jewish-Catholic relations, students benefit from anything that exposes them to actual relationships and the consequences of the teaching of contempt: meeting and hearing actual survivor and second-generation testimony is ideal, as educators well know, but museum visits and well-chosen video and written memoirs are also effective.[17] My students have the benefit of spending seven days in Poland studying the Holocaust and Jewish-Christian relations. They study with educators at the State Museum at Auschwitz-Birkenau; they learn about Jewish life in Krakow and Oświęcim before, during, and after the Holocaust; and they learn about Jewish-Christian relations in Wadowice and the contribution of Pope John Paul II to reversing the teaching of contempt. They have the privilege of hearing the witness of a Jewish Polish survivor. They view the exhibit "The Labyrinth," the art installation testimony of Marian Kolodziej, a Catholic survivor of Auschwitz.[18] There are visits to Jewish and Catholic cemeteries, and the contrasts tell the story of the Holocaust's devastation. Studying *in situ* changes students' understanding of *NA* and everything they thought they knew about the *Shoah*.

The Teaching of Respect

When we return from our journey to our familiar classroom, we need to plumb more deeply the teaching of respect in the post-*Shoah* decades in order to demonstrate and/or question the progress made since *NA* in repudiating the teaching of contempt. We look anew at *NA* and students analyze no. 4 attaching new meaning to each line, with images from their journey seared into their memories. *NA* is no longer something abstract and new that they learned in a class but an absolute necessity. When comparing their reading of *NA* at the beginning and the end of the semester, students report the following:

- "Before, *NA* was just text on a page. Now it makes a lot more impact following our experiences."

- "Before, it was shocking to learn about Jewish-Christian relations and why a document was needed. Now it is refreshing to know that we can go forward."
- "Before, I didn't understand in full why it was necessary for the Church to write it. I had no idea there were problems. Now it is clear why it was necessary and it makes more sense."
- "Before, I barely knew what it was talking about when we first read it. Now I see how important Jewish-Christian relations are as part of the Holocaust."

The brevity of a semester does not afford students enough time to interpret and integrate their encounter with Auschwitz-Birkenau. The reactions above capture their initial attempts to articulate their new and deepened appreciation for *NA* in the face of the Holocaust.

Students develop a deep sense of responsibility for preserving the voices of the survivors and the victims. They are keenly aware that soon the survivors will have all passed from us and they speak of their need to bear witness for them, having had the extraordinary opportunity to hear the witness of survivors in both America and in Poland and having walked the grounds hallowed by the blood of the innocent. They recognize that *NA* helped foster a dialogue that gave them the opportunity to recite *Kaddish* on the edge of the ash fields of Birkenau with a Jewish professor and a Catholic professor leading a group of students of different religious persuasions.

When we reread *NA*, no. 4, we compare it to *An Address to the Churches: The Ten Points of Seelisberg* and look at how other Catholic, ecumenical, and Jewish statements have approached the renewed relationship between Christianity and Judaism.[19] How far has the dialogue that *NA* tried to initiate come? Are we are on deeper religious and theological footing with our Jewish dialogue partners? Are Christians more prepared to accept and live the teaching of Seelisberg and *NA* and the subsequent documentary history? Do we still need Jewish-Christian dialogue? Do we need to teach *NA*?

Conclusion

Because I teach the Holocaust through the lens of Jewish-Christian relations, because I teach within the context of a Catholic college, I find that *NA* must be integral to the teaching of the Holocaust. Because my millennial students have not heard of *NA*, because Catholic or not many simply assume an exclusivist attitude on the part of Catholics and/or their own religion, the future of Jewish-Catholic relations must be built on constant attention to the foundation, to the basics taught in *NA* and Seelisberg. Many specialists are ready for deeper theological dialogue, but our students, their parents, and their religious educators still need to be taught the fundamental insights of *NA*. Other contributors to this volume have put it starkly, noting that if we do not do this basic work, we might find ourselves back in 1933. Elementary Catholic Sunday School students tell me that Jesus was a Catholic priest; a skilled, experienced

Jewish religious educator who was to work with me on a 7th-grade interreligious study of the Holocaust had absolutely no idea about Seelisberg, *Nostra Aetate*, and nearly 70 years of Christian efforts to build a teaching of respect; and a Catholic deacon asked me to highlight Catholic rescuers very early in the curriculum of the same 7th-grade program. *NA* as its own document and as a symbol of all the other documents, dialogue, and labor that has gone into constructing a teaching of respect has not reached the everyday Christian and Jew. We are all the poorer for it in our communities because we know how enriched we are when Jews and Christians enter into serious dialogue.

Allow me to conclude with the thoughts of one of my students who wrote in the immediate aftermath of our study at Auschwitz-Birkenau, "Was the experience of any students this past week 'good'? In many senses it was not good, but tough. Challenging. Troubling. In many other senses, it was a call to speak out. IN OUR TIME, we will speak out in many ways, using many different mediums. Thankfully our guided study has taken us from the 'teaching of contempt' to the 'teaching of respect' and right to the place where we engage others to learn more. IN OUR TIME."

Questions for Discussion

1. *In what ways should Christians consider the Holocaust as part of their own history?*

2. *Should schools teach the history of Christian anti-Judaism since relations between Jews and Christians are so advanced after The Address to the Churches (Seelisberg) and* Nostra Aetate?

3. *Why is it important to reflect on one's religious identity in the light of other religious traditions?*

4. *Why is it important for Christians to know the teaching of contempt and the teaching of respect? Aren't documents just words, while deeds are more important?*

5. *Can an understanding of the history of Christian anti-Judaism help us take new approaches to contemporary expressions of religious extremism?*

Further Reading

Boys, Mary. *Redeeming Our Sacred Story: The Death of Jesus and Relations between Christians and Jews* (New York: Paulist Press, 2013).

---------*Has God Only One Blessing? Judaism as a Source of Christian Self-Understanding* (New York: Paulist Press, 2000).

Donat, Alexander. *The Holocaust Kingdom* (Washington, D.C.: U.S. Holocaust Memorial Museum, 1999). Originally published in 1965 by Holt, Rinehart, and Winston.

Frederick, James, and Tiemeier, Tracey (Eds.). *Interreligious Friendship after Nostra Aetate* (New York: Palgrave, 2015).

Sherman, Franklin (Ed.). *Bridges: Documents of the Christian-Jewish Dialogue, Volumes 1 and 2* (New York: Paulist Press, 2011 & 2014).

Film and Video Resources

I am Joseph Your Brother (59 mins). Produced by Tal-El Productions. Available at http://www.jewishfilm.org/Catalogue/films/Joe.htm.

The Labyrinth: The Testimony of Marian Kołodziej (30 mins). Produced by December 2nd Productions. Available at Amazon.com.

The Last Days (87 mins). Directed by James Moll and produced by June Beallor. Available at https://sfi.usc.edu/education/documentaries.

Walking God's Paths: Christians and Jews in Candid Conversation (six discussion videos, 15 mins each). Produced by the Council of Centers on Jewish-Christian Relations. Available at http://www.ccjr.us/dialogika-resources/educational-and-liturgical-materials/curricula/958-wgp.

Notes

1. See http://www.ccjr.us/news-1/1367-na-statements for the full texts of seven anniversary documents issued in 2015 by a variety of interreligious, Catholic, Protestant, and Jewish groups.
2. Pew Research Center, "America's Changing Religious Landscape" (May 12, 2015), p. 11; available at http://www.pewforum.org/files/2015/05/RLS-08-26-full-report.pdf.
3. Paul Taylor and Scott Keeter (Eds.), *Millennials: A Portrait of Generation Next* (Pew Foundation, 2010), p. 101; available at http://www.pewsocialtrends.org/files/2010/10/millennials-confident-connected-open-to-change.pdf.
4. See http://ccjr.us/dialogika-resources/documents-and-statements/ecumenical-christian/567-seelisberg.
5. David Bentley Hart, "Christ and Nothing," *First Things* (October 2003); available at http://www.firstthings.com/article/2003/10/christ-and-nothing.
6. Many such documents can be found in Franklin Sherman (Ed.), *Bridges: Documents of the Christian-Jewish Dialogue, Vols. 1 and 2* (New York: Paulist Press, 2011 & 2014).

7. http://www.vatican.va/archive/hist_councils/ii_vatican_council/documents/vat-ii_decl_19651207_dignitatis-humanae_en.html.
8. http://www.vatican.va/archive/hist_councils/ii_vatican_council/documents/vat-ii_decree_19641121_unitatis-redintegratio_en.html.
9. http://www.vatican.va/archive/hist_councils/ii_vatican_council/documents/vat-ii_const_19641121_lumen-gentium_en.html.
10. http://www.vatican.va/archive/hist_councils/ii_vatican_council/documents/vat-ii_const_19651207_gaudium-et-spes_en.html.
11. http://www.vatican.va/archive/hist_councils/ii_vatican_council/documents/vat-ii_const_19631204_sacrosanctum-concilium_en.html.
12. John W. O'Malley, *What Happened at Vatican II* (Cambridge, MA: Harvard University Press, 2008).
13. John Connelly, *From Enemy to Brother: The Revolution in Catholic Teaching on the Jews, 1933–1965* (Cambridge, MA: Harvard University Press, 2012).
14. Ibid, p. 10.
15. In 1986, Gregory Baum argued that "the Church's recognition of the spiritual status of Jewish religion is the most dramatic example of doctrinal turn-about in the age-old *magisterium ordinarium*." See Baum's "The Social Context of American Catholic Theology" in *Proceedings of the Catholic Theological Society of America*, 41, 1986, p. 87. Students need to understand the force of the contrast that *NA* represents.
16. Mary Boys' *Has God only One Blessing? Judaism as a Source of Christian Self-Understanding* (New York: Paulist Press, 2000) and her more recent, *Redeeming Our Sacred Story: The Death of Jesus and Relations between Christians and Jews* (New York: Paulist Press, 2013) are resources for explaining this history and proposing new ways forward.
17. Of the many memoirs available, I have found Alexander Donat's memoir of survival, *The Holocaust Kingdom* (Washington, D.C.: The Holocaust Library, USHMM), particularly useful for illustrating the teaching of contempt and its effect on relations between Polish Jews and Christians. Steven Spielberg's Oscar-winning documentary, *The Last Days*, follows three Hungarian women's stories of deportation to and survival at Auschwitz-Birkenau. Their stories echo elements of the teaching of contempt and put students' questions about faith and God in the Holocaust into a personal context.
18. For a summary of the exhibit, see http://www.thelabyrinthdocumentary.com/about-the-film/synopsis.html.
19. Ideally, we examine *We Remember: A Reflection on the Shoah*, available at http://www.vatican.va/roman_curia/pontifical_councils/chrstuni/documents/rc_pc_chrstuni_doc_16031998_shoah_en.html; *Dabru Emet: A Jewish Statement on Christians and Christianity*, available at http://www.icjs.org/resources/dabru-emet; *A Sacred Obligation: Rethinking Christian Faith in Relation to Judaism and the Jewish People*, available at http://www.ccjr.us/dialogika-resources/documents-and-statements/ecumenical-christian/568-csg-02sep1; and *A Time for Recommitment: The Twelve Points of Berlin*, available at http://www.iccj.org/A-Time-for-Recommitment-The-Twelve-Points-of-Berlin.184.0.html. With the December 10, 2015, announcement from the Vatican's Commission for Religious Relations with the Jews, the *NA* anniversary document *The Gifts and Calling of God Are Irrevocable*, available at http://www.vatican.va/roman_curia/pontifical_councils/chrstuni/relations-jews-docs/rc_pc_chrstuni_doc_20151210_ebraismo-nostra-aetate_en.html, can now be folded into consideration.

PART 2: THE HOLOCAUST

The Holocaust by Bullets:
A Conversation with Father Patrick Desbois

Editor's Note

Father Patrick Desbois has devoted his life to researching the Holocaust, fighting antisemitism, and furthering relations between Catholics and Jews. A Catholic priest, he is the President of Yahad – In Unum, a global humanitarian organization he founded in 2004 dedicated to identifying and commemorating the sites of Jewish and Roma mass executions in Eastern Europe during World War II. Father Desbois also serves as director of the Episcopal Committee for Catholic-Judeo Relations under the auspices of the French Conference of Bishops.

What follows is an edited version of the presentation he gave during the 2015 Ethel LeFrak Holocaust Education Conference, The Holocaust and Nostra Aetate: Toward a Greater Understanding, held at Seton Hill University. Following Father Desbois' comments are responses he gave to questions asked from the audience. These also have been edited for clarity. Both should be read and studied in conjunction with the excellent materials on the Yahad – In Unum website,[1] especially the CBS 60 Minutes program devoted to the work of Father Debois and Yahad – In Unum[2] and the publication, The Holocaust by Bullets: A Study Guide for Educators.[3]

★ ★ ★

I am a French Roman Catholic priest. In July 1942, my grandfather, a member of the French military, was deported to the East by the Germans. He never spoke about his experiences there, even though growing up I asked him many times what had happened while he was a prisoner in Rawa Ruska, at the time a town located on the border of Poland and Ukraine, but he would never speak about it. Once, though, just once, he told me, "For us, the camp was difficult. There was nothing to eat but grass and dandelions, and little or no water. But for the others, it was even worse." I often wondered, "Who were the others?"

After my grandfather passed away – his name was Claudius – I decided to go to Rawa Ruska. It is in a part of Europe that often changed hands between Russia and Poland, but during World War II, it was part of Poland. Today it is part of Ukraine. From my own research, I knew that in Rawa Ruska the Germans shot 18,000 Jews. It happened during the time my grandfather was a prisoner there. When I first went to Rawa Ruska, it was still the Soviet period. Everybody I asked about what had happened in their town during the German occupation said, "We don't know. They killed them in secret. It was not public."

I found this very strange because as a child, I often heard my family, friends, and neighbors say that in our village in France during the war, the communist resistance had killed two Germans. Everybody knew about it then, and everybody knows about it now. So to say that during World War II the Germans had killed 18,000 Jews in Rawa Ruska and no one knew about it because it was done in secret seemed very strange to me.

I returned five or six times to Rawa Ruska, always asking the same question: What happened here during the German occupation? I always got the same response – that is, until a new mayor, who was not a Soviet, brought me along with 50 farmers to a place in the forest where the killing had been done. I will never forget the testimony of one of the farmers. He said that during the war a German soldier arrived in Rawa Ruska on a motorcycle. He was alone except for his dog. He looked all around the town, then left. Everybody was wondering why. Why did he come? What was he looking for? A few days later, German soldiers arrived with a group of about 30 Jews. The Germans forced the Jews to dig a huge hole, eight meters deep and many meters long.

We now know that before any killing would begin in a village or town, the Germans would send someone to that place who was a specialist in the digging of mass graves. His task was to survey the municipality and to inquire how many Jews still lived there. Then he would calculate, according to the number of people the Germans wanted to kill, how large the mass grave needed to be.

Eventually the Germans said to the Jews they had brought with them to dig the hole, "Now rest; you are tired from all the work." The Jews climbed out of the hole and sat on the grass. Then secretly, one of the soldiers went down into the grave and put explosives in the ground. After a while, the Germans told the Jews to go back to digging. Eventually, the Germans detonated the explosives while the Jews were in the grave, and the 30 Jews exploded into bits and pieces.

The farmer who spoke was not a historian, but he remembered various details. He remembered, for example, that the Germans were worried about the digging, so they put on a gramophone and would play German music. One day, the farmer said, he was forced to play the harmonica for the Germans, but his harmonica broke so he could no longer play it. Years later, with a metal detector, we found pieces of that farmer's harmonica. Another thing he remembered was that when the Germans became hungry, they asked the villagers for two chickens. Because they were afraid of being poisoned by the villagers, the Germans always killed the chickens themselves then grilled them so they could eat.

Another witness who came forward was a woman named Maria. She told me, "I was 14. A German ordered me to come, come!" She had to climb up into the trees and collect the pieces of the Jews' bodies that had ended up in the trees after the explosions, then put them in piles and cover them with tree branches so that other Jews would not see them. Later, the Germans brought trucks and trucks and trucks filled with Jews. In a day and a half, they shot 1,500 Jews, the last Jews of Rawa Ruska. They did this, she said, with only two shooters and three pushers. Why pushers? Because the leader of the *einsatzgruppen* told the soldiers to use only one bullet per Jew. It was one Jew, one bullet; one bullet, one Jew. This was so as not to waste ammunition. If it was a baby or an old person, they buried them alive. Afterwards, witnesses told us, the mass grave was moving for three days.

Finally, I had discovered the secret my grandfather did not want to tell us. I found out what he didn't want to say. I could have finished then and there, but when I went back to the car, ready to leave, the mayor of that city, a Slav, said to me, "Patrick, what I did for you for one village, I can do for you for 100 villages."

I'll never know why he said that, but when I got back to Paris, I decided to go to meet Cardinal Jean-Marie Lustiger (1926-2007) and tell him what I had discovered in Rawa Ruska while my grandfather was a war prisoner there. Cardinal Lustiger was born a Jew. In 1940, as a teenager and against the wishes of his parents, he became a Catholic. After the war and the Holocaust, he became a priest, then a bishop, and in 1981, the Cardinal Archbishop of Paris. After I told him what I had learned while I was in Ukraine, he said to me, "Patrick, I know the story, because my Jewish family in Poland was shot the same way in Bedzin."

Eventually, I went to New York where I met with Robert Singer of the World Jewish Congress. He did not know I could speak Hebrew, but I overheard him say to one of his colleagues, "We have been looking for these mass graves in Eastern Europe for years and this guy we don't even know finds them."

I later organized a meeting in Paris between Robert Singer and Cardinal Lustiger. Together, we built a non-profit organization called Yahad – In Unum. *Yahad* in Hebrew means "to give," and *In Unum* in Latin means "together." We made the decision that we will not say *Unum*, because we are not one, but "in one," and that "One" is God.

Many people think that I am doing the work I do alone, but I am not. Yahad – In Unum is doing this work. We are 25 people, young people, working full-time in Paris. Our first task was to get into archives and explore what is there. We have two people working in the *Bundesarchiv* in Germany. The people there are very gracious and very helpful to us. The *Bundesarchiv* is the archive holding information about the people accused of participating in Nazi Germany's crimes. We also have people working in Soviet archives. Most of the Soviet archives about what happened during World War II and the Holocaust are from the Soviet Extraordinary State Commission established in November 1942 and tasked with investigating war crimes against the Soviet Union. They began their investigations in 1942, and then later, as the Red Army made its way west, they opened mass graves when they found them. Sometimes they made a sketch or drawing to show where the mass graves were. The Soviet Commission also interviewed people. There are millions of pages of testimony, mostly written by hand, as well as sketches and other documents. As you can imagine, this is difficult material to read.

We gather documents from various archives. We translate these documents and classify them by village, town, and city. That is why in Yahad – In Unum there are 25 people working full-time. There is lots of work to be done. Once we collect the documents, translate them, organize the material, we build a file. When we have enough of a file, we then "go on the ground." That is, we visit sites in Eastern Europe. We send out about 17 teams per year. Currently, we are working in ten countries. People think we work only in Ukraine. I think that is because my first book, *The Holocaust by Bullets* (New York: St. Martin's Press, 2008), was about Ukraine, but we actually are working in ten countries. At the present time, we even have one team working in central Russia. We have other teams working in central Ukraine and central east Ukraine. We pause when winter comes because of the snow, but then we begin again, usually in March.

What do we find when we do our investigations "on the ground?" We discovered, as I said, that first the Germans decided where and when to kill people. We also discovered that one day a guy might be a shooter of Jews at a mass grave site, the next day he could be a driver, and the third day he could be a cook for his comrades. Every day was different, but what is the same is that the night before an action, the commanders picked out their men. They would say, "You, you, you, and you, tomorrow." We also now know that very frequently, the night before the action, the commanders would provide drink for the men they chose for "tomorrow." Not always, but frequently. It depended. When they did, there was a lot of drinking that went on.

The next morning, very early, 4:00 A.M., the men would dress, grab their guns and their bullets, and by 5:00 A.M. they were in a truck on their way to a village. They drove in the dark to the village or town. Why did they drive in the night? Because they wanted to arrive in the village or town exactly at the moment when people were waking up. That way nobody could run away; no one could escape.

And before all this, as I've already said, the orders were given to prepare the mass graves. Of course, the local people did not know that the big hole the Jews were digging was to be a mass grave for the Jews. The local people were told that it was a hole for potatoes – in the Soviet Union, they used to bury potatoes in deep holes to protect them from the cold, so it seemed believable to people.

During the night, the ghetto – the Jewish area – was encircled by the local authorities, the police. We have been able to prove that during the night before the killing, local police and other men raped Jewish women and girls. They would enter a ghetto and rape as many Jewish women and girls as they wanted before they began their killing work. In the morning when the Germans arrived to do their killing, the locals would brag about the number of girls they had raped. Frequently, the Germans would select the most beautiful girls they could find and take them as sex slaves. Sometimes the Germans raped girls near the site of a mass grave, then after, they killed them. We have proof about all this: eyewitnesses from the ghetto, survivors who gave testimony, as well as reports in archives that documented such things.

Once the Germans arrived, they surrounded the ghetto, then using loudspeakers, the Germans announced that the Jews must leave their homes, take with them their belongings, and assemble in the main square. The Jews were lined up five by five. Why five by five? Because it was easier to count them when they were in groups of five. Most of the Jews did what they were told, assembled with their belongings. If they did not, the Germans and the local police would go from house to house, from apartment to apartment, and force the Jews out – young and old, sick and healthy, men, women, and children. It could be very violent.

I will never forget a testimony I found in a German archive. It was from a Jewish family who did not leave their dwelling when they were ordered to do so. The Germans tried to force them out, but they refused to go. A German soldier saw a small baby in that house. He grabbed the baby and smashed the head of the baby on the wall. After that, the family went out into the street. That soldier wrote in an official report which we found in an archive, "I found the remedy for the uncooperative."

When the Jews were assembled in the main square waiting for what was next, a German official would arrive. He often would tell them that they were being sent to Palestine but that they had to walk to the trains or to the trucks carrying their belongings with them. Usually the Germans chose a place for their mass grave site that was in the direction of the local train station, so people really did think they were going to the train station, but they weren't.

At some point, the Jews would realize they were not going to the train station, that soon they would be shot. What did they do? They tried to destroy all they had with them that was valuable – money, jewels, other valuables – so as not to let the Germans have them. Later, years later, using a metal detector, we of Yahad – In Unum find what is left of these things that were thrown away. Sometimes we find

Star of David medallions and wedding rings, among other things. Throwing such things away was the last gesture of desperate people before they were sent to die. Believe it or not, in the many years since 1942 nobody had come back to find these things, which is why we of Yahad – In Unum found them.

Before the Jews were shot, they had to undress and sit for a time near the mass grave. In the winter, they also had to take off their warm coats, so they were freezing. Then they were assembled in groups of five or ten, forced to the edge of the hole or down into the hole, and shot. One bullet per Jew, not more. Most of the babies were buried alive or thrown in the air and shot by soldiers or local people – for fun. It was a horrible game. For the mothers it was terrible because they had to see their children massacred in front of their eyes. It was just an unbearable situation.

When the Germans arrived in a place, they always arrived in force and they always arrived with a cook. Why a cook? Because the Germans wanted to be able to eat on time. The cook had to be ready exactly at noon for lunch. The Germans always paused in their work so they could eat. It was incredible. The Germans would set up a long table, then they would come to eat, and when they were finished, they would go back to their work shooting Jews, Gypsies, communists.

I interviewed a woman who served the Germans their food. She told me the shooters would come two by two. She served the men big pieces of meat for lunch. By the end of the meal, another 1,500 Jews were dead. The people we interviewed are the people who were there: neighbors watching from windows and people the Germans forced to work for them. They all had stories to tell us about that time and what they witnessed in Rawa Ruska during World War II and the Holocaust.

Before they were shot, the Jews had to take off all their clothing. Everything, including what was in their bags and suitcases, was collected. Why was the clothing collected? Because often the Jews sewed their valuables – money, jewels, whatever was valuable – in their pockets and in the lining of their coats. The Germans learned that many people did this, so the Germans collected everything and sent it all back to the SS in Germany, who made a lot of money from the clothing and valuables they found.

On the 22nd of June 1941, Nazi Germany invaded the Soviet Union. From the first day of the invasion, the Germans began shooting Jews, Gypsies, and communists. They continued doing so until the last day they were in the Soviet Union. The topography of terror shooting in the former Soviet Union is large, spread over a vast territory: Ukraine, Belarus, Russia, and Poland, too. From the Baltic countries to the border of Azerbaijan, it is a continent of extermination.

We at Yahad – In Unum estimate the number of Nazi Germany's victims who were killed by shooting – and this is only Jews – at about 2.3 million. In addition, the Germans also shot Gypsies, communists, and disabled people. If the Germans came upon a house with a disabled person in it, they would shoot them in front of everybody. Yad – In Unum also has opened an investigation into Gypsy mass graves, that is, Roma graves. Most Roma were buried like animals and there are very few memorials for them, almost none. We also have interviewed Roma survivors of World War II and the Holocaust. They are mostly from Romania or Moldova. What we at Yad – In Unum have discovered is that these shootings – whether Jews, Gypsies, or communists – were public, ultra-public. Everybody wanted to see what was happening.

One day in a village we visited, we discovered there were 17 people who wanted to speak to us. I will never forget one woman. She told me, "I saw the shooting. I was a young girl." I said, "Could you show me where was your home?" She showed me her home. I said, "But from your home you can see nothing." Her home was far from the mass grave site. "Ah," she told me, "I didn't tell you the truth. My mother came back from the market and she told us – we were two children – that we have to come with her so we can see the shooting of the Jews." This woman told me, "For the first shooting, we had a good seat in a place where we saw everything." So you see, on this day, as the woman testified, the killing was ultra-public. People saw what was happening. She saw what was happening to the Jews.

In another village I interviewed someone who at the time of the war also was a young girl. She was about ten years old. On a particular day, the director of her school closed the school: "He gathered all the children and he said to them, 'No school this afternoon because we shall kill our enemies. You can go and watch. It will be the lesson for tomorrow.' Then, we 37 children ran to the mass grave site, but we arrived too early. There were no Jews and no Germans there, so we waited until the Jews and Germans arrived. The Jews sat under a tree. I remember asking my friends, 'Do you see your schoolmates from your school?' But there were so many people, we couldn't see everyone. It was awful. We cried a lot, but we stayed and watched as the Jews were shot." Even if people cried a lot, they still went to watch.

Among the many, many witnesses I found and interviewed, there was only one person I talked to who didn't stay and watch. For me, that says something. It means that if you were not Jewish or you were not Gypsy or not communist or not disabled, you were chosen for life, but they were chosen for death.

I remember another village where the shooting place was very far away from the village. I thought we would not find any witnesses because it was too far away. The Germans knew it was distant from the village, so do you know what the Germans did? They gave out binoculars to the people. Children would climb trees so they could look through the binoculars and see the shooting in the distance. I found 15 boys who were in the trees with binoculars watching what was happening. I never found a secret killing. All these shootings took place in public.

What I discovered is that people like to watch. It's like today, if a building is burning or if there's a car accident, people brake their cars so they can watch, so they can try to see what is happening. It was the same thing during World War II and the

Holocaust. People are curious; they want to see what is happening. This is the human condition.

For me, the question we have to raise today is, if it is not your group that is being targeted to be killed, does that mean that you should not be concerned because you are not in danger of being killed? We also have to think about this way of killing by bullets. In the Nazi East, it was not so much killing by camps. The Germans did have some camps in the Soviet Union, but most of the killing was done one by one. It was personal killing. This part of the genocide of the Jews is the act of genocide that was in danger of being lost from memory. Why do I say that? Because one day I was in Krakow, Poland. It was perhaps 25 years ago. I knew a Polish man, a friend who was an intellectual. He said to me, "Patrick, Hitler made a mistake." I said, "Oh, which mistake?" He responded, "He built Auschwitz." I said, "Why is that a mistake?" "Because," said my friend, "some Jews survived. When the Germans and their collaborators killed them in the forest, they didn't come back."

When you kill people one by one in the forest, in nature, they disappear. You will never find an Auschwitz in Syria. You will never find an Auschwitz in Iraq. You will never find an Auschwitz in Rwanda. Shooting, cutting off people's heads, bombing, that's the way the killers kill there. We have to teach a new generation about the Holocaust by bullets because it is a paradigm. Unfortunately, it is a model that works. We must be prepared to fight against such a model, such a genocide.

Questions & Answers

Question: Why should we remember the Holocaust today?
Father Desbois: We have to remember the Holocaust and teach about it because antisemitism is not dead. In Europe, there are many shootings and a lot of violence against the Jews. There is no synagogue in France that is safe. They are all protected either by the army or the police. There is no meeting of Jews in Paris that is not protected by the army or by the police. The ghosts of Nazi Germany are still around.

We also have to remember and teach about the Holocaust because we cannot be in this new millennium and go on killing one people so another can exist. On the continent of Europe there are still mass graves, and we cannot build democracies on top of mass graves. It demeans all of our values, Christian values and human values: dignity, respect, acceptance, tolerance. Today we must say such killing is finished.

Antisemitism, and today in parts of the Middle East, anti-Christianism is not dead at all. In too many cases, Islamists accept exactly the same ideology and take the same model that Nazi Germany used in the 1940s in the East during World War II and the Holocaust. They are determined to kill, and they kill in public, using all the media available to them to publicize this killing. ISIS (Islamic State of Iraq and the Levant) releases videos detailing how they kill. They kill so everybody can see.

Recently, ISIS killed four people publicly. We cannot accept that. Otherwise, we are like the neighbors in Ukraine during the Holocaust. It's not my group, it's not me. I'm not there. I sleep well. We simply cannot, whoever we are – Christian, Jew, or whoever – we simply cannot accept to allow such things to continue happening. We must find a way to protest, to stop these things.

Question: What happened during the Holocaust happened before the technology of today existed. But today these killings by ISIS are happening and are shown via social media all over the world. Why isn't there more of a response?

Father Desbois: Because humanity doesn't change. A human being is a human being. What happened during the Holocaust, what the *einsatzgruppen* did in Ukraine and other places, was public. We have photographs of their killing of Jews by shooting. Germans knew. Soldiers sent pictures to their lovers or to their families. It was public, but as long as it is not you, not your group, not your family, not your country, it is easy to close your eyes, to ignore what is happening to someone else.

Tomorrow if ISIS kills 200 French people, it is a catastrophe, but when they kill local people in Syria, Iraq, or someplace else, it's not a catastrophe because it is not us, not our people. It is the same human condition at work. The solidarity of the human race is very weak. People too often only identify with their group. That's the fragility of humanity.

It's why the mass killers say exactly who they want to kill. They want to destroy the Christians from the Middle East. They want to kill the Yazidi. But who cares about the Yazidi? They want to kill the Shiite, but you are not Shiite, so who cares? That's why we at Yahad – In Unum try to push people to act and not only to think. It's why we are always saying, "Join us" or "Join our organization." Remember, Syria and Iraq are not far from Paris, only three or four hours by plane, and from here in the eastern United States, perhaps only ten hours or so. We are connected as human beings, but we must recognize that connection.

Question: When you interview individuals, do they ever express any regret or remorse for having been a bystander, for having watched what happened to the Jews and others during World War II and the Holocaust?

Father Desbois: First, you have to remember that these people were in the Soviet Union during the war and then for more than 40 years after. In the Soviet Union you had no freedom. In the Soviet Union you couldn't act, you couldn't think for yourself. In the Soviet Union, if you began to have feelings of remorse, you were finished. People always ask me, "Do people have remorse? Do they confess to you?"

You can have remorseful feelings if you are free. But when you have no freedom, like a Soviet person, you cannot have that. You must understand, in the Soviet Union there was absolutely no freedom.

Question: What is genocide?

Father Desbois: Genocide is a human disease. It took place in your country – I am thinking about how America treated its native population. It took place in Germany, and it spread all over Europe and the Soviet Union. Genocide is now in the Islamic world. It is a human disease. Genocide is the attempt to kill and murder large numbers of people just because of who they are, not because of what they have done. To accomplish genocide, you need people who are very smart, very normal, very educated to organize it and to carry it out.

What too often happens during genocide is that people change; they transform. Instead of helping their neighbors, they denounce their neighbors. They kill and rape. They maim and murder people just because of who people are – Jews during the Holocaust, Yazidis today, Tutsis twenty years ago.

Genocide is like a disease. It can spread. That is why we have to teach about the Holocaust and other genocides. Pope John Paul II – now St. John Paul II – frequently said, "Antisemitism is a sin against God and humanity." We have to teach that antisemitism is a sin. We have to name it first, then treat it. We have to say to young people, "One day you will be a journalist, or a member of the military, or a social worker, and you may find yourself in a place where it is legal to kill people just because they are 'the other ones.' You have to be prepared to resist the temptations to treat others as less than human. You have to recognize that some people are transformed when they get power, including the power to kill and rape and murder."

Often there are a few people who refuse to take part in such actions, such killings, a few who say, "No, we won't do it. We will try to save people." It is always a very small minority, but nevertheless they try to do something to help people whose lives are in danger.

Soon all the witnesses of the Holocaust will disappear. The Holocaust will be just a historical fact, that's it. We have to teach about the Holocaust so we can learn how to fight against mass violence today. We have to help our young people to develop the ability to think critically, to observe and to read events critically, if we are going to develop the ability to resist potentially genocidal acts.

What I have learned is that anybody can be a killer and anybody can be a rescuer. Before I began this work, I thought people who saved Jews were always smiling, nice people, and I thought people who killed Jews were always terrible and awful. But what I discovered is that those who saved and those who killed have the same face, so to speak. Whether killers or saviors, these people have the same smile, offer the same welcome. What makes the difference for what one shall become, either a killer or a savior? That is what we must discern then teach, so that our students, too, can discern and develop the qualities of character that when they are put to the test, they will choose to help rather than to harm. This is not easy to do.

Question: Can you say more about why there is so much sexual violence in genocide?

Father Desbois: I have no explanation for this, only a statement. When I began to say that there were sex slaves in many camps of the SS and the German army in the Nazi East, historians yelled at me in public meetings. Why? Because they said the SS were forbidden to touch a Jewish girl, even though we know that Himmler said it was okay for his men to rape Jewish girls in the Soviet Union. Why is this? Because he said the war in the East was so difficult, so all the Nazi rules did not apply there.

We know that pure ideology cannot completely drive genocide. You need also to capitalize on the sexual instinct and the money instinct. You must let your soldiers take money and girls as they want. Otherwise they will not do their job. It's part of the cleverness of the leaders of genocide to let their men do what they want. Himmler knew the Gestapo had Jewish sex slaves and he let them have them. Sex, money, ideology. All three are needed. Without them, Himmler could not get his people to do what he wanted them to do.

Question: How is it that you care so much when so many people could care less about what happens to others?

Father Desbois: You know, for me, it all goes back to my family. Very simply, my family trained me, encouraged me to care about others. We had a small shop and if my mother saw that we were not caring about the people who came into our shop, it was a big problem for us. My mother taught me that I must welcome the beggar like I would welcome a prince. If I failed to do that, if I made a small difference in how I greeted people, believe me, I had a problem with my mom. So you could say that I've been trained to care about others since I was a child.

We also have to train young people to care. It's the only way, and it is a big challenge for us. Otherwise, our young people – our children and grandchildren, our students – will see only their small world, a world that is safe for them, and that's it. They won't see the big world.

We always face the temptation to be in solidarity only with the people who are like us. But humanity is bigger than just us. Humanity is not just one group. For those of us who are Christians, we take Jesus as our model, and he did not care only about his own group, the Jews. No, he cared about everyone – Jews and Romans, Samaritans and others. He never said, "I don't care about you. You are blind, you are poor; I don't care. You are rich; I don't care." No, he was caring about everybody, those who were on the road and those who were on the side of the road. For us Christians, Jesus is our model. I learned this at home in my family, who were a very great influence on me. But for sure, it is not easy. The temptation is not to care. Look at the news on TV. Look at social media. Still, we have to try. This is what it means to be a human being: to care about others.

Question: Do the people you meet in Eastern Europe, in Ukraine, or in Russia speak freely to you? Do they express their opinions to you freely, or are they careful?

Father Desbois: These are good questions, for sure. You have to understand: because you live in America, you can speak freely, you can ask any question you want. I also can speak freely here, ask any question I want. However, in some places in Eastern Europe or in Russia, if you ask certain questions, you could risk having the police immediately arrive at your door. One does not ask such questions as, "What do you think of Putin?" It is too risky. During 75% of their lives, people in these regions were trained to keep silent. When you are under total political oppression you try to survive, and the first rule of survival is silence.

Question: What can you tell us about the Holocaust survivors you meet? How do they deal with the trauma they experienced and now have to live with? How do they cope?

Father Desbois: Survivors are amazing, but they have their limits. Let me give you an example. One guy in France whose mother was a Jewish survivor of the Holocaust said that his mother wanted to give her testimony to us. I said, "Okay, but I can only videotape her if you are not in the room." He said, "No, I want to be in the room," but I said, "No," and the mother agreed with me. As it so happens, during the war she was hidden under the ground on a farm with her baby. At some point the Germans came searching the farm; she was hidden in the ground beneath the area they were searching. Suddenly, the baby began to cry and she was forced to smother the baby, or they both would have been discovered and killed for sure. Her son did not know about this and his mother did not want to tell him, even these many years later. As a result, I never completed the interview on videotape. For me, this is an example of a survivor having a limit.

Remember this: you don't have to be a survivor to give testimony. Today you are a witness as a result of what you have seen and heard. The question I ask you is, "Now that you are a witness, what will you do? What will we do?" We must do something. Otherwise, we are like Ukrainians who say, "How very sad," but then do nothing.

One day I was in Los Angeles. It was a big crowd who came to hear about the work we at Yahad – In Unum were doing. At the end of the evening, a lady approached me. She said, "Ah, Father, I will never forget you." And I said to her, "No, don't forget the victims. Me, it's nothing. It's nothing." She looked at me strangely. I said to her, "It's my message. Absolutely, don't forget the victims. And don't just think about all this. Do something for victims today." Merci.

Discussion Questions

1. Read all or selected parts of The Holocaust by Bullets: A Priest's Journey to Uncover the Truth Behind the Murder of 1.5 Million Jews. Identify three (3) or four (4) significant reasons why Father Desbois set out on his "journey to uncover the truth." What is "the truth" he wants to uncover? In what ways has he succeeded? In what ways has he failed?

2. Why, in your view, has it taken so long for eyewitnesses to speak up about what they witnessed and endured during WWII and the Holocaust?

3. What is the significance of historical sites in terms of revealing "the truth" about what happened to the Jews during the Holocaust? Be concrete and specific.

4. Is the work of Father Desbois and Yahad – In Unum relevant today? Explain.

Further Reading

Browning, Christopher. *Ordinary Men: Reserve Police Battalion 101 and the Final Solution in Poland* (New York: HarperCollins, 1992).

Desbois, Patrick. *The Holocaust by Bullets: A Priest's Journey to Uncover the Truth Behind the Murder of 1.5 Million Jews* (New York: Palgrave Macmillan, 2008).

Hogan, David J. (Ed.). *The Holocaust Chronicle: A History in Words and Pictures* (Lincolnwood, IL: Publications International, Ltd., 2000).

Lower, Wendy. *Hitler's Furies: German Women in the Nazi Killing Fields* (New York: Houghton Mifflin Harcourt Publishing, 2013).

Snyder, Timothy. *Bloodlands: Europe Between Hitler and Stalin* (New York: Basic Books, 2010).

Szczepinska, Urszula. *The Holocaust by Bullets: A Study Guide for Educators* (Paris: Yahad – In Unum, 2015). Available at https://issuu.com/yahadinunum/docs/study_guide_review_may_15_v3/25.

Film and Video Resources

(The) Hidden Holocaust. Produced by CBS News: *60 Minutes*. Available at http://www.cbsnews.com/news/hidden-holocaust-60-minutes/.

Holocaust by Bullets with Father Patrick Dubois (9 mins). Produced by Nazareth College. Available at https://www.youtube.com/watch?v=weIr_XaEr0I.

Notes

1. Available at http://www.yahadinunum.org/?lang=en.
2. Available at http://www.yahadinunum.org/yahad-in-unum-featured-on-60-minutes-2/?lang=en.
3. Available at http://issuu.com/yahadinunum/docs/study_guide_review_may_15_v3/5?e=16014843/13341379.

Wartime Rape: Understanding Women's Experiences during the Holocaust

Alysa Landry

Recipient of the 2015 Ethel LeFrak Outstanding Student Scholar of the Holocaust Award

"War tends to intensify the brutality, repetitiveness, public spectacle, and likelihood of rape. War diminishes sensitivity to human suffering and intensifies men's sense of entitlement, superiority, avidity, and social license to rape."
Rhonda Copelon, "Surfacing Gender" in Dombrowski (Ed.), *Women and War in the Twentieth Century*, p. 347.

Wartime Rape

In an essay that appeared in a 2010 anthology about the sexual assault of Jewish women during the Holocaust, Nomi Levenkron writes the following: "Armies have always marched over the bodies of countless women – women they raped, prostituted, inseminated, and enslaved."[1] Yet history is devoid of these accounts, writes Levenkron, a legal advisor in Tel Aviv. In her essay, she explores the repression and silencing of women's rape stories, along with the reasons Jewish women were targeted for rape during the Holocaust.

While peacetime rape is considered a crime against women – or the men to whom they "belong" – sexual assault is routine in war. In war, Levenkron writes, "when a man's life isn't worth a tinker's damn, a woman's life and her autonomy over her body are worth even less."[2] Rape during war is often considered a byproduct of armed conflicts, a soldier's wage, but Levenkron argues that rape has wider implications and that it is a metaphor of war itself: "The soldier invades the woman's body just as he invades her country; he crushes her body as well as her right to autonomy and control over her life."[3] Susan Brownmiller, an American journalist and feminist, also compares rape to war: "The body of a raped woman becomes a ceremonial battleground, a parade ground for the victor's trooping of the colors … vivid proof of the victory for one and the loss and defeat for the other."[4]

Accounts of violence during the Holocaust are full of rape stories, though researchers only recently have isolated the study of women's experiences during World War II. That study includes women's testimonies of rape and sexual torture, atrocities that occurred more than half a century before the United Nations declared rape a war crime. An inquiry into rape during the Holocaust also reveals a horrifying irony: just as the murder of Jewish women and other people considered racially inferior was legal, so, technically, was rape. Yet *Rassenschande*, or race defilement, was considered a heinous crime.

SS leaders were guilty not only of the murder of 6 million Jews – or two-thirds of Europe's Jewish population – but also of an appalling sexual hypocrisy. Under the control of Adolf Hitler, Heinrich Himmler, and the Nazi Party, German soldiers used sex as both a force of destruction and an act of creation. Sex was used simultaneously as a tool to wipe out an entire "inferior" ethnic group and to raise up an "ethnically pure" Aryan race. In this essay, I explore the Nazis' use of sexual intimacy – and of women – as a double-edged sword. They used sex to further prove Jewish women's worthlessness and, through the *Lebensborn* (or "fount of life") program, to propagate the "superior" Aryan race.

Sex as Power

In a 2011 story printed by CNN, journalist Jessica Ravitz describes accounts of sexual assault found in the archives at the University of Southern California's Shoah Foundation Institute for Visual History and Education. Of the 52,000 video testimonies, 1,700 included references to sexual assault, including sexual harassment, abuse, molestation, and rape. The story also reveals that assaults weren't isolated to concentration camps, but that they occurred during deportation, in ghettos, during forced marches, in hiding, and in refugee camps. Sexual assault even came at the hands of liberators and those giving aid.[5] In perhaps one of the greatest acts of betrayal, rape was perpetrated by rescuers, relatives, and the very people who volunteered to hide women and children in their attics.[6]

Yet those who endured sexual abuse likely were a minority, arguably making the incidents insignificant in the broader study of the Holocaust. In fact, Ravitz writes, sexual assault does not fit into the narrative of the Final Solution, whose purpose was the systematic extinction of the Jews. Rape is not an image that exists side by side with yellow stars, ghettos, cattle cars, concentration camps, gas chambers, and crematoria, Ravitz writes, but the testimonies are undeniable and the memories are significant to the women who endured such violence.

During the Holocaust, racial laws expressly prohibited soldiers from engaging in sex with the "conquered population," yet the prohibition likely made Jewish women's bodies more desirable.[7] These "inferior" women became invisible, which meant their suffering was insignificant and the Germans could be completely indifferent to it. In a 2008 article rejecting the myth that laws forbidding racial mixing would prevent the rape of Jewish women, Helene Sinnreich points out that rape was created by political conditions and it began immediately with German occupation: Jewish women were "abducted off the streets and during search of their homes for valuables. Sometimes forced labor preceded sexual abuse and in some cases, rape was the primary motive for entry into a home."[8] Women were raped by a wide range of individuals, Sinnreich writes: perpetrators, bystanders, and even fellow victims. Yet the stories do not "fit neatly into the standard narratives of the Final Solution precisely because [rape] contradicted central policy."[9] In order to justify rape, officers classified Jewish women as "sub-human and therefore not as sexual beings,"[10] yet dehumanizing women did not deter rape, but enabled perpetrators. In fact, rape "accorded with Nazi goals to subjugate and destroy inferior races,"[11] or, as Christoph Schiessl says, "in wartime, the distinction between killing and other forms of violence gets easily lost."[12]

In an essay about racial persecution against Jewish women, Brigitte Halbmayr uses the term "sexualized violence" to describe what occurred. Sexual assault was not about the sexuality of the perpetrators, she writes, but violence committed via sexuality. It is a "show of power on the part of the perpetrator and includes many forms of violence with sexual connotations, including humiliation, intimidation, and destruction."[13] Violent acts are sexualized if they are directed at the most intimate parts of a person's body and against that person's "physical, emotional and spiritual integrity." Such acts include any bodily attacks or "unauthorized crossing of body boundaries," yet the goal of all forms of sexualized violence is "the demonstration of power and dominance through the humiliation and degradation of the other."[14]

In concentration camps, the SS had complete power over their prisoners, including the "extreme exploitation, abuse, and dehumanization, often leading to annihilation" that characterized daily life. Wolfgang Sofsky calls concentration camps places of "absolute power"[15] where "sexualized violence took place not only in the form of breaking rules but often in their implementation." Yet rape was not part of the genocidal process of the Holocaust. Instead, it was "part of the continuum of violence that resulted from genocide. Rape was not an instrument of genocide, but was the byproduct of intentional annihilation."[16]

Myrna Goldenberg points to a "catalog of horrors" endured by women during the Holocaust, including beatings, nakedness, starvation, and sexual humiliation.[17]

Women survivors reported prolonged nakedness, examination of their genitals, full-body shaves, and rough physical treatment,[18] but they also reported mutilation such as having breasts cut off, being raped in public, and other examples of sexual victimization as a commodity of war. Rape during the Holocaust is a "complex issue," Goldenberg writes;[19] it was not a weapon of war as it has been in other cases of genocide, but rather it had a "profoundly demeaning and useless dimension."[20] While wartime rape is often used as a physical manifestation of the domination of victims, rape during the Holocaust was unnecessary. The implementation of the Holocaust itself was evidence of the Germans' physical and political superiority; therefore, acts of sexual violence against Jewish women were "redundant tools of terror and dominance."[21]

The many accounts of sexual violence during the Holocaust reveal four types: rape, sexual slavery, sex in exchange for some commodity, and sexual humiliation. At the root of these sexual abuses is this dichotomy: the Nazis saw Jewish women "both as sexual objects and as a biological danger, as it is women's wombs that bear future generations."[22] This dichotomy is further evident in a study of the *Lebensborn* program, in which the SS used Aryan women's wombs to ensure future generations of genetically superior people.

Sex for Procreation

The SS was dominated by "extreme racism" that created distinctions between the master race (*Herrenrasse*) and the inferior race (*Untermenschen*), the Aryan race and lower races, or those worthy of life and those unworthy of life.[23] This racism also determined who was worthy of reproduction. In Nazi Germany, millions of "impure" people, including Jews, Gypsies, homosexuals, and blacks, were targeted for death while, at the same time, the SS introduced a plan to replace the inferior population with a new breed of genetically superior Germans.

As many as 20,000 children were bred in the *Lebensborn* program, helping to usher in the future of the Master Race, though many didn't know the truth of their birth circumstances until years or decades later. The *Lebensborn* program, according to a 2000 Newsweek article, was "one of Nazism's most troubling social experiments."[24] In 1933, the Nazi Party made it illegal for Aryan women to have abortions. At the same time, Himmler's SS built 20 *Lebensborn* homes in Germany and other European countries where Aryan women could deliver their illegitimate children. These children, along with others who were kidnapped from Poland or other occupied lands, were raised as Germans and turned over to Nazi foster parents.

The purpose of *Lebensborn* was to further the Aryan race by "whatever means were available."[25] To be accepted into the program, women had to possess the right characteristics: blonde hair, blue eyes, proof they had no genetic disorders, and the ability to prove the identity of the baby's father, who had to meet similar criteria. Most of the women were not married and the children were conceived in "all the usual ways: love affairs, one-night stands, and so forth."[26] The result of this "mad system of eugenics" was "beautiful blond children," "pure white" people void of any "Jewish aspects" such as dark hair or pointed noses – and suitable to populate the world as part of the Aryan Master Race.[27] Women with Scandinavian features were prized for their "Viking roots" and sought after by SS officers, who coerced or offered them gifts in exchange for sex.

In a 2004 *Daily Mail* article, journalist Andrew Malone describes *Lebensborn* as "a breeding programme to safeguard the future of the Thousand-Year Reich by providing pure future generations to replace those lost by war."[28] At the same time German soldiers were raping Jewish women and killing their children, SS officers were stealing blonde-haired, blue-eyed children from their families and operating "breeding clinics" where pure German SS officers were told to mate with suitable women. "As the Nazis wreaked mayhem across Europe, these Aryan babies were born into privilege and power," Malone writes. SS officers fathered children with local women even if they were already married. These women, in turn, "wanted for nothing, with the finest food, homes and clothes supplied to ensure the next generation of Nazis grew accustomed to enjoying the spoils of war."[29]

In short, German women were rewarded for bearing children while Jewish women were sexually degraded and victimized, often destroying their ability or desire to have children. The irony is that sex in Nazi Germany was used on both sides of the equation: as a tool for both genocide and reproduction, to annihilate one population and build up the other.

The Hypocrisy of Rape during the Holocaust

In 1948, the United Nations General Assembly defined genocide as acts committed with "intent to destroy, in whole or in part, a national, ethnical, racial or religious group."[30] Those acts include imposing measures intended to prevent births within the group. Although all Jews were targeted for death during the Holocaust, women were particularly vulnerable to genocidal acts because they endured "gender-specific traumas" like sexual assault and "reproductive abuse."[31] Traumas that targeted women included sexual victimization, pregnancies, abortions, forced prostitution, childbirth, and the killing of newborn babies in camps. In many cases, women found that their very survival depended on their willingness to trade sex for food or other commodities – or submit to sexual humiliations on threat of death.

Ironically, gender-specific trauma, including rape and sexualized violence, "feminizes the victim," Monika Flaschka writes in her essay, "Only Pretty Women Were Raped." A rapist chooses his target because he recognizes her as a woman, yet even in the face of what one survivor called "sex from morning to night,"[32] the environment in concentration camps actually "challenged women's identities as women,"[33] damaging them emotionally and psychologically. According to Flaschka,

"Upon entry into the camp, their heads were shaved, they were given formless clothing, and starvation frequently caused cessation of menstruation and loss of body weight, including in the breast and hips, two regions stereotypically associated with femininity and attractiveness ... all of these changes prompted women to question their own identities."[34]

In many cases of sexualized violence, Jewish women targeted for rape had characteristics of "physical attractiveness."[35] Even in concentration camps, where rape was "evidence of the inhumanity of the Nazi regime,"[36] women who survived by trading sex for food or leniency often were younger, more feminine, and more physically attractive.

In the *Lebensborn* program, attractive women also were targeted for sex, though the outcome was the opposite. While Jewish women's femininity was removed, Aryan women were encouraged to celebrate the characteristics that made them women, including the ability to reproduce. Aryan women played a specific role in the Third Reich and in Hitler's idea of an "ideal German Community."[37] They were expected to focus on their roles as wives and mothers, fulfilling the "domestic ideal." They were instructed to increase the population and upgrade the species. *Lebensborn*, according to family therapist Gisela Heidenreich, was "the opposite example of the Holocaust."[38] For Jewish women, the Holocaust meant death; for Aryan women, *Lebensborn* meant life.

During the Holocaust, it can be argued that Jewish and Aryan women faced similar fates. Each population was targeted because of femininity and their ability to reproduce – the very things that identified them as women. Although rape wasn't expressly considered a weapon of war during the Holocaust, it was indeed a weapon – a double-edged sword. And when sex is used as a weapon, all women are victims.

Questions for Discussion

1. *What does it mean to say that rape is a weapon of war? In what way or ways is rape an act of genocide? Explain the difference between rape as a weapon of war and as an act of genocide.*

2. *What makes the use of rape during the Holocaust similar to or different from the use of rape in other cases of genocide?*

3. *Give some examples of how women's experiences during the Holocaust were different from men's. Why do researchers focus on these different experiences? What insights do we obtain about genocide through this study?*

Further Reading

Goldenberg, Myrna, and Amy H. Shapiro (Eds.). *Different Horrors, Same Hell: Gender and the Holocaust* (Seattle and London: University of Washington Press, 2013).

Hedgepeth, Sonia M., and Rochelle G. Saidel (Eds.). *Sexual Violence against Women during the Holocaust* (Waltham, MA: Brandeis University Press, 2010).

Herzog, Dagmar (Ed.). *Brutality and Desire: War and Sexuality in Europe's Twentieth Century* (London: Palgrave Macmillan, 2009).

Rittner, Carol, and John K. Roth (Eds.). *Teaching about Rape in War and Genocide* (London: Palgrave Macmillan, 2016).

---------*Rape as a Weapon of War and Genocide* (St. Paul, MN: Paragon House, 2010).

Sinnreich, Helene. "'And it was something we didn't talk about': Rape of Jewish Women during the Holocaust." *Holocaust Studies: A Journal of Culture and History*, 14(2), Autumn 2008, pp. 1-22.

Film and Video Resources

Worse Than War (120 mins). Produced by PBS. Available at https://www.youtube.com/watch?v=w7cZuhqSzzc.

Rape as a Weapon of War (25 mins). Directed by Ev. Available at http://vimeo.com/18809745.

Sexual Violence as a Weapon of War and Genocide (9:30 mins). Produced by Facing History and Ourselves. Available at https://www.facinghistory.org/resource-library/video/sexual-violence-weapon-war-and-genocide.

Notes

1. Nomi Levenkron, "Death and the Maidens: Prostitution, Rape, and Sexual Slavery during World War II," in *Sexual Violence against Jewish Women during the Holocaust*, eds. Sonia M. Hedgepeth and Rochelle G. Saidel (Waltham, MA: Brandeis University Press, 2010), p. 13.
2. Ibid.
3. Ibid, p. 14.
4. Myrna Goldenberg, "Jewish Women's Experiences and Artistic Expressions of the Holocaust," in *Holocaust Education: Challenges for the Future*, ed. Carol Rittner (Greensburg, PA: Seton Hill University, 2014), p. 108.
5. Jessica Ravitz, "Silence Lifted: The Untold Stories of Rape During the Holocaust," CNN (June 24, 2011).
6. Marissa Fox-Bevilacqua, "Silence Surrounding Sexual Violence during Holocaust," *Haaretz* (June 16, 2014).
7. Levenkron, p. 14.
8. Helene Sinnreich, "'And it was something we didn't talk about': Rape of Jewish Women during the Holocaust," *Holocaust Studies: A Journal of Culture and History*, Autumn 2008, p. 7.
9. Ibid, p. 1.
10. Ibid, p. 2.

11. Ibid, p. 3.
12. Ibid.
13. Brigitte Halbmayr, "Sexualized Violence Against Women during Nazi 'Racial' Persecution" in *Sexual Violence Against Jewish Women during the Holocaust*, eds. Sonia M. Hedgepeth and Rochelle G. Saidel (Waltham, MA: Brandeis University Press, 2010), pp. 29-44.
14. Ibid.
15. Ibid, p. 32.
16. Ibid, p. 31.
17. Goldenberg, p. 105.
18. Ibid, p. 107.
19. Ibid, p. 108.
20. Ibid.
21. Ibid.
22. Levenkron, p. 15.
23. Halbmayr, p. 33.
24. Joshua Hammer, "Hitler's Children," *Newsweek*, March 20, 2000.
25. Mark Landler, "Results of Secret Nazi Breeding Program: Ordinary Folks," *The New York Times*, Nov. 7, 2006.
26. Ibid.
27. Andrew Malone, "Stolen by the Nazis: The Tragic Tale of 12,000 Blue-Eyed Blond Children Taken by the SS to Create an Aryan Super-Race," *The Daily Mail*, Jan. 9, 2009.
28. Ibid.
29. Ibid.
30. See http://www.un.org/en/preventgenocide/adviser/pdf/osapg_analysis_framework.pdf.
31. Janet Liebman Jacobs, "Women, Genocide, and Memory: The Ethics of Feminist Ethnography in Holocaust Research," *Gender & Society*, April 2004, p. 230.
32. Sinnriech, p. 15.
33. Monika J. Flaschka, "Only Pretty Women Were Raped: The Effect of Sexual Violence on Gender Identities in Concentration Camps," in *Sexual Violence Against Jewish Women during the Holocaust*, eds. Sonia M. Hedgepeth and Rochelle G. Saidel (Waltham, MA: Brandeis University Press, 2010), p. 80.
34. Ibid.
35. Ibid, p. 77.
36. Ibid, p. 79.
37. See http://www.ushmm.org/wlc/en/article.php?ModuleId=10005205.
38. Landler.

The New Normal — A Street Boy

George D. Schwab

Latvian Jewish survivor of the Holocaust; Professor of History Emeritus, Graduate Center, City University and City College of New York (CUNY); President Emeritus, National Committee on American Foreign Policy, New York, NY

Editor's Note
The following essay is an excerpt from the author's forthcoming memoir about WWII and the Holocaust. It is his story – the story of a lonely 13½-year-old boy who, in May 1945, had just been liberated after four years in a ghetto and in Nazi German concentration and labor camps. He writes about his desperate attempt to suppress his horrifying experiences by immersing himself in the pleasures of life.

Emaciated and limping Jews, non-Jews, British soldiers, military vehicles, and army ambulances with Red Cross banners swarmed all over the huge U-boat base in Neustadt/Holstein, where many of us survivors huddled on the soccer field. The dreaded SS men in their unmistakable green uniforms, German army soldiers, and sailors were nowhere to be seen. I recognized Jewish survivors barely able to drag their feet breaking into naval canteens and helping themselves to whatever was on the shelves and on the floor. I followed suit and barely managed to drag by the handle a familiar-looking can filled with substitute marmalade. I dragged it aimlessly, for I had no idea where to go and what to do. Suddenly Jule (an older inmate who, from time to time, advised me on how to maneuver in the quagmire and, at a critical moment, saved my life on the day of liberation) appeared as if I had willed his return and told me that two former *Reichsbahn* (the German equivalent of Amtrak) inmates had quartered themselves in a clean room in one of the barracks on the base. There I found a clean bunk bed for myself. I sat down and enjoyed the treat created from their bread and margarine and my marmalade. Although afflicted by hunger, I was able to consume only small portions, for my stomach apparently had shrunk considerably. Jule had a much larger appetite but did not stuff himself. Many who did died.

After a short while, we heard knocks at the door. Several former Polish inmates, probably *kapos*, entered the room, looked around, liked what they saw, and ordered us to vacate the premises. Notwithstanding his dog bites and physical weakness, Jule and the two other roommates read the intruders the riot act and the Poles vanished. After nearly a week of resting, sleeping, obtaining some food from the British and meeting former camp buddies with whom we daydreamed about the future, which had appeared bleak, I suddenly collapsed on May 8th – the day of the official end of World War II in Europe. A British military ambulance rushed me to the town's hospital, where I remained for several weeks recovering from general bodily weakness.

I was raving madly from hunger as I was only given small amounts of warm porridge and water several times a day and was told that this was the best cure for my condition. Jule, also hospitalized and suffering terribly from the dog bites, came to visit me. On one occasion when I was delirious, craving food, I remember screaming at him. He just stared at me for some time and left.

After gradually regaining strength, I was returned by a British military ambulance to the base that, in the meantime, had been converted into a huge displaced persons (DP) camp. Just before leaving the hospital, I ran into the former Jewish *kapo*, the sadist Kurt Kendziorek, who informed me that he, too, would be released from the hospital later in the day and that I should convey his greetings to our mutual friends. On my return to a large barrack that had been turned into a rehabilitation quarter, I was reunited with a number of former camp inmates whom I immediately informed of the cruel Kendziorek's imminent arrival. As expected, they rapidly organized a welcoming party at which he was clobbered with fists and chairs. Bleeding profusely, Kendziorek was returned to the hospital. That was my last encounter with that walking horror.

Because I was still weak and emaciated, I rested a lot and watched older former inmates play poker and blackjack with German currency. The money, I was told, came from selling cigarettes on the black market in town – cigarettes obtained from British soldiers. I borrowed some money and began to play as well and had beginner's luck.

With loot in my pockets, I, too, began to make my way to town – passing the railroad station that was packed with unarmed, unshaven, filthy-looking German soldiers in unkempt uniforms. What a wonderful sight it was to observe these so-called *Übermenschen* begging us survivors for bread and cigarette butts. In town, I struck up an acquaintanceship with a German-Jewish gentleman who was married to a German woman. In the foyer of their small apartment, they had a huge dog that allegedly once belonged to Heinrich Himmler. She was very protective of her puppies and did not like me to come close to her and her offspring. On one of my visits, the gentleman sat me down in his living room and asked me questions about my background and wartime experiences, which he recorded on pads of paper.

Those few weeks came to an abrupt end when I once more collapsed in the barrack and was immediately returned to the hospital. The diagnosis was identical to the one rendered before, general bodily weakness. In the course of my recovery, which took more than a week, I was visited by Soviet officers accompanied by their British counterparts. I was urged by the Soviets to return to my homeland, Latvia, where I would be reunited with family and friends. The British urged me to accept the invitation, but I categorically refused, remembering Mamma's directive never to return to Latvia but to move west to England or America. As I later learned, those who accepted the offer were sent to deep Russia. Those that did not die there succeeded in returning to Latvia in the 1960s and 1970s.

For reasons unknown to me, the British military ambulance did not return me to the DP camp. Instead, I was driven some five kilometers from Neustadt to a Latvian children's home in a suburb-like setting called Haffkrug. I was well-received as a son of Latvia. Everyone spoke Latvian, sang Latvian songs, danced Latvian folk dances, and talked much about returning to the homeland. Some of the Latvian staff people claimed to have known Papa and to have been patients of his. The head of the home was a woman who often traveled to Lübeck where, among others, she met with General Dankers, a name that did not mean a thing to me. According to the head of the children's home, the general wanted to meet me, which, fortunately, did not come to pass (I subsequently learned that he was a notorious antisemite.) Yet, despite the warmth with which I was received, I did not truly feel that I belonged in that milieu where the focus was on returning to Latvia. On a day when the head of the children's home was visiting Lübeck, I made my way back on foot to the DP camp in Neustadt; I never returned to the children's home.

Once more I was assigned to the rehabilitation barrack where some new faces greeted me. Jule, in the meantime, had left for Kiel where his wife, Genia, had been liberated. As before, the former Jewish prison inmates were busy playing cards and were engaged in black marketeering. With some money left over from my previous success, I resumed playing cards and my luck held.

Some of my older camp buddies talked me into traveling to nearby Lübeck. There, I was told, they would "beat off their troubles" (in Yiddish: *obschlogen die tsores*). Not yet 14, still weak, and not fully physically mature, I did not yet understand the meaning of getting rid of one's troubles. I thought it meant going to movies and cabarets. Not daring to reveal my ignorance, I did not ask questions and agreed to go with them to Lübeck.

The trip was nothing like what I had expected. A short walk from the railroad station led to a street by the name of Klemens, I believe, which had 12 numbered buildings – six on each side of the street. In the doorways and windows on the main floor of buildings I and IA stood or sat very attractive young girls inviting us in. My three buddies soon disappeared, and I was left alone to fend for myself. Not really knowing what to do and politely refusing invitations, I walked back and forth on the street, just looking around and trying to quiet my pounding heart. I was struck by the contrast of the women sitting in the windows of houses XI and XII with those in I and IA. The former appeared to be in their 40s or 50s and terribly overweight. On the return trip to Neustadt, my buddies compared notes and cruelly snickered at me for not having joined them.

I was hiding my shame that I was a sissy. In addition to not being fully grown, I did not yet have pubic hair to speak of. Nevertheless, I agreed to join them on their next outing, even though I was sure that I would not go back. After considerable prodding and teasing, I went along on their next trip. I paid some 20 marks to a young attractive brunette. Showing understanding of my innocence and fright, she patiently and lovingly introduced me to a phenomenally enjoyable experience. Finally, I understood the meaning of *obschlogen die tsores* ("beat off their troubles").

I entered the bordello a child and left feeling a man ready to conquer the world. On the train trip back to Neustadt, I joined my buddies in laughter and in comparing notes. Merriment notwithstanding, deep down I was despondent, wondering whether my mother had survived and where she might be and what I should do without her and Papa and Bubi. I sensed that she was alive but had no clue how to find her in war-torn Germany. Mail service to the United States and England had not yet been restored. With pockets full of money, and even some hidden under my bed in the bunk, I had the urge to strike out and see the world, remembering stories my parents, relatives, and friends told about their travels.

My frame of reference was, of course, stories I had heard from Aunt Hermine – her stories overshadowed those of my other relatives, including my parents, even though they shared some of the excitement when they were in Berlin frequenting *Kabaret der Komiker*, dinner parties with diplomats, dancing in Paris nightclubs. President Hindenburg insisting that Aunt Hermine, whom he called *meine Garbo* ("my Garbo"), be seated next to him, and so on. One unforgettable story was of a dinner party with diplomats at the residence of Aunt Hermine and Uncle Xavier[1] (a Chinese envoy to Germany), which Papa and Mamma attended. The gossip about fellow diplomats was scathing – so much so that nobody dared get up to use the facilities for fear of becoming the target of gossip. Another story I never forgot, and Mamma told it over and over again, was about when she, Papa, uncles, and aunts were on a trip to Paris from Berlin with some relatives joining from Vienna – they were dazzled by the food at Maxim's. Mamma asked to be shown the kitchen and was horrified to see cats on the counter. I also remembered the brand names of cigarettes Aunts Hermine and Tanja smoked – Went Patent and Diplomat. What had also impressed me was Aunt Rita's luggage: on arriving in Libau for a visit, she brought her suitcase that I marveled at because of the beautiful labels of hotels she had stayed at in Rome, Venice, Zurich, and elsewhere – places I was sure to visit. Aunt Tanja, who also lived with her husband Karl in Berlin, noted that Berlin was only a village in comparison with Paris and Paris a village in comparison with London.

Remembering also my parents mentioning distant relatives living in Hamburg, it occurred to me to take a train to that city on the pretext of looking for them and seeing the city to broaden my horizons. I arrived at Hamburg's bustling main railroad station (*Hauptbahnhof*) in late September or early October with a small suitcase. Wandering in and around the station, I was shocked to see the destruction all around me – which reminded me of the destruction of Libau, but even worse. I was at a total loss about where to go, what to eat – in short, what to do. Apparently noticing my dilemma at the station, the police approached me and asked for identification papers; I presented those I had obtained in Neustadt's DP camp. After consultations with higher-ups at a police station, I was driven to a Jewish children's home in the Hamburg suburb of Blankenese, the city's equivalent of Greenwich, Connecticut. A few child survivors were already there and more were scheduled to arrive. Fellow survivors from Libau Hirsh Dorbian and Joske Genton arrived somewhat later, and I made new friends with the half-Jewish Rolf Redlich who hailed from Berlin, Wolfgang Teichtahl who originally came from Vienna, and Szlamek Bresler from Poland.

On the large estate overlooking the Elbe River stood three solidly constructed buildings and a gatehouse where the estate's caretaker lived with his wife and dog that had belonged to the Warburgs. The owner of the estate, I learned, was a banker by the name of Max Warburg, whose family had been dispossessed of the estate by the Nazis; he regained it immediately after the war. Not living there, the family made it available to some Jewish organizations – the American Joint Distribution Committee and British Relief Unit – for the purpose of sheltering a small number of child survivors.

What a relief life on this tranquil and scenic estate was. Originally I was placed in the guest house, which was on a small hill, and then was moved to the White House – the main building. The three-story structure even had an elevator. The children's home was administered by the American Joint Distribution Committee. I remember Selma who hailed from the Bronx proudly wearing a handsome American military uniform, as did Charlotte, even though she was from Metz, France. Other staff included Egon Fink from the U.S. and Hilda of the British Relief Unit who wore a British military uniform. From time to time we were visited by an imposingly tall and heavy high Joint official in American military uniform by the name of Rothman.

In the rear of the White House was a barrack where, after morning calisthenics and breakfast, we studied the Hebrew language, Jewish history, the Jewish-Arab struggle over the Holy Land, the geography of the region, and the Jewish-British struggle over Jews being permitted to enter Palestine. Instructors were members of the Jewish Brigade, including Zvi and Ben Yehudah, both in clearly identifiable British uniforms. We were heavily indoctrinated with Zionist ideology and for the need for us to prepare to enter the Holy Land. To reach it, Jews had to evade the British blockade for which we were being prepared mentally and physically by keeping our bodies in shape. This illegal immigration was known as *alijah bet* in contrast to the very small in number legal immigrants who received British certificates – I believe 1,500 a month. To me, who had been brought up in an assimilated home, welcoming the sabbath was very meaningful. Following the festive meal, we folk-danced and sang Hebrew songs, which I enjoyed immensely. Some of the dances called for boys to invite girls and vice-versa. I was particularly attracted to bosomy Rosi from Czechoslovakia who later left for a *kibbutz* in Palestine.

The war years – during which time I was persecuted for being Jewish – coupled with the Jewish education I was now receiving – continued to sensitize me to Jewishness. Without becoming religious, including not adhering to dietary laws, I was beginning to be impressed by the richness of Jewish history and my cultural heritage. In short, I was on the way to becoming a proud Jew prepared to fight for the liberation of the biblical Jewish homeland of Palestine.

Even though the material covered in the classes I attended in the barrack near the White House was interesting and influenced my evolving mindset, I, as in Libau, continued to have difficulties warming up to school routine. Unlike most of the kids who listened to the teachers, some of us – out of boredom – shot spitballs at them. Obviously aware of our wartime experiences, they did not get too upset and counseled us on the value of education in general and what it would mean for building a Jewish state.

In Blankenese, I was finally able to scribble some words to relatives in England and the United States telling them that I was alive. My "announcements" were sent by military mail. Addressing my uncle in London, I simply wrote on the envelope, Mr. Robert Schwab, London, England, neglecting to indicate that it should be sent to Shell Oil where he was one of the directors. Obviously he did not receive any of my semi-illiterate epistles. Nor did my scribbles reach my cousin Nuta and her husband, Dr. Eli Bruskin, in Hartford, Connecticut. Addressing letters to the husband of my cousin Manja, David Alder, in Salt Lake City, Utah, I ascribed to him the title, director of Shell Oil. On receiving several of my announcements, the manager of the Shell gasoline station in Salt Lake City looked up the name David Alder in the phone book. There, he was listed as the owner of an insurance agency. On telephoning David Alder, the Shell manager asked whether the name George Schwab meant anything to him. David confirmed that I was his wife's cousin. Thus contact with some of my relatives was established by way of Salt Lake City.

In the meantime, Mamma, who had been liberated by the Soviets in March 1945 in the small town of Chinov, not far from Stolp and Lauenburg, heard that there were many Jews in Lodz, Poland, and decided to travel there in the summer of 1945 in the hope of obtaining information about my fate. On leaving a trolley car in Lodz, she was recognized by a woman who called out "*Frau* (Mrs.) Dr. Schwab." That lady from Libau, Mrs. Dorbian, informed her that I was alive and living in the British zone. Overwhelmed by the news, Mother neglected to ask where in the British zone. Back in Lauenburg, where she was working as a nurse in a Soviet hospital, Mamma packed her few belongings and with some money in her pocket made her way to Berlin, a city she knew from visits in the late 1920s and early 1930s. There she rented a room in Schöneberg and visited the American Joint Distribution Committee. Because she was a fair-skinned, blue-eyed blonde unable to speak Yiddish, the Joint assumed she was a German, and on her numerous visits refused her pleas for help to locate her son who had survived four years of hell.[2]

At last one lady at the Joint said that she believed Mamma's story and would help her locate her son. On Mamma's behalf, she sent letters by military mail to our relatives in England and the United States, which they received; this lady of the Joint also succeeded in establishing telephone contact between my mother in Berlin and me in Hamburg. We both cried and promised to look for ways to reunite.

Once a week we were able to speak by way of a military telephone. In the meantime, our U.S. relatives especially began to bombard us with packages containing clothing, cigarettes, chocolate, canned meats, coffee, and so on. In addition, every letter I received by military mail contained a five- or ten-dollar bill. My cousins wrote that the cigarettes and coffee were not meant for me but to be used by me to exchange for things I needed.

Discipline at the school was not strict. Under the pretext of looking for relatives and seeing the city, I soon made my way to Hamburg's *Reeperbahn* – the amusement part of town also known as the Red Light District. Bribing a bouncer with two cigarettes, I was admitted to a dance parlor whose name I believe was Alhambra or Alcatraz. There I had a beer or two and, like the man of the world I imagined myself to be, smoked a few American Camel cigarettes that scratched my throat. I could hardly stand smoking, but as a man I felt compelled to do so. To be "with it" was the name of the game. The immersion into a world of pleasure helped me at least temporarily overcome memories of my painful past and sad present. Beneath my happy-go-lucky facade, I was emotionally unsettled. My emaciated looks notwithstanding, which had been aggravated by a recent appendectomy in a hospital in the Altona district of Hamburg, older women invited me to dance – I hardly knew how – and asked me for cigarettes and chocolate, which I dispensed with alacrity. At the time I was convinced that this dive, where I was always warmly welcomed, was the height of elegance in cosmopolitan, bombed-out Hamburg.

I also hired a driver who claimed that his family owned a factory that produced parts for machines and employed 200 people in Hamburg-Harburg. The owners offered to sell it to me for ten pounds of coffee and 40,000 cigarettes. There was no way I could muster the quantities asked for, nor did I know anything about owning a factory, or for that matter, any kind of business. I was just eager to have a good time, enjoying being a man of the world on the verge of turning 14.

At about the same time, Jule reappeared on the scene. He was now the driver for Norbert Wollheim, a German-Jewish gentleman who headed the Jewish community in the British zone. He lived with his wife in Lübeck. On their way to Bergen-Belsen's DP camp, Norbert and Jule would, at times, pick me up in Blankenese and together we would drive to the camp. There I was introduced to, among others, Yosele Rosensaft, head of the large Jewish part of the DP camp. The huge camp also had a Polish district, where it was dangerous for Jews to be seen – especially after dark when some were beaten for no other reason than being Jewish. I was told that Jews were even shot at. As Poles were widely known for their rabid antisemitism, that section of the camp was, of course, avoided by Jews during the day, as well.

Norbert spoke Yiddish with a German accent that I was able to follow. It was akin to the Yiddish spoken in my part of Latvia, which, as already noted, I had picked up during the war. It was different with Yossele's Yiddish, which I had difficulties following. Both Jule and Norbert understood him and translated his questions about Blankenese, which I answered in a Yiddishized German. On one of the return trips, Norbert invited me to stay overnight at his home in Lübeck where I was told I would meet his wife. She was very attractive and they lived in a lovely section of town. On another occasion, Jule brought me to Kiel where he lived with Eugenia in the nearby DP camp at Eckernförde. The reunion was warm and wonderful.

One day at Blankenese, I received an invitation to appear at the Joint's suite on the second floor of the White House. Apparently some staff members were suspicious of my Jewish heritage and thought that I was perhaps a German in disguise. I was asked about my background, wartime whereabouts, and eyewitnesses at Blankenese who could identify me as a survivor, something I was immediately able to provide.

On several occasions during my weekly conversations with Mamma, she mentioned that after we would be reunited, in the not-too-distant future she hoped, we would join our relatives in the United States who expected us. On learning that my plan was to go to Palestine, she assured me that once reunited we would jointly decide what would be best for us. One day I was informed by Selma and Charlotte that I would shortly be reunited with Mother, but because U.S. military vehicles had to obtain permission from Soviet authorities to travel in the Soviet zone of occupation, the reunion could not take place overnight. The month of my departure was finally set for May 1946, and it was Selma in U.S. military uniform who accompanied me in a military vehicle with an American military driver.

On the course of that drive, which took many hours, I began to wonder whether reunification would spell the end of my independence. As a man of the world, I would refuse to live the way I lived back in Latvia, under control of a strict governess and a relatively strict mother, both of whom would supervise all my activities, especially piano lessons, and above all, make me to go to school. It suddenly occurred to me that living with Mamma might not be such a good idea after all.

At last we arrived at Naumann Street in Schöneberg, a very nice working-class district in the center of Berlin, which was in the American sector and not bombed out. Selma and I walked up the stairs – Mamma was waiting at the door. In the hallway, Mamma and I exchanged kisses. To introduce the new me, I asked an unexpected first question: "What is the nightclub situation like in Berlin?" Apparently not startled by the question, Mamma replied, "It is an interesting question. As a woman alone in Berlin, I could not investigate it. Now that you are here, we will be able to explore it together." Disarmed by Mamma, I was satisfied with the answer.

In the coming weeks, Mother showed me around the Berlin she knew. I was eager to see where Aunts Tanja and Hermine lived in the Charlottenburg district of the city – respectively on Oliver Square and Bleibtreu Street, immediately off the *Kurfürstendamm*, the city residence of Aunt Hermine and Uncle Xavier. The official residence of the embassy was in Krumme Lanke, a suburb. Grandaunt Marta had lived for a while in Grunewald, also a suburb.

Although parts of Berlin were bombed out, sections on the *Kurfüstendamm* near the zoo were relatively intact. There we went to cafés and movies, sometimes two or three a day. We also visited the Chancellery, which was heavily damaged, and even went into Hitler's office. In the same area near the Potsdammer Square and the Brandenburg Gate, we viewed the semi-destroyed Ministries of Propaganda and Air Force. Seeing Berlin, especially in the context of a largely destroyed evil capital of a former brilliant city where the devil revealed himself to be a coward and took his own life, was a dream come true. As survivors, Mamma and I walked with our heads high and joyfully watched the so-called German *Übermenschen* in rags, begging for food and cigarettes and scrounging in search of cigarette butts. Although we could not bring back those we loved, at least we could see the Germans get what they deserved for their passionate support of Hitler and his fellow criminals.

Between May 1946 and February 1947, the month we left for the United States, Mamma convinced me to accompany her to a performance of Pagliacci with a world-renowned tenor from Italy whose name, I believe, was Beniamino Gigli. To my great surprise, I immensely enjoyed the performance. The story of the clown, the music, and the singing captivated me. Nearby on the Friedrich Street in the Soviet sector was a well-known café where, according to Mamma, a famous Gypsy violinist by the name of George Boulanger played Gypsy music, which she thought I would enjoy as well, and she was right. I began to reevaluate Mamma and gradually came to the conclusion that she was much more "with it" than I had given her credit for in Latvia.

To help me forget the deep hurt that the war had caused, including the nightmares that haunted me for years, Mamma did not mind accommodating me and my passion for exploring what Berlin still had to offer. She suggested that we visit the DP camp in the Berlin suburb of Schlachtensee. There she had a few friends she wanted me to meet and wanted to investigate the school. Among others, we met Max Kaufmann of Riga whom I remembered from Libau and the Riga concentration camp. He was writing a book on the Jewish catastrophe in Latvia and extensively interviewed Mother and me about our wartime experiences. It was published in Germany in 1947 under the title *Die Vernichtung der Juden Lettlands (The Destruction of the Jews of Latvia)*.[3] On visiting the DP camp's school, I saw a good number of boys and girls of all ages with whom I thought I could be friends. Thus, I was surprised – but did not mind – that the head of the school placed me in the highest grade, notwithstanding the fact that I was the youngest and still quite illiterate. Nevertheless, I was looking forward to this new experience – learning, of course, was not uppermost in my mind.

Daily during the week, I commuted to Schlachtensee. More subjects were taught, and even though we learned Hebrew, the students were not excessively exposed to preparing for illegal immigration to Palestine. That is not to say, however, that Palestine as a destination for us Jews was removed from consideration. *Alijah* to Israel was much talked about, followed by talk of leaving for the United States. Mamma, remembering how impressed I was by American movies before the war, reinforced this by not talking about the United States excessively, but inviting me to accompany her to American movies, which I loved, especially those depicting skyscrapers and other wonders of New York. I also admired the tempo of the people.

To my astonishment, students took school seriously. When once I lobbed a spitball at the teacher, I was reprimanded by him as well as by my peers. Because I was eager to get back to town to continue exploring Berlin with Mamma and visiting friends who lived in town, especially the Kahns who resided with their young daughter on Friedrich Street in the Soviet sector, I rarely participated in the variety of cultural activities offered at the camp.

Nevertheless, I enjoyed my classmates, especially the three well-dressed older Polish girlfriends who appeared very sophisticated and spoke mostly Polish with one another: Renia Laks, Rachelka Feigenbaum, and Tunia Rybak. Like me, they enjoyed what Berlin had to offer. Considering myself a man of the world, I saw no reason why we should not join forces and enjoy things together. On several occasions I asked to join them on their exploits in town. I remember Renia, probably 17 at the time, snickering at this nearly 14-year-old jerk, as she called me, with whom she and the other two would have nothing to do socially. Others I became friendly with included Feliks Freidenreich, Roma Lichtengthal, Itzke Lewin, Arnold Kerr, and the Zycer brothers.

School was tolerable. Most enjoyable were class outings to Sansoucci in Potsdam, the castle of Frederick the Great, the Berlin zoo in the center of town, visits to museums, and the theater where we saw Schiller's *The Robbers* and Brecht's *Threepenny Opera*. I was overwhelmed by the music.

Although still thinking of going to Palestine, I began to waver under the influence of American movies, my cousins in the U.S. telling us that they had applied for visas and paid the Joint Distribution Committee for second-class tickets for us to cross the Atlantic aboard one of the Queens. In the meantime, parcels with food, clothing, and letters with dollar bills continued to reach us. On several occasions, Mamma said that there was no future for us in Europe and Palestine, where we had no relatives. Repeating from time to time the proverb that "a man without an education (*Bildung* in the German embraces education and culture) is no man," she told me that in the United States I would receive a proper education under normal circumstances. At the same time, Mamma promised that once I reached 21, I would be able to decide whether to immigrate to Palestine or not.

Although I was conflicted, New York did exert a strong pull. I also felt responsible for Mamma, who I knew had suffered enormously during the war. We all had been brought up to always smile, "no matter how deep the hurt may be."

Unbeknownst to me, Mamma had registered us with the Joint to leave for New York. Late in the year, they notified Mamma that we were scheduled to leave early in 1947. We assumed that we would board one of the Queens either in France or England. The news of embarking from either country was exciting, and my passion for leaving for Palestine receded. I informed my classmates of the latest developments and learned that Renia Laks, her sister Chris Lerman, and brother-in-law Miles Lerman (future chairman of the U.S. Holocaust Memorial Museum in Washington, D.C.) had received identical notices.

As it turned out, the Joint did not honor the tickets purchased for us to sail on one of the superliners. As we later found out, the difference in cost between sailing on a luxury liner and troop transport was considerable, so the Joint, in an effort to aid as many refugees as possible to reach the shores of the United States, lumped us in with the rest. Thus, in late January, together with the Lermans and Renia, we boarded a passenger train for Bremen. There, we were placed in a transit camp only to learn that our trip had been postponed because of a coal miners' strike in the United States. Using this opportunity to visit friends in the Bergen-Belsen DP camp, Mr. and Mrs. Lerman set off, leaving Renia with us. A few days later the news reached us that we were about to embark. Mother, in the absence of the Lermans, took it upon herself to persuade the authorities that Renia had been left in Mother's custody and had to sail with us no matter what. After permission was granted, the Lermans returned, breathless, just in time before we all sailed together for New York.

Aboard the *S.S. Marine Perch*, Miles and I bunked together, as did Mamma and Chris. Renia was placed with a younger group of girls. The stormy weather on the

Atlantic caused the ship to roll right and left and the front to descend between the waves that smashed onto the deck – we all were seasick. In tranquil moments, we met on deck. The night before our arrival in New York in February, I was determined to stay on deck all night as rumor had it that the lights of New York were visible for tens of miles out to sea. That was not the case, and so it turned out to be my first disappointment. When we finally docked in the afternoon at a Hudson River pier in the West 40s, I was disappointed once more: The West Side Highway was poorly lit, the street under it looked dilapidated and had hardly any lights, there were no skyscrapers in sight, and the terminal was cold and not very clean. We parted with the Lermans, vowing to stay in touch, and disembarked.

To our great surprise, we were warmly welcomed by Aunt Ida Schonberger (née Firkser), whose first husband, Bernard Schwab, fell victim to the influenza epidemic that followed the Great War. She lost her second husband, an American citizen, on a luxury cruise from the United States to Europe. Also at the pier were Raja (née Taub and a relation by marriage) and Gustav Smith, a German Jew who had come to Libau after Hitler's accession to power and married Raja there. The couple had immigrated to the United States shortly before the outbreak of World War II.

The taxi trip on the West Side Highway to Brooklyn was a disappointment, as well. I missed seeing skyscrapers and the reputed lights of New York. The bridge to Brooklyn was spectacular, but the trip to Brooklyn's Borough Park section was unbelievably dull: no tall buildings, nondescript small houses, and poorly lit streets. Arriving at Aunt Ida's three-story townhouse, we were heartily greeted by Aunt Ida's third husband, a lovely and warm rabbi. His world, as Mother told me, was different from Mother's and mine, as well as from that of Aunt Ida in Libau and those of her two worldly husbands. We were also welcomed by Aunt Ida's daughter, Ellen Licht (née Schwab), from her first marriage; her husband Barney; and her son Bernard. They occupied the second floor of the house. For the next six weeks, the large living room on the main floor did double duty: a living room during the day and our bedroom at night.

That same evening we were visited by Aunt Ida's sister Marcia Schwartz, originally from Libau, whom Mother knew well, and her husband Bernie, who was in the clothing business and presented me with an Eisenhower jacket that I proudly wore for years. Aunt Ida's son, Harry Schwab, came over, as did Rabbi Schonberger's daughter Gerri and her husband Leo, also a businessman. They planned to introduce us to a Manhattan restaurant we would surely enjoy. We also had welcoming letters with enclosures from cousins Manja and Nuta. I soon forgot my disappointments, welcomed the warmth with which we were received, and looked forward to exploring New York at age 15 years and three months.

Questions for Discussion

1. What are the titles of other memoirs written by Latvian survivors of the Holocaust?

2. Why do you think some Holocaust survivors find it very difficult to do more than "tell the facts" about their experiences during the Holocaust? From your reading of survivor memoirs, what is often left unsaid by a survivor? Why do you think that is so?

3. If you had a chance to ask George Schwab a question about his experiences during the Holocaust, what would you ask him? Why?

Further Reading

Eliach, Yaffa (Ed.), *We Were Children Just Like You* (Brooklyn, N.Y.: Center for Holocaust Studies, 1990).

Greenfeld, Howard. *After the Holocaust* (New York: HarperCollins Children's Books, 2001).

Kaufmann, Max. *Churbn Lettland: The Destruction of the Jews of Latvia* (Konstanz, Germany: Hartung-Gorre Verlag, 2010).

Schwab, George. "The Destruction of a Family" in *Muted Voices: Jewish Survivors of Latvia Remember*. Ed. Gertrude Schneider (New York: Philosophical Library, 1987), pp. 145–155.

Film and Video Resources

Analysis of Nazi Massacres in Latvia by Scholar David Marwell (3:23 mins). Produced by Facing History and Ourselves. Available at https://www.facinghistory.org/resource-library/video/analysis-nazi-massacres-latvia-scholar-david-marwell.

Elie Wiesel: Universal Lessons of the Holocaust (8:21 mins). Produced by Yad Vashem. Available at https://www.youtube.com/watch?v=D_kuKXRLEnY.

The Holocaust Comes to Libau (96 mins). Produced by Chabad. Available at http://www.chabad.org/multimedia/media_cdo/aid/2247315/jewish/The-Holocaust-Comes-to-Libau.htm.

Notes

1. His full name was Xavier Kinginthai; for short, Dr. King Lee.
2. Mamma's looks and fluency in German and Russian got her into trouble with the Soviets when she tried to intercede with a Russian officer to treat leniently an SS man who was thought by camp inmates to have been humane and helped them survive. According to eyewitness Gertrude Schneider, "Mrs. Klara Schwab of Libau … spoke [to] the Soviet officer in charge … in flawless Russian [who] accused her of being a spy – she was a blonde woman and even good looking then – and threatened to kill her if she continued to ask that Schultz's life be spared." Gertrude Schneider, *The Unfinished Road: Jewish Survivors of Latvia Look Back* (New York & London, 1991), p. 24.
3. It was reprinted in Germany in 1999, and an authoritative English translation appeared with a new Foreword, Preface, and Introduction in 2010.

1943. New York. De Profundis: Cain, Where is Abel Thy Brother?
Image Courtesy of The Arthur Szyk Society

Figure 1

Injustice Illuminated: The Holocaust Art of Arthur Szyk

Irvin Ungar

Founder and CEO of Historicana; Curator of The Arthur Szyk Society, Burlingame, CA

Figure 2

Let us begin at the end. The Polish-Jewish artist Arthur Szyk (Figure 1: Portrait of Arthur Szyk, Paris, 1930s; photo by Louvre Studios) died in 1951 at the age of 57 in New Canaan, Connecticut. During the last year of his life, he illuminated Thomas Jefferson's well-known statement (Figure 2: *Thomas Jefferson's Oath*; New Canaan, 1951), "I have sworn upon the altar of God eternal hostility against every form of tyranny over the mind of man." Szyk (pronounced *Shick*), who was born in Łódź, Poland, in 1894, admired the great American Presidents – Jefferson, Washington, and Lincoln – and the ideals of freedom they represented for humanity at large. They helped inspire his lifelong commitment to fighting tyranny and oppression directed against his own people, the Jews of Europe: Arthur Szyk was the leading anti-Nazi artist in America during World War II. This essay, dedicated to the hallowed memory of Europe's martyred Jews, will illuminate the injustices that Szyk attacked, both as a fighting artist for democracy – FDR's "soldier in art"[2] and a "one-man army"[3] against fascism – and as a consciously Jewish artist resolved "to serve his people with all of his art and all of his talent."[4]

In 1933, the very year Hitler came to power, Arthur Szyk was invited to attend an exhibition of his works on freedom at the Library of Congress in Washington D.C., where he was awarded the George Washington Bicentennial Medal by the U.S. Congress. On a cold and snowy December day, newspaper photographers greeted Arthur Szyk and his wife Julia. The artist was already quite famous in America and Europe; he had previously been decorated for his many works on freedom by the governments of Poland and France. One outstanding example of those works, the 38 paintings of his American Revolution series, *Washington and His Times*, was completed years before Szyk ever visited the United States, for a simple reason: the European artist loved the story of American democracy.

While in the U.S., Szyk answered questions about life in Europe and about his varied careers as a WWI soldier, director of art propaganda for Poland in its war against the Bolsheviks, successful book illustrator, editorial artist, campaigner for democracy, fighter against antisemitism, and defender of Jewish rights. In a 1934 newspaper interview in New York, Szyk emphatically stated, "An artist, and especially a Jewish artist, cannot be neutral in these times … Our life is involved in a terrible tragedy, and I am resolved to serve my people with all my art, with all my talent, with all my knowledge."[5]

In July 1934, after seven months in America, Szyk returned to Łódź, Poland. Conscious of his commitment to serve his people with all of his art and all of his talent, he began to illustrate his magnum opus: a modern interpretation of the Passover *Haggadah*, the great book of freedom in Jewish tradition. In its telling of the enslavement of the Israelites in ancient Egypt and of their Exodus, Szyk's *Haggadah* was to be different from all others, for Szyk saw Adolf Hitler of Germany (Figure 3: *Hitler as Pharaoh*; c. 1933) as the new Pharaoh – and the

Figure 3

Nazis as the new Egyptians– who had come to degrade, restrict, punish, dehumanize, and annihilate the Jews of Europe.[6]

In his *Haggadah*, Szyk painted a "wicked son" who looks very German, with a positively Hitler-esque black mustache. He painted swastikas on the Egyptians and a Nazi armband on the wicked son – political details which his publisher required him to paint over or remove prior to the *Haggadah*'s publication in London in 1940.

Szyk's *Haggadah* dedication to King George VI (Figure 4: *Dedication to King George VI, The Haggadah*; Łódź, 1936) carries a distinctive political message: "At the feet of your most gracious Majesty I humbly lay these works of my hands shewing forth the afflictions of my people Israel." The question raised here is, Why would Szyk dedicate his *Haggadah* to the King and therefore to England? For two reasons: first, Szyk planned to leave Poland to supervise the printing of his *Haggadah* in England; second, and more important, Szyk saw England as the best candidate to lead the potential fight against the Nazis. Therefore, he optimistically dedicated his book of freedom to the British King and his kingdom.

Figure 4

But Szyk had a conflict of interest when dedicating his *Haggadah* to England. In 1936, the British passed the first of a series of laws (the "White Papers") that restricted the movement and emigration of Jews from Europe, limiting their immigration to Palestine. So how was Szyk to remain emotionally and intellectually honest in dedicating this great book of freedom to the British, who on the one hand opposed the Nazis but on the other hand prevented European Jews from finding security and freedom in Palestine? Szyk found a solution. On the bottom right of the Dedication page, he paints modern European Jews (whom he hopes will have an Exodus of their own), and at the bottom left he paints the word "Zion" on the gates of Jerusalem. In the middle, he paints a British military ship standing sentry between the Jews who desperately want to leave Europe for Zion, the Land of Israel, but who are restricted from doing so by the British Mandate in Palestine. Additionally, Szyk paints himself standing beside his people, dressed in military uniform as "a soldier in art." While the *Haggadah* is a religious book used at the Passover *seder*, for Arthur Szyk it is also a political book about opposing tyranny and oppression and fighting for freedom in every age, and particularly at that very hour.

Szyk completed additional Dedication pages for the *Haggadah*. One from 1938 is dedicated to the Jews of Austria and Germany after the Anschluss and Kristallnacht. While not published in the *Haggadah*, these works show that Szyk remained vigilant regarding the plight of his people and committed to calling attention to their immediate suffering. Again, Szyk paints himself in military dress, wearing the three medals bestowed upon him by Poland, France, and the United States.

In September 1939, the Germans and Russians invaded Poland, starting World War II. Szyk's biting caricatures and graphic satire immediately denounced the brutality of both the Germans and Russians (Figure 5: Arthur Szyk, *Father, Do Not Forgive Them, For They Know What They Do*; London, 1939). His art continued to appear in newspapers and in prominent exhibitions, such as *War and "Kultur" in Poland* (London Fine Art Society, January 1940), where he also highlighted the heroism of the Poles and the suffering of the Jews.

"FATHER, DO NOT FORGIVE THEM, FOR THEY KNOW WHAT THEY DO."

Figure 5

In 1940, the Polish government-in-exile (which relocated to London) and the British government supported Arthur Szyk's move to North America. The two governments hoped that he might bring the face of the war in Europe to the Western hemisphere. Szyk arrived first in Canada, where newspapers announced his arrival. Several articles mention that Hitler had personally placed a price tag on Szyk's head (Figure 6: "Famed Polish Artist Has Price on His Head," *The Halifax Herald*, July 13, 1940), so powerfully effective was his anti-Nazi art. At an exhibition in Toronto, Szyk was recognized for his art in the service of humanity. Reporters quoted him as saying, "Art must be mobilized – like everything else."[7] At the same time, Szyk's *Washington and his Times* series – purchased by the President of Poland – hung in President

Figure 6

THE HOLOCAUST AND *NOSTRA AETATE*: TOWARD A GREATER UNDERSTANDING

Franklin Roosevelt's White House, a gift from the people of Poland to the people of the United States.[8]

In late 1940, Szyk immigrated to America. Almost immediately his art appeared everywhere, warning the people of America about the Nazi threat and later seeking to mobilize American war efforts. In his painting *A Madman's Dream*, Szyk portrays Hitler upon a throne surrounded by his Axis supporters.[9] The world is practically in his lap, the Jewish *untermensch* at his feet, with Uncle Sam and John Bull (the U.S. and Great Britain) before him as prisoners in chains – an insane but possible future that Szyk depicted clearly for the American public, well before the U.S. entered the war. In another image published in *American Mercury* magazine,[10] Szyk warns that if America does not pay attention Nazism will overthrow democracy. To drive home the point, he shows the Statue of Liberty with Hitler's face, also titled *A Madman's Dream* (Figure 7: *A Madman's Dream*; New York, 1940), holding a swastika instead of the light of freedom. This drawing also appeared well before the U.S. entered the war.

A Madman's Dream

Figure 7

In July 1941, Szyk's *The New Order* was published in New York. It was the first anti-Nazi book of its kind, attacking the Nazis' racist new order. Contemporary art critic Thomas Craven wrote:

> Szyk's designs are as compact as a bomb, extraordinarily lucid in statement, firm and incisive of line, and deadly in their characterizations … He concentrates his powers on people – on Hitler and his gang, fixing the guilt where it belongs and creating an immortal record of inhuman conduct and organized savagery.[11]

Throughout its pages, *The New Order* presents images of the defenseless, huddled Jews of Europe, vulnerable in their involuntary status as *de facto* enemies of the Third Reich.

After Pearl Harbor was bombed, the United States declared war on Japan (and on Germany three days later). It was Arthur Szyk's somber portrait of Admiral Yamamoto "the aggressor" that appeared on the cover of *Time* magazine, introducing the American public to the face of its violent enemy. Newspapers such as the *New York Post*, the *Chicago Sun*, and *PM*, and magazines such as *Collier's*, *Esquire*, *Look*, and *Liberty* also published Szyk's wartime art. Members of the American press applauded Szyk as a one-man army conducting a personal war against Hitler (Figure 8: "One-Man War Against Hitler," *Click* magazine, August 1942). The American military even called Szyk "a citizen-soldier of the free world."[12]

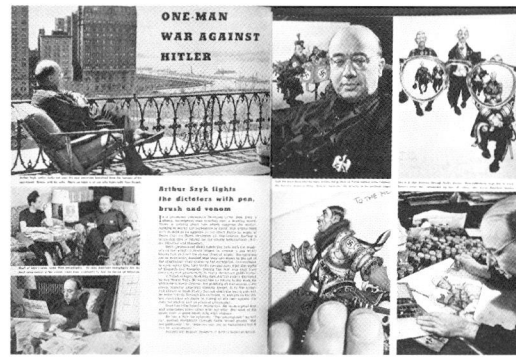

Figure 8

Eleanor Roosevelt wrote about Szyk in her newspaper column "My Day," and in one of his works, Szyk inscribed his portrait of the American President to "Mrs. Franklin D. Roosevelt, from Arthur Szyk, FDR's 'soldier in art'" (Figure 9: *FDR's "Soldier in Art"*; New York, 1944, inscribed 1946).

While Norman Rockwell illustrated covers for *The Saturday Evening Post*, Szyk, an illustrator of a very different kind and the leading propagandist for the Allied cause, illustrated the covers of *Collier's* magazine. His *Arsenal of Democracy* (Figure 10: Cover of *Collier's* magazine, September 12, 1942) appeared on the cover of the Labor Day issue of *Collier's*, motivating Americans to go to work supporting the war effort. (Note how he depicts the deadly Nazi serpent winding its way around the pillars of democracy.)

Figure 9

Figure 10

THE HOLOCAUST AND *NOSTRA AETATE*: TOWARD A GREATER UNDERSTANDING

Figure 11

As Szyk fought two wars – one against the Axis and the other on behalf of his Jewish brethren (Figure 11: *To Be Shot as Dangerous Enemies of the Third Reich*; New York, 1944) – his *modus operandi* was clear: "The Jewish artist belongs to the Jewish people, and it is his mission to enhance the prestige of the Jews in the world ... His task is to reveal to the world of our glorious past and our tragic present."[14] His Holocaust-era masterpiece *De Profundis* (Figure 12: *De Profundis: Cain, Where is Abel Thy Brother?*; New York, 1943) does just that. Going beyond Picasso's *Guernica* or Chagall's *White Crucifixion*, Szyk shows the suffering of his people and calls out for justice for the victims of Nazism and accountability for the perpetrators. His very human rendering shows lifeless Jews, many of them with eyes wide open, one pointing up to the biblical reference to the first murder: "Cain, where is Abel thy brother?" (Genesis 4:9). The inferences are clear: what happened while we looked away? Who is accountable for this massive crime against humanity? Within the "C" of Cain, Szyk paints a swastika; within the "A" of Abel, a Jewish Star of David. Within his visual indictment of mass murder, Szyk places Jesus of Nazareth holding the Ten Commandments, as if to say, were Jesus alive in 1943, he too would be killed as a Jew, murdered alongside his people. The original art, a 12" x 16" pen-and-ink drawing on board, was published in a full-page advertisement in the *Chicago Sun* in February 1943. Surprisingly, the accompanying text was written not by any Jewish group but rather the Christian Textbook Commission (of Protestant Digest, Inc.). The advocacy group announced to the world that "2,000,000 sensitive human beings are being tortured, starved, butchered, in an orgy of hate reaped by Hitler but sown in the very soil of Christian civilization, sown in the texts of intolerance ... accusing Christian textbooks in America of hate-breeding falsehoods about Jews and poisoning the lips of children by their anti-Semitic statements." Thus, Arthur Szyk's art fought hatred and mass murder abroad as well as poisonous antisemitism at home in America.

Figure 12

In April 1943, on the first day of Passover, German tanks entered the Warsaw

Ghetto to liquidate its residents. Szyk chronicled the heroism of his brethren in the Warsaw Ghetto Uprising that year with *Repulsed Attack*, and two years later with the full color *Samson in the Ghetto* (Figure 13: *Samson in the Ghetto*; New York, 1945), which he dedicated "to the German people, Sons of Cain, be ye damned forever and ever, Amen." By the time he completed *Samson in the Ghetto*, Szyk had learned of the Nazi transports from the Łódź ghetto and knew his mother and brother were dead – they were murdered at the Chelmno killing center.

Amid the mounting genocide of his people, Szyk channeled his rage toward "Action – Not Pity," words he used when dedicating his work *Tears of Rage* (Figure 14: *Tears of Rage*; New York, 1942, as published in the *New York Times*, February 8, 1943): "To those of my people who fight for the right to die with their boots on: my pride, my love, my devotion …" He added a scathing aside in parentheses: "To those of you who tuned in late …" This artwork, sponsored by the Committee for a Jewish Army of Stateless and Palestinian Jews, appeared both in the *New York Times*[15] and the *Washington Post*[16] in 1943. The Committee was one of several non-sectarian groups organized by Peter Bergson, a Palestinian Jew in America whose activism took aim at the American government as well as those American Jews whom the Bergsonites saw as too passive in their efforts to rescue their brethren in Europe. The Committee drew great support from the non-Jewish community, counting among its leaders Congressman Will Rogers, Jr., of California, Senator Guy Gillette of Iowa, journalist Pierre Van Passen, and a young Marlon Brando. Among its ranks were Jews such as screenwriter Ben Hecht, actor Edward G. Robinson, and producer

Figure 13

Figure 14

Billy Rose. Together with director Moss Hart and musical director Kurt Weill, Rose produced the 1943 pageant "We Will Never Die." Held in five cities, this theatrical enactment dramatized for the American public the urgent need to rescue European Jewry from certain death. Szyk's art was part of this effort, too. His work was designed for mass reproduction, whether as poster stamps (Figure 15: *Save Human Lives* poster stamps), for supporters of Bergson's organizations (among them, The Emergency Committee to Save the Jewish People of Europe), or as program covers for fundraising rallies and events.

Szyk's illustration for Ben Hecht's *Ballad of the Doomed Jews of Europe* (Figure 16: Arthur Szyk

Figure 15

and Ben Hecht, *Ballad of the Doomed Jews of Europe*; New York, 1943) appeared in *The Answer Magazine* (April 1943), and subsequently the text was published in an ad by the Bergson Group in *The New York Times* on September 14, 1943. This brilliant composition criticized U.S. State Department's indifference to the suffering and dying Jews of Europe:

> Four Million Jews waiting for death.
> O hang and burn but – quiet Jews!
> Don't be bothersome; save your breath –
> The world is busy with other news.
> Four million murders are quite a smear
> Even our State Department views
> The slaughter with much disfavor here
> But then – it's busy with other news…

Figure 16

In this image, Jews facing their imminent extermination plead with the international community to intervene. A desperate woman uses a telephone to call for help but the nations of the world (represented by a soldier) pointedly don't pick up.

In 1944, with the unspeakable murder of Europe's six million Jews continuing unabated, Szyk declared, "Every Jew now alive is the legatee of those who died to uphold the sanctity of the Name or dignity of his origin."[17] In his artwork, Szyk transformed the yellow badge of shame into a yellow badge of honor – *ahl kiddush haShem*, for the sanctification of God's Name.

When the Nazis were at last vanquished in 1945, misery continued for those Jews consigned to the Displaced Persons Camps of Germany and Austria when they wished to evacuate to Palestine. Bergson's American League for a Free Palestine, which counted Szyk as one of its vice-chairmen, raised awareness of the confining conditions of those refugees. Szyk's art on the cover of a Bergson journal (*Lullaby for Dying Children*, 1945) shows a Holocaust survivor holding his dying son, who clutches in his small hand a paper representing the same restrictive emigration policies (dictated by the British Mandate in Palestine) that Szyk had decried back in 1936.[18]

Szyk's 1946 work *Pilgrims* highlights the similarities between the 17th-century ship *Mayflower* (bearing English Puritans headed for America) and a modern "illegal" passenger ship (bearing European Jews headed for Palestine). Both carry refugees seeking to break free of the British yoke and religious persecution. The artist further slammed the British in *Just One Step Backwards Please* (1947), where Jews attempt to escape the DP camps in order to safely reach the Land of Israel, rebuffed by a fearsome monster (an ugly John Bull, the symbol of Great Britain).

The declaration of Israeli statehood on May 14, 1948, was an unalloyed joy for the artist. Szyk's wife Julia wrote in her memoirs:

> When Israel was declared independent we were at home with some friends and heard the news over the radio. Arthur cried for joy. It was a dream of his life that had come true. He was the happiest man in the world. He sat down the next day and made the Declaration of Independence of Israel. It was a magnificent scroll with all the dreams of his youth. Palestine was always his personal concern. Those who fought for it were like his own children. He felt like they belonged to him.[19]

And while Szyk enthusiastically created works of art to support Hadassah and its youth *aliyah*, Israel Bonds, the United Jewish Appeal, the Magen David Adom (the Israeli Red Cross), and stamps for the Jewish State, he remembered and cherished the six million Jewish martyrs slaughtered during the *Shoah*. In the 1948 work *Zachor* (remembrance), a simple pen-and-ink drawing of a flower measuring only a few inches high, Szyk acknowledges, through the biblical quote of Deuteronomy 26:8, the eternal need for *both* God and man to extend "a strong hand and outstretched arm" in constant vigilance and guardianship on behalf of the Jewish people.

In his foreword to the catalogue for the 2002 exhibition "The Art and Politics of Arthur Szyk" (U.S. Holocaust Memorial Museum, Washington, D.C.), former museum chairman Rabbi Irving "Yitz" Greenberg, writes of Szyk, "Arthur Szyk is a role model of the engaged artist ... who above all, represents the artist as witness – against evil, and for liberation [...] Szyk affirmed the universal cause of democracy even as he upheld – often militantly proclaimed – a distinctive Jewish history, culture, and identity ... (his) witness rises to the level of prophecy – prophetic as to the Jewish future but, like the biblical prophets of old, carrying a powerful message for all of humanity." (See Figure 17: Frontispiece for *Ink and Blood: A Book of Drawings*; New York, 1944).[20]

Reflecting on his friend's many contributions to the various Jewish causes of the 1940s, Ben Hecht writes of Arthur Szyk:

Figure 17

> His Hebrews under fire, under torture, exterminated in lime pits and bonfires did not change. They remained a people to be loved and admired. Their faces, fleeing from massacre now, were tense and still beautiful. There was never slovenly despair or hysterical agony in Szyk's dying Jews, but only courage and valor. If there was ever an artist who believed that an hour of valor was better than a lifetime of furtiveness and cringe, it was Szyk. Just as the Irgun produced the first fighting Jew since Bar Kochba, Szyk put him on paper for the first time. He died still drawing for the Jews.[21]

And consider Szyk's own words, in the final dedication page of his *Haggadah*. Here, instead of a dedication to the King of England, there is a dedication of another kind, to his own people. He writes, "I am but a Jew praying in art. If I have succeeded in any measure ... if I have gained the power of reception among the elite of the world ... I owe it all to the teachings, traditions, and eternal virtues of my People."[22]

Discussion Questions

1. How did Szyk's Jewish heritage inform the content and the form of his art and his activism in the 1940s?

2. How does Szyk's use of text (captions, scripture, dedications, etc.) help the viewer interpret his complex images?

3. Which symbols and motifs do you find most effectively communicate Szyk's ideals of freedom? Of Jewish identity and survival? What symbols might he use today?

Further Reading

Ansell, Joseph P. *Arthur Szyk: Artist, Jew, Pole* (Oxford: The Littman Library of Jewish Civilization, 2004).

Luckert, Steven. *The Art and Politics of Arthur Szyk* (Washington, D.C.: United States Holocaust Memorial Museum, 2002).

Sherwin, Byron, with Irvin Ungar. *The Szyk Haggadah* (New York: Abrams Books, 2011).

Ungar, Irvin. *Justice Illuminated: The Art of Arthur Szyk* (Chicago: The Spertus Museum, 1998).

Widmann, Katja, and Johannes Zechner. *Arthur Szyk – Drawing Against National Socialism and Terror* [bilingual German/English edition] (Berlin: Deutsches Historisches Museum, 2008).

Film and Video Resources

Arthur Szyk: Soldier in Art (14:44 mins). Produced by Illuminated Productions. Available at http://szyk.org/documentary-films.

Father John Pawlikowski Reflects: Nostra Aetate *and Arthur Szyk* (5:40 mins). Produced by Illuminated Productions. Available at http://szyk.org/documentary-films.

L'Chayim: The Art of Arthur Szyk (58:45 mins). Produced by The Jewish Broadcasting Service. Available at https://www.youtube.com/watch?v=hkt3UjpATpI .

Soldier in Art: Arthur Szyk: America's Weapon Against Nazi Germany (9:45 mins). Produced by Illuminated Productions. Available at szyk.org/documentary-films.

The Work of Arthur Szyk: An Interview with Irvin Ungar, Curator of The Arthur Szyk Society (5:46 mins). Produced by Facing History and Ourselves. Available at http://szyk.org/documentary-films.

Justice Illuminated: The Art of Arthur Szyk (online exhibition). Produced by The Arthur Szyk Society. Available at http://justiceilluminated.szyk.org.

Notes

1. The text was in a letter from Jefferson to Dr. Benjamin Rush, September 23, 1800.
2. See Arthur Szyk's 1946 inscription to Eleanor Roosevelt on his 1944 work, FDR's *"Soldier in Art."*
3. See *Click* magazine's August 1942 photo essay, "One-Man War against Hitler," as well as Morris Schreiber's article "One Man Army," *American Hebrew* (September 11, 1942).
4. Interview with Arthur Szyk in *Jewish Daily Bulletin* (New York; February 18, 1934).
5. Harry Salpeter, "The Human Touch," *Jewish Daily Bulletin* (New York; February 18, 1934).
6. While Szyk was working on his *Haggadah*, he also drew caricatures of Hitler. In one 1935 work, the German leader stands atop the Reichstag wrapped in sheep's clothing, making the Nazi salute with one hand and holding an olive branch in his other hand (basically, "don't trust a wolf in sheep's clothing"). Szyk also liked to quip, "Don't trust a wolf that promises to be a vegetarian!"
7. *The Ottawa Journal* (July 31, 1940).
8. "Art Must Be Mobilized, Declares Great Polish Painter," *Ottawa Journal* (July 31, 1940); "Claims 'Fighting Art to be Powerful Weapon of War,'" *Citizen* (Ontario; August 1, 1940); "Only Human," *Daily Mirror* (New York; April 10, 1941).
9. *Coronet* magazine (January 1942), p. 19.
10. *The American Mercury* (November 1941), p. 575.
11. On the dustjacket of *The New Order*.
12. "Szyk Honored for Anti-Axis Cartoons," *Jewish Times* (Baltimore; August 21, 1942), p. 12.
13. This portrait of FDR appeared on the cover of *Reader's Scope* magazine, November 1944. It was later inscribed to Eleanor Roosevelt in 1946. The original work of art resides at the Roosevelt Library in Hyde Park.
14. "An Artist's War on Hitler," *The Southern Israelite* (Atlanta, Georgia; April 21, 1944).
15. *The New York Times* (February 18, 1943).
16. *The Washington Post* (May 17, 1943).
17. *The Answer Magazine* (August 29, 1944), p. 19.
18. *The Answer Magazine* (December 1945).
19. Unpublished manuscript, in the collection of Irvin Ungar, Historicana.

When Theology and Racism Mix: Catholicism, Antisemitism, and National Socialism

Kevin P. Spicer, C.S.C.

James J. Kenneally Distinguished Professor of History, Stonehill College, North Easton, MA

In 1920s Germany, one might categorize the relationship between Catholics and Jews as difficult at best. Even though many German Catholics had little direct contact with Jews, especially in the rural countryside, they often viewed Jews negatively, believing caricatures of them in the public mind were true. In 1933, less than one percent of the total German population identified themselves religiously as Jews. This one percent comprised just shy of 500,000 persons out of a population of 66 million.[1] Religious and confessional tensions among Catholics, Protestants, and Jews also served as natural barriers.[2] At times, such religious divides easily enabled Catholics, for example, to embrace ludicrous representations of non-Catholics, especially Jews. Though in their pastoral letters, sermons, and religious instructions most bishops and priests did not actively promote violence against Jews, they still routinely made comments that negatively marked them.[3] Often minimized by historians as anti-Judaism, such statements regularly surfaced the ubiquitous deicide charge and placed an emphasis on Jews' rejection of Christ as messianic savior.[4] Over centuries, Catholics' perennial labeling of Jews as "Christ killers" made this and similar charges seem firmly rooted in fact and, in turn, invited additional attacks on Jews' collective character.[5] As historian Olaf Blaschke argues, "The Crucifixion, for example, was not just a historical event but bore a profound meaning and carried a timeless message of eternal salvation which – as is evident from any passion play – differentiated between Christians and Jews: 'The crucifying Jew as the personification of evil and the crucified Jesus as the embodiment of good.'"[6] In part, such a negative dichotomy fueled discrimination against and persecution of Jews in all levels of society, especially as other forms of antisemitism – economic, social, and racial – reared their ugly heads.

The Holy See did little to offer Catholics guidance to combat such a prejudicial characterization of Jews. Evidence of this fact is found in the Sacred Congregation of the Holy Office's March 25, 1928 inconsistent pronouncement that both disbanded *Amici Israel*, translated "Friends of Israel" – a clerical organization, which promoted understanding between Judaism and Catholicism[7] – and repudiated "any hatred of the people once chosen by God."[8] Despite the support of many leading churchmen for *Amici Israel*, certain officials within the Holy Office could not tolerate *Amici Israel's* request to reform the Good Friday supplication prayer that referred to Jews as "perfidious." Such a change, they believed, might stir the Church toward acknowledging the continued validity of the covenant between God and Israel, a point that most Catholics were unwilling to accept.

The public document that disbanded *Amici Israel* did not abate the Church's negative outlook on Jews. As the German historian Hubert Wolf has shown, subsequent statements by individuals associated directly with Pope Pius XI served to lessen the credibility of the Holy Office's condemnation of antisemitism. Such action took place after a British newspaper, *Jewish World*, published an article that criticized the disbandment of *Amici Israel*. Upon learning of the article's contents, Pope Pius XI and the Holy Office charged Father Enrico Rosa, a Jesuit and editor of *Civiltà Cattolica*, with the task of offering a rebuttal. In the journal's May 1928 issue, Rosa presented two forms of antisemitism: an unacceptable form that was "un-Christian," racist, and hate-filled, and an acceptable form that monitored and offered a "healthy evaluation of the danger emanating from the Jews" to the society and the Church. Rosa then explained that the latter form included Jewish domination in many sectors of the economy and public life.[9]

Rosa's arguments reflected the Church's official stance toward Jews in the 1930s. Many churchmen held Jews as chief among those modern non-Christian forces that embraced the tenets of the Enlightenment and worked to secularize European society. Not all Jews, however, were automatically counted among this number. Bishops and priests primarily included only those individuals whom they believed had betrayed the basic tenets of the Jewish faith by exhibiting a so-called pernicious influence on Christian society. Still, due to the ingrained anti-Judaism within the Catholic tradition, Church leaders regularly looked upon all Jews suspiciously. The 1919 German translation and publication of the fictitious *Protocols of the Elders of Zion* that purported to document a plan for Jewish world domination – a publication that immediately followed the Bolshevik Revolution and the short-lived though impactful 1918-1919 German Revolutions – also provided further fodder for anyone in Germany inclined to view Jews negatively.[10]

Over the centuries, the process of the vilification of Jews by bishops, priests, theologians, and lay Catholics unequivocally had an impact on all Christians in Western society. Such language enabled Christians to view Jews as "the Other" – Christ killers who fundamentally were not to be trusted. History has demonstrated that there were clear social and political repercussions from such teaching: discrimination, ghettoization, expulsions, pogroms, and murder. At times, Church leaders directly or indirectly encouraged the promulgation of edicts or laws enacted by Christian states and their Christian leaders against Jews.[11] Ultimately, the last stop on this path of persecution and murder was the Holocaust.

Christianity's historical progression on this Holocaust trajectory was "twisted" in that it provided the germ from which varied strains of hatred of Jews grew and from which outside sources nourished.[12] As the Catholic ethicist John Pawlikowski has argued,

> I have always opposed drawing a simple straight line between classical Christian antisemitism and the Holocaust. Clearly the Nazi program depended on modern philosophy and pseudo-scientific racist theories. But we cannot obfuscate the fact that traditional Christianity provided an indispensable seedbed for the widespread support, or at least acquiescence, on the part of large numbers of baptized Christians during the Nazi attack on the Jews and other marginalized groups. Christian antisemitism definitely had a major role in undergirding Nazism in its plan for Jewish extermination.[13]

Theologian Mary C. Boys concurs with Pawlikowski by qualifying "seedbed" with the richly descriptive word "fertile" to describe the role of Christianity's anti-Judaism in the Holocaust. Boys further explains that "it seems undeniable that the teachings of Christianity about Judaism played their own nefarious role in the Holocaust."[14] Yet, if we accept this linkage, it becomes impossible for us simply to label Catholicism's anti-Jewish writings and teachings as anti-Judaism. Rather, the misunderstanding and hatred such teachings instilled and continue to instill among Christians and other groups toward Jews reaches far beyond the limited definition of this term. The direct linkage of early Christian anti-Jewish teaching and its negative unfolding over the centuries into the economic, social, and secular realms is better labeled "Christian antisemitism," as Pawlikowski does above. Such terminology solidifies the affinity between earlier forms of Christian anti-Judaism and nineteenth and twentieth-century antisemitism.[15] Eminent historian Peter Pulzer supports such an association by writing that "a tradition of religiously-inspired Jew-hatred – or at least of unfavorable stereotyping – was a necessary condition for the success of anti-Semitic propaganda, even when expressed in non-religious terms and absorbed by those no longer religiously observant."[16] Pulzer concurs with the conclusions of German historian Hermann Greive, who produced two notable works that illustrate this very point.[17] Similarly, in his discussion of "redemptive antisemitism," noted historian of the Holocaust Saul Friedländer concludes, "The centrality of the Jews in this phantasmic universe [of Jew haters] can be explained only by its roots in the Christian tradition."[18]

Evidence of such Christian antisemitism may be found more regionally, for example, in the 1927 guidebook, *Our Lay Apostolate: What It Is and How It Should Be*, which was used to train and offer guidance to members of lay Church associations throughout Germany. Authored by Monsignor Maximilian Kaller, future bishop of Ermland, the chapter on the "Apostolate of Prayer for the Conversion of Israel," began by stating that Catholics have "a very strong dislike of Jewry."[19] Without fully clarifying this statement, Kaller continued to address this topic by differentiating between religious and secular Jews. According to Kaller, "enlightened 'modern' Jewry … is actually a shameful stain on the Jewish people. Stock market and business, art and theater, literature and press and, above all, politics are widely subjected to its destructive influence. This 'modern' Jewry undermines everything that is Christian and any religion and morality; it is composed of cynical egotism, sophisticated business sense and unscrupulous disdain of morality." For this reason, Kaller argued, Catholics had to defend themselves against this "Jewish danger" and overcome it "by any and all permissible means." By offering a caricature of the "modern" Jew, Kaller was clearly accepting the anti-liberalism and anti-socialism that was prevalent among German Catholics. This form of ideology identified Jews as the creators and proponents of a socialism that yearned for the removal of Christian values from public life.[20] Nevertheless, Kaller also stressed that Catholics, in conscience, could never adopt an antisemitism that preached "a struggle against the Jewish race" and sought "to destroy all Jews without exception or at the very least" expel them. According to Kaller, such antisemitism used "the Christian religion as a cloak for un-Christian feelings and political machinations." Instead, he reminded Catholics, they were obliged to love all individuals, including Jews, and had "to be resolute in rejecting and combating seduction." Interestingly enough, Kaller ended this section of his book by reminding his readers of Jesus' Jewish ancestry and by highlighting the fact that the Jewish people were the chosen people of God.[21]

Kaller's characterizations of Jews helped reinforce in Catholics negative stereotyping of Jews. Even if Kaller exhorted Catholics to respect and love the religious orthodox Jew and to reject and defend themselves against the actions of the so-called "modern" Jew, further on in his presentation he encouraged Catholics to pray for the salvation of Israel. In doing so, Kaller chose language that was also critical of the religious orthodox

Jew, the very same group he had singled out in a positive light and had contrasted with the "modern" Jew. The prayer Kaller cited read, "O God … we plead with you to turn a compassionate gaze on the remnants of the house of Israel, that they may acquire the knowledge of Jesus Christ, our only savior, and have a share in the precious grace of salvation. Amen. Father forgive them; for they do not know what they do!" In addition, Kaller encouraged Catholics to pray the last line of the prayer three times in succession, following the consecration of the Eucharist during Mass.[22]

Kaller's text was not the only publication that might have influenced the opinion of German Catholics towards Jews. The textbooks used by Catholics during their childhood religious education also contained comments on Jews in reference to biblical history. Texts such as the *Little School Bible* and *Bible History* identified Jews as the people who "demanded" Christ be put to death on the charge of blasphemy. These texts made it possible for Catholics at an early age to develop an aversion for their Jewish neighbors.[23] However, it is still difficult to determine the level of contempt Catholics had for Jews in their everyday lives. In addition, what is even more challenging is the fact that many Catholics who lived through the Weimar Republic and under National Socialism now deny having harbored any hostile feelings or ill-will towards their Jewish neighbors. This seems evident in an interview I conducted with Gertraud Tietz, a Berlin Catholic. When asked how priests and teachers in Catholic religious education classes portrayed Jews, Tietz, in retrospect, answered assuredly that although her teachers, mostly members of the laity, inferred that Jews had crucified Christ, they never made this issue the direct theme of a religion class, nor did they dwell on this point. Neither, according to her, did her teachers or priests teach her to hate Jews directly.[24] However, the handed-down assertions of her teachers of blaming the Jews for Christ's death defined, at least partially, the atmosphere in which an argument for antisemitism seemed reasonable.

To a greater degree, however, Kaller's understanding of the "modern" Jew revealed that Catholics, despite whatever education they may have received, were already confronted with more than just traditional religious prejudices against Jews before the 1930s. Kaller's notion of the "modern" Jew clearly incorporated into it secular antisemitic ideas, all of which viewed Jewish influence as detrimental to a Christian-based society. In the 1920s and 30s, racial antisemitism, which the extreme right-wing *Völkisch*, a nationalistically racial movement, publicly validated, elevated both pre-existing religious and secular prejudices against Jews to a national status. Consequently, according to *völkisch* philosophy, blood rather than religion became the determining factor in ascertaining Jewish identity. As a result, this line of thought not only affected thousands of Jews who had already converted to Christianity, but it also challenged the view that most Catholics held of Christians who, for centuries, were of Jewish heritage and of Jews in general, whether religious or secular, who were residents of their community.

During the Weimar Republic, the German Catholic hierarchy regularly did challenge the racial teaching of *völkisch* writers, especially those in the National Socialist camp. As early as March 21, 1931, Christian Schreiber, bishop of Berlin, exhorted Catholics to reject the National Socialist teaching that placed "race higher than religion."[25] Again, during a 1932 Christmas radio address, Schreiber called on Catholics to build bridges that transcended "all differences of parties, of ideology, of race and of religion."[26] Still the Catholic Church rejected racial teaching primarily because it came into conflict with Catholic dogma and teaching, not because it was harmful or offensive to Jews.

During the Weimar Republic, some leading clergymen such as Cardinal Michael von Faulhaber of Munich also responded positively to Jewish concerns. For example, in October 1920 following an attack by National Socialists on the character of Rabbi Dr. Leo Baerwald of Munich, the Central Association of German Citizens of Jewish Faith informed the cardinal of a statement they planned to print and distribute in support of the rabbi and against the Hitler party.[27] In response, Faulhaber wrote to the Association letting them know of his solidarity with Rabbi Baerwald since he too had "personally been in the same situation." Faulhaber added, "I can only wholeheartedly assent to the desire of the Central Association to teach the public speakers, and even more the press, more diligence."[28] Faulhaber would remain in regular contact with Rabbi Baerwald throughout the Weimar Republic and into the Third Reich.[29] Such regular contact and concern led Rabbi Baerwald to publicly condemn the treatment of Catholics in Mexico. Cardinal Faulhaber was so delighted by this action that he even wrote to the Holy See's *Osservatore Romano* and encouraged them to publish an article highlighting Rabbi Baerwald's action as "bold" and "courageous."[30] In 1927, during a gathering of Catholic clergy in Munich, Faulhaber himself condemned antisemitism by exhorting his priests "to avoid everything that smacks of antisemitic coloring."[31] Most probably, Faulhaber's involvement in *Amici Israel* encouraged him and other clerics to take such actions.

Despite these overtures, Faulhaber in his own writing revealed evidence of lingering traditional antisemitism. In his unpublished autobiography, for example, Faulhaber described individuals who participated in a real-estate deal with family members as being "worse than Jews."[32] He also negatively characterized Jews as "dominating commercial life in their oriental caftans" when recollecting a visit to the Jewish quarter in Łódz, Poland while a supervisor of military chaplains during the First World War.[33] Still, Faulhaber did not allow such feelings to color his sermons and public statements. Nevertheless, Faulhaber, like the majority of his fellow Catholic bishops and priests, truly believed that Jews as a people needed to be converted and that such conversion was part of the Church's mission. Though the Holy See today does not openly support such efforts of mass conversion, at that time it viewed such a venture as part of its global mission and as essential to fulfilling

Christ's commission here on earth. Of course, the Holy See wished its bishops and priests to bring all people to full membership in the Catholic Church, not just Jews, but Jews were always a concern as if the Holy See anticipated universal Jewish conversion as part of God's plan. Consequently, Faulhaber directly helped promote missionary work among Jews by sending to Palestine a recent Jewish convert to proselytize there.[34]

The ultimate goal of the Catholic Church at that time was to gather the people of the earth together and lead them to Christianity and full membership in the Catholic Church. Even though most Catholics understood this missionary goal, most lived and functioned within their limited world and milieu, not giving it much thought. Thus, when they interacted with people of different religious traditions, they chose to accept those people along with their beliefs as part of civic life. In these situations, the Catholic hierarchy was always concerned with Catholics losing their faith or being led astray. Still, because of the biblical injunction to "love your neighbor," the Catholic hierarchy also believed that Catholics needed to be involved in works of charity for those who were not of their faith. As Father Carl Sonnenschein, a prominent Catholic priest and writer in the Weimar Republic, had attested, there was no monopoly on doing works of charity. According to him, any group – whether Roman Catholic, Protestant, Salvation Army, Quaker, or Jewish – that worked to alleviate their neighbors' plight must show respect for all. In this way, anyone who endeavored to work in this fashion fulfilled the second great commandment of God: love your neighbor. In addition, Sonnenschein emphasized that this love of neighbor was not only limited to an individual's particular denomination or people, but instead was "formulated beyond ethnic boundaries by Christ" and therefore extended "beyond the boundary of denomination" as demonstrated in the Gospel's Good Samaritan story (Luke 10:25-37).[35] However, one problem seemed to linger: Who would be included in the category of neighbor?

Father Sonnenschein was not the only priest who addressed the question of "Who is one's neighbor?" In 1923, a newly ordained priest for the archdiocese of Munich and Freising, Father Josef Roth, decided to venture into the public arena and offer his own thoughts on the subject. Roth's own worldview was far removed from Father Sonnenschein's. Following his service as an infantryman in the Great War, Roth had become deeply involved in the German right-wing movement.[36] Feeling compelled to do even more for the right-wing movement, Roth gathered together his views on the "Jewish Question" and wrote a series of three articles that he subsequently submitted for publication to the National Socialist *Völkischer Beobachter*. Over the course of June 1923, the *Beobachter* published Roth's writing under the nondescript headline, "Catholics and the Jews." Two months later, Franz Eher, the NSDAP publishing house, collected these articles and published them as the tract *Catholicism and the Jewish Question*.[37]

Preceding Hitler's *Mein Kampf* by only a few years, Roth's work dealt with the Jewish question in almost equally harsh terms as Hitler. For example, Roth argued that Catholics had to move beyond their "catacomb antisemitism" and embrace the full teaching of their religion, which revealed an inherent antagonism between the Christian religion and Judaism. According to Roth, and in contrast to many theologians, it was not anti-Christian to profess racial antisemitism, but rather a religious "duty." Jews, he stated, transmitted immorality through their Jewish blood, which Catholics must resist. Consequently, for Roth, the Christian command to love one's neighbor excluded Jews, because from the very beginning every Jew was "already a latent danger for the Christian religion and morality" and for that reason "the Jewish race on account of the demoralizing influence inherent in its nature" had to be "eliminated from the public life and religion" of the German *Volk*. Roth assured his readers that this was the only true way to show genuine "love of neighbor toward Jews." If any Catholic had qualms about this practice, Roth assured them that the struggle to defend their homeland against Jewish national influence was "not a violation of the Christian love of neighbor," but a patriotic duty. Otherwise, he argued, Christ would also have to be "considered as un-Christian when he drove the traders and money-lenders from the temple." Furthermore, it was a "distortion of the command of Christian love of neighbor to demand that one should allow all unworthiness unhindered." Thus, he assured his readers that antisemitism today was "an act of self-defense. All Christian moral conditions for just self-defense" were present in their "stance against Jewry."[38]

Roth also insisted that "something must be done by Christianity and individual Catholic Christians to save, preserve, and protect its sacred goods by the elimination of Jews from public life." This, however, could not be accomplished by merely having the swastika as a "house ornament," nor through "new German names for the months" or "tasteless antisemitic treatises and slogans." "Little use" would be served if Germans only attempted to limit the "influence and activity of Jews" generally or by simply conducting "boycotts" against their businesses. Rather, he insisted, Germans needed to strike hard and elevate the Germanic *Volk* to eliminate "the worst influences." Germans could only accomplish this by duplicating the methods of the Inquisition and by totally eliminating the Jews' "rights as citizens." This solution would include expelling them "from all state offices," denying them "licenses for any trade and commerce," and prohibiting them from "any literary and propaganda activity."[39] Roth's proposed exclusionary measures against Jews were later echoed in the actual legislation that Hitler's government enacted during the course of the Third Reich.

Roth was not the only one among Catholic clergy who publicly and forthrightly expressed their antisemitism. There were more than 130 such clergymen who openly supported National Socialism and its racist ideology. Perhaps the most extreme was

Father Richard Kleine. As a priest of the Hildesheim diocese, since 1919 Kleine had served as a religion teacher at the Duderstadt Gymnasium.[40] Known affectionately as "Papa Kleine" by the thousands of students whom he taught over the years, Father Kleine was also greatly respected by his colleagues and continued to remain a presence in the Gymnasium, even years after his official retirement in 1957. Upon his death on April 1, 1974, the *Südhannoversche Volkszeitung* declared him "a good and well-respected human being and priest" who despite "the growing terror of anti-Christian and anti-Church forces in the National Socialist regime that wanted to remove him from office" anchored himself "more firmly in it."[41]

Though Kleine might have been a kind and dedicated priest to his "fellow Aryan Germans," he certainly did not display the same attitude toward anyone who fell outside this racial category. Kleine was a zealous adherent of National Socialism and devoted admirer of Adolf Hitler. He endeavored to reform his Church according to National Socialist principles and actively worked to graft the racial teaching of National Socialism into Catholicism. He even founded a National Socialist Priests' Group and solicited the help of Dr. Karl Adam, a priest of the Rottenburg diocese and a noted professor of systematic theology at the University of Tübingen, to assist him with his work.

After a year of intense discussion, in April 1941, Father Kleine felt he could trust Adam enough to reveal to him his work within the Catholic division of the Institute for the Study and Eradication of Jewish Influence on German Church Life Institute in Eisenach.[42] This revelation did not bother Adam in the least. Rather, he confided to Kleine that he lived and died "for the conviction that Christianity viewed and realized as a life force has been and remains the only viable form for the German people. Of course, its core must be freed from all Jewish-Hellenistic and, especially, from all medieval feudal and canonically ossified appendages."[43]

Adam's letter assured Kleine that they were nearly in agreement over how they viewed the current state of the Church and theology in Germany. Therefore, in his reply Kleine felt confident to assure Adam that the Eisenach Institute's Catholic division was specifically working to address the very points that he had raised, namely uncovering the "true" roots of Christianity that, in Kleine's view, existed far apart from Judaism. To this end, he invited Adam to join their work.[44] At the same time, Kleine sent him his essay, "Was Jesus a Jew?," which he had been circulating since 1939.[45]

In "Was Jesus a Jew?," Kleine did not follow the path of many *völkisch* theologians, who argued that Jesus was not Jewish but was born of Aryan ancestry. Instead, Kleine attempted to avoid answering this question directly. According to Kleine, as the offspring of his mother Mary and the paternal Holy Spirit, Jesus remained free of any negative Jewish traits. He explained, "the Church expressly denies that Mary stands in the succession of sinful depravity; therefore, all the more reason that what is so hereditarily corrupting in Jewry is excluded from her and also from Jesus."[46] Thus, even though Kleine technically did not say that Jesus was not Jewish, he did everything possible to separate him from his Jewish ancestry.

Kleine also labeled all Jews, including those who left their Jewish faith to follow Jesus, as troublesome. He wrote, "Indeed, even the baptized Jews, the Jewish Christians, by questionable behavior and, indeed, from the nature of their Jewish behavior, caused such serious difficult danger for the early Church that one must speak of this as the first great test of the Church; the *Acts of the Apostles* and the letters of the apostles are full of the reverberations of this struggle of life and death."[47] Further on in the essay, he clarified this point by explaining, "There are many bitter experiences for the Church … in cases where this precaution that the Jew remains a Jew after baptism just as a negro remains a negro, and the German a German was not minded." Kleine quickly caught himself and noted that, "Of course, we cannot think poorly of the supernatural effect of grace." For after all,

> a beneficial effect may be expected, even though only outwardly, from a drastic intervention in the east-Jewish ghettos in Poland, although one should never fail to see that this race can never be allowed to come close to our people or even to intermingle with them. The German *Volk* must in all circumstances be separated hermetically from Jewry, even if baptized. Also, in the Christian churches of our *Volk* the Jewish-Christians are unbearable. One could bring them together in Jewish-Christian parishes. We have already experienced in the case of the Poles who live in Germany, that – and indeed not only on account of their native Polish language – they remain an alien element in our parishes and feel so themselves. How much greater, then, is our distance from Jewry! Already in the early Church, the Jewish-Christians … led a special existence that created many and great difficulties for Christians from other peoples. … Only when a neat separation arose in Jewish-Christian communities could the Church there experience the strength of its mission for the peoples of this earth and was able to make itself felt.[48]

Kleine's arguments about Jesus' Jewish origins stimulated Adam's thinking. The theology professor was not content to allow the dialogue to end in a minor correspondence between the two individuals. Consequently, he wrote in 1943 "Jesus, the Christ, and We Germans,"[49] in which he repeated many of Kleine's original assertions about Christ, including his emphasis on Mary's Immaculate Conception as the means of exempting Jesus' inheritance from any negative Jewish traits.[50] In essence, Adam put Kleine's basic argument into publishable theological language and context.

Kleine's feeling of the urgency of his "mission" only intensified. On January 31, 1943, the German army finally showed that it was not invincible when General Field Marshal Friedrich von Paulus surrendered the *Wehrmacht's* sixth army to the Soviets following the failed battle of Stalingrad. Days later, on February 18, in the Berlin Sport Palace, Josef Goebbels, the Reich's Minister of Propaganda, delivered an address in which he declared a campaign of total war for Germany. Amid this chaos and almost apocalyptic atmosphere, Kleine prepared to do his part by authoring the essay "The Sermon on the Mount as a Challenge to Fight against Jewry." He believed such a publication would serve the effort of bringing a religious final solution to the "Jewish question." On April 25, 1943, Kleine wrote to Karl Dungs, a former Catholic priest and now chair of the Eisenach Institute's Catholic division, and asked to present his work at the next gathering in Vienna.[51] Dungs consented.[52]

On August 11, 1943, in Vienna, before his colleagues, Kleine presented "The Sermon on the Mount as a Challenge to Fight against Jewry." According to him, "the essential stumbling block between the National Socialist Reich and the Christian churches" was the relationship of Christianity to Judaism. For him, the inherent hostility between the two was not an "academic question" to be pondered, but a fact intrinsic to the Gospels themselves. Now, he argued, it was the task of Christian preachers "to comprehend the struggle of Jesus Christ against Judaism in all its depth and significance" and to give it an "appropriate, passionate expression in our preaching." In that vein, he exhorted his listeners, "it must be our most urgent task to present the Christian message from the viewpoint of the struggle of Jesus Christ against Judaism." Thus for Kleine, Jesus had first set forth his campaign against Jews in the Sermon of the Mount. Indeed, according to Kleine's exegesis of the well-known Gospel passage, Jesus himself initiated the campaign against the Jews at the very start of his ministry.

Those in attendance received Kleine's paper positively. Dungs was so impressed that he asked Kleine for permission to copy and distribute it among the Institute's membership. Of course, Kleine gave his consent.[53] Through such a work, Kleine had exceeded his earlier commitment to study the evils of Judaism and eradicate all Jewish influence in the Catholic Church. And Kleine did not display his zeal and dedication merely through writing and publishing. He traveled extensively through the Reich, meeting, speaking, and motivating like-minded individuals to work for the same cause. In April 1943, he admitted to his friend Adam that in the last nine months he had traveled more than 5,000 kilometers in an effort to disseminate his beliefs.[54]

Conclusion

The various foregoing examples of individual bishops and priests above illustrate the difficult relationship that existed between Catholics and Jews. Although priests such as Josef Roth and Richard Kleine represent a small right-wing group within the Catholic clergy, their thinking reveals the extent of antisemitism within German Catholicism. Despite cordial relations between some Church leaders and local Jewish communities, the clergy's view of Jews as "the Other" and "untrustworthy" did not go away. Instead, such belief, rooted in centuries of Christian antisemitism, remained strong. If it was not in the forefront of clerical consciousness, it was at least beneath the surface, existing there like the tip of a spear, sharpened by centuries of prejudice and ready to be hurled at the world.

Indeed, there were noble, enlightened individuals such as Father Dr. Engelbert Krebs, professor of dogmatic theology at the University of Freiburg, who in *The Early Church and Judaism* (1926) and subsequent publications, criticized attempts to separate Christianity from its Jewish origins while at the same time condemning antisemitism.[55] However, individuals such as Krebs were few and far between. While most bishops and priests were unwilling to support outward hatred toward any group, they still typically viewed Jews as threats to Christian society and moral order. In turn, these same clergymen neglected to condemn antisemitism in any bold or lasting way. Even Cardinal Faulhaber who was a trained biblical theologian of the Old Testament and who regularly corresponded with various Jewish religious leaders, failed to stand in solidarity with persecuted Jews. Evidence of this may already be seen in November 1932 when Faulhaber wrote to Rabbi Dr. Lehmann of the Jewish Reform Community of Berlin to thank him for the kind words concerning a recent pastoral letter on "The Ten Commandments in the Life of the German People and Other Peoples."[56] Rabbi Lehmann quickly wrote back to Faulhaber to thank him for his letter and asked if he might reprint the letter that spoke so eloquently about the "worth of the Old Testament and the overcoming of hatred through love" in his synagogue's newsletter.[57] In turn, Faulhaber responded with a politely worded negative answer, stating that his remarks were private between the rabbi and himself. The Cardinal then added, "In this regard I have enough experience that such statements just as the ones I spoke from the pulpit to protect the Jewish community following a pogrom against Jews in Munich or recorded in my letter to [Gustav] Stresemann result in a series of written abuses and newspaper articles. The letter contains nothing new and will provoke agitation in the many who have written to me without receiving an answer."[58]

In 1934, after Hitler came to power, Faulhaber would offer a similar response when some Jewish leaders attempted to interpret his 1933 Advent sermons on the importance and significance of the Old Testament as a defense of Jews against National Socialist attack. Faulhaber publicly rejected this interpretation and thus made it known that he would not publicly defend Germany's Jews.[59] Ultimately, the rest of the German hierarchy and the Vatican itself followed suit as if all had been felled by the same wind of indifference and prejudice.

Questions for Discussion

1. *Is there a link between Christian antisemitism and National Socialist racial antisemitism?*

2. *Does the term "Christian antisemitism" legitimately express the anti-Judaism found within the doctrine and tradition of the Catholic Church?*

3. *How representative are priests like Josef Roth and Richard Kleine of German Catholic religious leaders under National Socialism?*

Further Reading

Connelly, John. *From Enemy to Brother: The Revolution in Catholic Teaching on the Jews, 1933-1965* (Cambridge, MA: Harvard University Press, 2012).

Ehret, Ulrike. *Church, Nation and Race: Catholics and Antisemitism in Germany and England, 1918-45* (Manchester, UK: Manchester University Press, 2012).

Phayer, Michael. *The Catholic Church and the Holocaust, 1930-1965* (Bloomington, IN: Indiana University Press, 2000).

Spicer, Kevin P. "Catholic Life under Hitler," in *Life and Times in Nazi Germany*. Ed. Lisa Pine (London: Bloomsbury Press, 2016).

---------*Hitler's Priests: Catholic Clergy and National Socialism.* (DeKalb, IL: Northern Illinois University Press, in association with the U.S. Holocaust Memorial Museum, 2008).

---------(Ed.). *Antisemitism, Christian Ambivalence, and the Holocaust* (Bloomington, IN: Indiana University Press, in association with the United States Holocaust Memorial Museum, 2007).

---------*Resisting the Third Reich: The Catholic Clergy in Hitler's Berlin* (DeKalb, IL: Northern Illinois University Press, 2004).

Film and Video Resources

Heil Hitler: Confessions of a Hitler Youth (30 mins). Produced by HBO Films. Available at https://www.youtube.com/watch?v=JJ6umV7CVY8.

The Longest Hatred: A Revealing History of Anti-Semitism (150 mins). Produced by Frontline, PBS. Available at Amazon.com.

The Cross and the Star: Jews, Christians, and the Holocaust (52 mins). Produced by First Run Features. Available at Amazon.com.

Notes

1. Tim Kirk, *The Longman Companion to Nazi Germany* (NY: Longman, 1995), pp. 73, 167.
2. Olaf Blaschke, *Offenders or Victims? German Jews and the Causes of Modern Catholic Antisemitism* (Lincoln, NE: University of Nebraska Press and the Vidal Sassoon International Center for the Study of Antisemitism/The Hebrew University of Jerusalem, 2009), p. 41. Also see the essays in Olaf Blaschke (Ed.), *Konfessionen im Konflikt: Deutschland zwischen 1800 und 1970: ein zweites konfessionelles Zeitalter Göttingen* (Vandenhoeck & Ruprecht, 2002).
3. On this point, see Walter Zwi Bacharach, *Anti-Jewish Prejudices in German-Catholic Sermons* (Lewiston, NY: Edwin Mellon Press, 1993).
4. On this point, see Frank J. Coppa, *The Papacy, the Jews, and the Holocaust* (Washington, D.C.: The Catholic University of America Press, 2006), pp. x-xi. On the history of the deicide charge, see Jeremy Cohen, *Christ Killers: The Jews and the Passion: From the Bible to the Big Screen* (New York: Oxford University Press, 2007), and Robert Michael, *A History of Catholic Antisemitism: The Dark Side of the Church* (New York: Palgrave MacMillan, 2008). On the discussion of the responsibility for Jesus' death, see Mary C. Boys, *Redeeming Our Sacred Story: The Death of Jesus and Relations between Jews and Christians* (Mahwah, NJ: Paulist Press, 2013), and John Dominic Crossan, *Who Killed Jesus? Exposing the Roots of Anti-Semitism in the Gospel Story of the Death of Jesus* (New York: HarperCollins, 1995).
5. Alfons Heck of the Mosel Valley region of the Rhineland who grew up under National Socialism recalled in his memoir, "All Catholic children knew that the Jews had killed Christ, which seemed worse than being a Protestant"; see Alfons Heck, *A Child of Hitler: Germany in the Days When God Wore a Swastika* (Phoenix, AZ: Renaissance House, 2001), p. 14.
6. Blaschke, *Offenders or Victims?*, p. 34. Here Blaschke quotes from Bacharach, *Anti-Jewish Prejudices*, p. 59.
7. Among the members were Cardinal Michael von Faulhaber, archbishop of Munich and Freising; Cardinal Karl Joseph Schulte, archbishop of Cologne; Herman Wilhelm Berning, bishop of Osnabrück; Ludwig Maria Hugo, bishop of Mainz; and Johannes Leo von Mergel, bishop of Eichstätt. For the complete membership list, see *Pax Supra Israel*, Archiv des Erzbistums München und Freising (AEM) Nachlass (NL) Faulhaber 6284.
8. "De Concociatione Vulge 'Amici Israel' Abolenda," *Acta Apostolicae Sedis*, XX, 1928, p. 104. See also Hubert Wolf, "The Good Friday Supplication for the Jews and the Roman Curia (1928-1975): A Case Example for Research Prospects for the Twentieth Century," in *The Roman Inquisition, the Index and the Jews: Contexts, Sources and Perspectives*. Ed. Stephan Wendehorst (Leiden: Brill, 2004), p. 252.
9. Hubert Wolf, *Pope and Devil: The Vatican's Archives and the Third Reich*. Trans. Kenneth Kronenberg (Cambridge, MA: Harvard University Press, 2010), pp. 116-117.
10. Michael Kellogg, *The Russian Roots of Nazism: White Émigrés and the Making of National Socialism, 1917-1945* (Cambridge: Cambridge University Press, 2006), pp. 63-66.
11. On antisemitism and its link to Christianity, see Robert Michael, *Holy Hatred: Christianity, Antisemitism, and the Holocaust* (New York: Palgrave MacMillan, 2006), and Marvin Perry and Frederick M. Schweitzer, *Antisemitism: Myth and Hate from Antiquity to the Present* (New York: Palgrave Macmillan, 2002).
12. Here I adapt the model proposed by Karl Schleunes to explain the origins of the Holocaust. See Schleunes, *The Twisted Road to Auschwitz: Nazi Policy Toward German Jews, 1933-1939* (Champaign, IL: University of Illinois Press, 1970).
13. John Pawlikowski, "Historical Memory and Christian-Jewish Relations," in *Christ Jesus and the Jewish People Today: New Explorations of Theological Interrelationships*. Eds. Philip A. Cunningham, Joseph Sievers, Mary C. Boys, Hans Hermann Henrix, and Jesper Svartvik (Grand Rapids, MI: William B. Eerdmans Publishing Company, 2011), p. 22.
14. Mary C. Boys, *Redeeming Our Sacred Story*, p. 140.
15. On the origin of the word "antisemitism," see Moshe Zimmermann, *Wilhelm Marr: The Patriarch of Antisemitism* (Oxford: Oxford University press, 1987).
16. Peter Pulzer, *The Rise of Political Anti-Semitism in Germany & Austria*, Revised Ed. (London: Peter Halban, 1988), p. xxii.
17. Hermann Greive, *Theologie und Ideologie: Katholizismus und Judentum in Deutschland und Österreich, 1918-1935* (Heidelberg: Lampert Schneider, 1969), and *Geschichte des modernen Antisemitismus in Deutschland* (Darmstadt: Wissenschaftliche Buchgesellschaft, 1983).

18. Saul Friedländer, *Nazi Germany and the Jews/Vol. I: The Years of Persecution, 1933-1939* (New York: HarperCollins, 1997), p. 85. Also quoted in Richard Steigmann-Gall, *Antisemitism, Christian Ambivalence, and the Holocaust*. Ed. Kevin P. Spicer (Bloomington, IN: Indiana University Press, 2007), p. 289.
19. Maximilian Kaller, *Unser Laienapostolat: Was es ist und wie es sein soll* (Leutesdorf am Rhein: Johannesbund, 1927), p. 264. On June 14, 1927, the work had also received the Church's Imprimatur.
20. On this point, see Heinz Hürten, "Judenhaß-Schuld der Christen? Kirche und Antisemitismus im Wandel der Jahrhunderte," in *Wie im Himmel so auf Erden. 90. Deutscher Katholikentag vom 23. bis 27. Mai 1990 in Berlin/Vol. II: Dokumentation* (Paderborn: Bonifatius, 1990), p. 1500.
21. Kaller, *Unser Laienapostolat*, pp. 264-265.
22. Ibid, pp. 266-267.
23. The *Biblische Geschichte* reads, "The Jews demand the death of Christ on account of blasphemy." See Bischöflichen Ordinariat zu Berlin (Ed.), *Biblische Geschichte für das Bistum Berlin* (Berlin: Herder, n.d.), pp. 235-236, and Bischöfliches Ordinariat zu Berlin (Ed.), *Kleine Schulbibel für das Bistum Berlin* (Freiburg: Herder, n.d.), pp. 76-77.
24. Interview with Frau Gertraud Tietz, Berlin (December 19, 1996).
25. Pastoral Directives, March 21, 1931, in Gotthard Klein, *Berolinen Canonizationis Servi Dei Bernardi Lichtenberg. Sacerdotis Saecularis in Odium Fidei, Uti Fertur, Interfecti (1875-1943)/ Vol. II: Summarium – Documenta* (Rome: Congregation de Causis Sanctorum, 1992), p. 39.
26. *Germania* (December 25, 1932).
27. Zentral Verein Deutscher Staatsbürger Jüdischen Glaubens, Ortsgruppe Munich to Faulhaber (October 1, 1920), AEM NL Faulhaber 6281.
28. Faulhaber to Zentral Verein Deutscher Staatsbürger Jüdischen Glaubens, Ortsgruppe Munich (October 4, 1920), AEM NL Faulhaber 6281.
29. See evidence of their correspondence in AEM NL Faulhaber 6281.
30. Faulhaber to Baerwald (May 20, 1928), AEM NL Faulhaber 6282.
31. The October 1927 instruction was discussed in *Deutsche Israelitische Zeitung* (February 28, 1929).
32. AEM Faulhaber Autobiographie, f. 13.
33. AEM Faulhaber Autobiographie, f. 364.
34. See the correspondence concerning Olga S. in AEM NL Faulhaber 6281 and 6284.
35. Carl Sonnenschein, "Caritaspflicht," in *Notizen aus den Weltstadt-Betrachtungen, Vol. II*. Ed. Maria Grote (Frankfurt: Josef Knecht, 1951), p. 87.
36. SA-Führer Fragebogen (June 15, 1935), Bundesarchiv Berlin (BArch B) SA-Personalakte (PA) Roth.
37. *Völkischer Beobachter* (June 6-8, 1923).
38. Josef Roth, *Katholizismus und Judenfrage* (Munich: Franz Eher, 1923), pp. 2, 4, 6.
39. Ibid, p. 10.
40. Generalvikariat Hildesheim to Kleine (January 14, 1919), Archiv des Eichsfeld-Gymnasiums, Duderstadt (AEGD) PA Kleine, f. 10.
41. "Oberstudienrat i.R. Richard Kleine zum Gedenken," Newsletter of the Duderstadt Gymnasium, reprint of the April 2, 1974 obituary from *Südhannoversche Volkszeitung*, AEGD PA Kleine.
42. Kleine to Adam (April 6, 1941), Diözesanarchiv Rottenburg (DAR) NL 67 Adam, Nr. 33, f. 28. On the Eichsfeld Institute, see Susannah Heschel, *The Aryan Jesus: Christian Theologians and the Bible in Nazi Germany* (Princeton, NJ: Princeton University Press, 2008).
43. Adam to Kleine (May 12, 1941), Johann Adam Möhler Institut für Ökumenik, Paderborn (MIO) NL Kleine.
44. Kleine to Adam (June 3, 1941), MIO NL Kleine.
45. For example, see Kleine to Pircher (November 12, 1939), MIO NL Kleine. In March 1940, Kleine attempted to publish this article in *Der Neue Wille*. Though the editors of this Catholic weekly published other articles by Kleine, they refused to publish it. See Hübner/*Der Neue Wille* to Kleine (March 28, 1940), MIO NL Kleine.
46. Richard Kleine, "War Jesus ein Jude?," cir. 1939, MIO NL Kleine, f. 12.
47. Ibid, f. 7.
48. Ibid, ff. 9-10.
49. Adam, "Jesus, der Christus und Wir Deutsche," *Wissenschaft und Weisheit* 1/2, Nr. 10 (1943), pp. 73-103 and 3, Nr. 11 (1944), pp. 10-23.
50. Adam, "Jesus, der Christus und Wir Deutsche," 2, Nr. 10, p. 91.
51. Kleine to Dungs (April 25, 1943), MIO NL Kleine.

52. Dungs to Kleine (May 31, 1943), MIO NL Kleine.
53. Kleine to Dungs (August 19, 1943), and Dungs to Kleine (October 22, 1943), MIO NL Kleine.
54. Kleine to Adam (April 20, 1943), MIO NL Kleine.
55. Robert A. Krieg, *Catholic Theologians in Nazi Germany* (New York: Continuum, 2004), pp. 131-140.
56. Faulhaber to Lehmann (November 14, 1932), AEM NL Faulhaber 6281.
57. Lehmann to Faulhaber (November 27, 1932), AEM NL Faulhaber 6281.
58. Faulhaber to Lehmann (November 29, 1932), AEM NL Faulhaber 6281.
59. See Mary Alice Gallin, "The Cardinal and the State: Faulhaber and the Third Reich," *Journal of Church and State*, 12, 1970, pp. 385-404, and Theodore S. Hamerow, "Cardinal Faulhaber and the Third Reich," in *From the Berlin Museum to the Berlin Wall: Essays on the Cultural and Political History of Modern Germany*. Ed. David Wetzel (Westport, CT: Praeger, 1996), pp. 145-168.

BALLAD OF THE DOOMED JEWS OF EUROPE

FOUR MILLION JEWS waiting for death.
Oh hang and burn but—quiet, Jews!
Don't be bothersome; save your breath—
The world is busy with other news.

Four million murders are quite a smear
Even our State Department views
The slaughter with much disfavor here
But then—it's busy with other news.

You'll hang like a forest of broken trees
You'll burn in a thousand Nazi stews
And tell your God to forgive us please
For we were busy with other news.

Tell Him we hadn't quite the time
To stop the killing of all the Jews;
Tell Him we looked askance at the crime—
But we were busy with other news.

Oh World be patient—it will take
Some time before the murder crews
Are done. By Christmas you can make
Your Peace on Earth without the Jews.

*April 1943. New York. Ballad of the Doomed Jews of Europe by Arthur Szyk and Ben Hecht
Image Courtesy of The Arthur Szyk Society*

PART 3: *NOSTRA AETATE*

The Unfinished Reforms of *Nostra Aetate*: Five Areas for Further Consideration

Dennis McManus

Professor, Program for Jewish Civilization, Georgetown University, Washington, D.C.;
Professor, St. John's Seminary, Boston, MA

Introduction

Significant reforms in the Catholic Church are never achieved quickly or without considerable effort. Very famously, for example, the cult of Simon of Trent, a supposed child saint featured in blood libel literature of the late medieval period, was inaugurated by Pope Sixtus V in 1588, nearly a century after the boy's alleged murder in 1475.[1] The "blood libel," or belief that Jews kill Christian children to use their blood, usually in the making of Passover *matzohs*, was popular throughout the medieval period. Yet it fell finally to Alessandro Maria Gottardi, Archbishop of Trent (1963-1987) at the time of the Second Vatican Council, to suppress the cult definitively in his own city.

Still, it must be asked how a blood libel such as this one could have a nearly 500-year life span, stretching across no fewer than 50 papacies until, in our own day, Giovanni Baptista Montini as Pope Paul VI (1963-1978) ended it completely? The answer is simple: a reform as consequential as how the Catholic Church understood Jews and Judaism depended on a change of theology as profound as what *Nostra Aetate* provides us. In short, until the Church examined the roots of her theology of Judaism, her liturgy and doctrine would remain unchanged. Accordingly, the Archbishop of Trent's decree of suppression for the cult of Simon was signed on

October 29, 1965, the day following the promulgation of *Nostra Aetate* by Paul VI at the Second Vatican Council.[2]

It should come as no surprise, therefore, that extreme traditionalists in modern-day Trento still gather to observe the feast day of the blood libeled "Simonino," since these are the same Catholics who broke from Rome in 1998 under Marcel Lefebvre's leadership.[3] The theological understanding of Jews offered by Lefebvre's Priestly Society of St. Pius X – as can be found on its official website – still rejects the principal teachings of *Nostra Aetate*.[4] The ancient adage of the Fathers, *lex orandi, lex credendi*, or "the law of praying establishes the law of believing,"[5] reminds us that our liturgical celebrations often control both our expression of faith and our formation in it. There could be no clearer example of this principle than in the case of the cult of Simon of Trent. While the Society of St. Pius X, as the present face of the Levebvrist movement, maintains a pre-Vatican II theology of Jews and Judaism, the post-Conciliar liturgy of Paul VI has chosen to recast its expression on the basis of *Nostra Aetate*.[6]

Our effort here will be to examine the unfinished reform of the Catholic Church relative to the implementation of *Nostra Aetate* in five areas of her life and thought: (1) the development of an ecclesiology in which the Church, considered as subject, prays, teaches, and acts with an awareness of her own roots in the Judaism of Jesus and his people; (2) the reform of the Rites of Paul VI, otherwise known since July 7, 2007 as the "Ordinary Form" of the Roman Rite; (3) the "Extraordinary Form" or permissible celebration of the Rites of 1962;[7] (4) the preaching of bishops, priests, and deacons about Jews and Judaism; and (5) the Church's obligation to extend the meaning of *Nostra Aetate* into her ecumenical and interreligious affairs.

A *Nostra Aetate* Ecclesiology of the Church as "Subject"

One of the great contributions that *Nostra Aetate*, no. 4, made to the inner life of the Church was to state that "Since the spiritual patrimony common to Christians and Jews is thus so great, this sacred synod wants to foster and recommend that mutual understanding and respect which is the fruit, above all, of biblical and theological studies as well as of fraternal dialogues."[8] In this one pivotal sentence, the Council offers an important theological proposition: that when it comes to interreligious affairs, a shared spiritual patrimony and the possibility of dialogue are related as cause and effect. From within Catholic ecclesiology, then, dialogue with Jews is born not in self-defense, but in self-definition around a deeply shared Judaism now impossible to deny or extricate from the Church's own interiority. Though every pope since Vatican II has affirmed the unique influence of ancient Judaism's spiritual patrimony on the life of the Church, none have explored it or defined it in any depth.[9] So, the question remains: How does this shared patrimony affect the identity of the Church within herself, that is, relative to her own subjectivity and identity?[10]

The notion that the Church, so adeptly described in the summary images of *Lumen Gentium*, no. 6, where she is variously sheepfold, vineyard, edifice, or temple, Jerusalem and mother, could also be described as mystically "self-aware" or properly as a "subject" has its roots in the patristic theologies of Ambrose of Milan and Origen.[11] In our own day, Hans Urs Von Balthasaar, among others, devotes some consideration to this intriguing notion in the first volume of his theological aesthetics, *The Glory of the Lord*.[12] There, he proposes that a kind of subjectivity exists in the Church as a whole, even if realized mystically and proleptically, rising first within the individual.[13] And while modernity offers us new analogues in which to understand the interiority of the Church through the wide expansion of behavioral science and the inevitable deepening of human interiority through first-person narratives in the theo-dramatics of the modern period, perhaps it is the ancient patristic notion of *anima ecclesiastica* – or the ecclesiasticizing of an individual's consciousness – that helps most here in understanding the ecclesial contribution of *Nostra Aetate*, no. 4. In effect, through correspondence with grace, every Christian believer is fully enfolded into the greater collective self of the Church, aware of her bridal configuration to Christ. The *novum* of *Nostra Aetate*, no. 4, becomes clear, however, when we realize that the Church's configuration to the Messiah can only be Jewish at its origins and therefore wholly formative of her liturgy, self-discourse, and evangelization. What Walter Kasper has observed, however, about the progress of dialogue between the Church and Jews, can also be said about this aspect of the Church's dialogue with herself: "We are only at the beginning of the beginning."[14]

The true model for a credible *anima ecclesiastica*, ancient or modern, must be Mary, whose profound interiority in the acceptance of the Word makes her the *urs* Christian in respect of this same consciousness. However, it is doubtful that the Church can develop this Jewish aspect of interiority without first a comparable growth in an ecclesiology as framed, for example, by Augustine. For the Jews, he taught, are *ecclesia ante ecclesiam* or "the Church before the Church."[15] Thus, the close interconnection of Mary as a woman and a Jewish believer and the Church as bride and body of Christ is the inevitable starting point for an ecclesiology of *Nostra Aetate*.

Nostra Aetate and the Reformed Liturgy of Paul VI

There could be no doubt that by 1975 certain texts and Rites of the Roman liturgy were dramatically revised in light of the Council's condemnation of anti-Judaism and antisemitism. Perhaps the most symbolic of such prayers was the Good Friday Liturgy's *Pro Conversione Iudaeorum* ("For the Conversion of the Jews"), present in the *Missale Romanum* since the reform of Pius V in July of 1570. As Annibale Bugnini, then secretary of the Concilium appointed for the revision of the Rites on January 3, 1964, remarked, "In the ecumenical climate of Vatican II, some expressions in the *Orationes sollemnes* of the Good Friday service had a bad ring to them. There were urgent requests to tone down some of the wording."[17] It would appear that Paul VI's thinking in the revision of this prayer was indeed influenced by the second-to-last draft of the text of *Nostra Aetate*.[18] As a result, we can assume that many of the previous anti-Jewish expressions or patristic compositions included in the Roman liturgy, especially in Holy Week, were excised with the teachings of *Nostra Aetate* in mind. This was certainly the case, for example, with the removal of Melito of Sardis' deicidal line in his hymn for Holy Saturday Matins, which accused the Jews of killing Christ as God.[19] The newly revised Office of Readings for the same day has omitted Melito's offending expressions, while retaining the balance of his lyrically typological homily about the death of Jesus.[20]

But can we say that even the Liturgy of Paul VI has been completely renewed in light of *Nostra Aetate* and that deeper ecclesiology referred to above? Are there still passages in today's Roman Liturgy that appear to conteract the letter or even the spirit of *Nostra Aetate*? A few examples may suffice to illustrate how the liturgical Concilium, lacking a full understanding of the implications of *Nostra Aetate*, chose to revise sometimes only a "superficial" anti-Judaism throughout the Church's Rites. In addition, the reformers may have actually introduced new schemes that merely disguised the problem of anti-Judaism under the protective banner of what were thought to be one or more modernizing principles. For example, while excision of problematic texts was widely used as a tool for reform in the Liturgy of the Hours, not all such instances were recognized, as in the case of the opening passage of Cyril of Jerusalem's catechetical instruction on the Church as the bride of Christ, found in the Office of Readings for Thursday of the 17th Week in Ordinary Time:

> The first assembly, that is, the assembly of Israel, was rejected, and now in the second, that is, in the Catholic Church, God has appointed first, apostles, second prophets ...[21]

Surely Cyril's obvious rejectionism (along with his implied supercessionism) violates the doctrinal claims of *Nostra Aetate*, no. 4, specifying that, in fact, God has not rejected the Jews and that they may not be thus presented in the Liturgy, as if this claim followed in some way from an acceptable reading of the Sacred Scriptures.[22]

Other liturgical questions might also be raised relative to the construction of the revised liturgical calendar. Why, for example, was the feast of the Circumcision – one of the few liturgical observances of the key moments in the covenantal initiation of Jesus – dropped from the 1969 General Roman Calendar of Paul VI? Its centuries-old celebration on the eighth day following Christ's nativity was itself an echo of its original Jewish observance, legitimated throughout the Bible without countless other Jewish males thereby made full members of the covenant of Abraham. In reintroducing in its place a previously entitled feast day centering on the motherhood of Mary, it may be asked whether the removal of this feast doesn't both de-historicize and de-Judaize Jesus at a time when reaffirming his Jewish identity is key to the reforms suggested by *Nostra Aetate*, no. 4.

More broadly, the elimination of nearly one dozen other feasts of Jewish figures from the Old Testament which the liturgical calendar of 1570 celebrated within the Roman Rite (such as the Maccabean martyrs on August 1) only reinforces the impression that the Concilium was either guided by a simplistic concept of anti-Judaism – possibly due to the late signing of *Nostra Aetate* (October, 1965) as the final document of the Second Vatican Council, lagging far behind the liturgical reform already begun with the signing of *Sacrosanctum Concilium* as the first document produced by the Council in December 1963 – or that it lacked any coherent sense of the problem to begin with. It is noteworthy that despite the widespread presence of overt anti-Judaism in the euchologies of many Eastern Church liturgies, their liturgical calendars still reflect a profound inclusion of Jewish and non-Jewish figures from the Old Testament.[23]

Other deep structure questions can also be raised in connection with the revision of the Sunday Lectionary, whose first and third readings for any given Sunday or Solemnity of the Lord are, by design, meant to be understood basically in a typological fashion. In short, the revisers of the Lectionary for Mass used a so-called "principle of harmony" to justify their pairing of an Old Testament reading with a gospel pericope that suggests a dominantly typological interaction between the two. The Lectionary Introduction describes this technique, linking it inexplicably to "the hermeneutical principles whose understanding and definition have been facilitated by modern biblical research" (no. 64). The "principle of harmony" is then more fully defined:

> 67. The best instance of harmony between the Old and New Testament readings occurs when it is one that Scripture itself suggests. This is the case when the doctrine and events recounted in texts of the New Testament bar a more or less explicit relationship to the doctrine and events of the Old Testament. The present Order of Readings selects Old Testament texts mainly because of their correlation with New Testament texts read in the same Mass, and particularly with the Gospel text.[24]

What lies unexamined in the "principle of harmony" identified by the reformers is that the multiple meanings of Old Testament texts, even considered from within the ancient four-fold schema of literal, typological, moral, and spiritual senses, are thereby reduced to corresponding only with their partner text in the gospel of the day. In fact, however, the Hebrew Scriptures carry both an original, literal meaning that conveys God's self-revelation in its own context, as well as a secondary meaning that interacts typologically with subsequent revelation. This important point was treated at length in the Pontifical Biblical Commission's 2002 document, *The Jewish People and Their Sacred Scriptures in the Christian Bible*.[25]

There, the Commission was at pains to offer two reminders to a post-*Nostra Aetate* Church about how the Old and New Testament are to be read, especially in a liturgical context. First, the Commission stated that the "writings of the New Testament acknowledge that the Jewish Scriptures have a permanent value as divine revelation. They have a positive outlook towards them and regard them as the foundation on which they themselves rest" (no. 8). In short, the Old Testament does not derive its truth or legitimacy from the New, but from being the Word of God. Second, readers are warned that reductionistic readings of the Old Testament, no matter the context, lead to what the Commission terms "one-sidedness" and introduce a serious risk that the original meaning and authority of the Old Testament text is lost rather than fulfilled inside of the New: "On the part of Christians, the main condition for progress along these lines lies in avoiding a one-sided reading of biblical texts, both from the Old Testament and the New Testament, and making instead a better effort to appreciate the whole dynamism that animates them, which is precisely a dynamism of love (no. 86)."[26]

As a result, the issue raised above about the application of the reformers' principle of harmony in the arrangement of readings from the Bible within all of the liturgical books of the Roman Rite, and not simply in the Lectionary for Mass, remains a lively one. What is at stake is the liturgy's acknowledgement of the full import of the Jewish Scriptures both in terms of the revelation they contain and in relation to the fullness of that revelation to come in Christ. Any diminishment of the Jewish character of the Scriptures, even by this style of liturgical reductionism, seems out of keeping with *Nostra Aetate* and its subsequent interpretation by the Church in *The Jewish People and Their Sacred Scriptures in the Christian Bible*.

While there can be no calling into question of the principle of "fulfillment theology" so rightly recognized by the Commission's document (see section I.b.6) and profoundly appreciated in then-Cardinal Joseph Ratzinger's *Preface* to the Commission report of 2001,[27] it remains fair to ask whether its current application throughout the Rites is consistent with the spirit of Conciliar teaching as found in *Nostra Aetate*.

Nostra Aetate in the Revision of the Extraordinary Form of the Roman Rite

A final note is appropriate on the establishment of the "Extraordinary Form" of the Roman Rite in light of the demands of *Nostra Aetate*. Because the July 7, 2007, *motu proprio* of Benedict XVI, *Summorum Pontificum*, allowed the widespread celebration of the Roman Rite as found in the liturgical books of 1962, the Church in some sense is asked to reconsider how these very same texts and Rites are to be read in light of

Nostra Aetate. The restoration of a broader use of this more limited observance of the Roman Rite has retrieved along with it the anti-Jewish texts of the liturgy, originally reformed after the Council of Trent, but subsequently excised or recomposed in the reform of Paul VI from 1965 to 1974. Should the present celebration of the Rites of 1962, as allowed under *Summorum Pontificum*, be re-examined through the lens of *Nostra Aetate*?

Perhaps a way forward was offered by Pope Benedict himself when on February 5, 2008, he altered the text of the Good Friday bidding prayer for the Jews in the *Missale Romanum* of 1962. His deputy in charge of religious relations with the Jews, Cardinal Walter Kasper, wrote a detailed explanation of how the Ratzinger revisions to this most symbolic of all prayers about the Jews in the Missale Romanum remains, in fact, in line with the reforms of *Nostra Aetate*.[28]

Just over two years earlier, the Pope had also recommitted himself to implementing the goals of *Nostra Aetate* on the occasion of its 40th anniversary, when he remarked that there was still "need to overcome past prejudices, misunderstandings, indifference and the language of contempt and hostility [and to continue] the Jewish-Christian dialogue … to enrich and deepen the bonds of friendship which have developed."[29] As a result, the Pope's first principle of the reform of the Rites of 1962 in the Extraordinary Form – the elimination of negative language about Jews – should be taken as an already-proven method.

A second principle that Benedict cited in *Summorum Pontificum* was the addition of new texts, even to the *Missale* of 1962, as an admission that the liturgy, even in its post-Tridentine form, should continue to grow at least in both the addition of Mass propers to the sanctoral cycle and in the introduction of new prefaces.[30] While this predictably horrified some critics, it also affirmed the same principle that was used in the liturgical reforms of Paul VI.

Taken altogether, then, three usable guidelines can be derived from Pope Benedict's own reform of the Rites of 1962: (1) the excision of negative language about Jews and Judaism from existing texts, (2) the addition of new prayers to the corpus of the euchology, and (3) the recomposition of existing prayers where their theological content or style is judged inadequate for one or another pastoral or doctrinal reason. If judiciously applied to the Extraordinary Form, these three "Benedictine" principles could well result in a properly post-*Nostra Aetate* liturgy that also meets the Pope's original intentions in this secondary liturgical reform following that of Vatican II.[31]

The Preaching of Ordained Ministers in the Liturgy

Since the promulgation of *Nostra Aetate* on October 28, 1965, the Catholic Church both universally and locally has issued an impressive set of statements about the implementation of this key document in Catholic-Jewish relations. No fewer than ten important documents have been published to assist ordained preachers in their all-important ministry.³² A most recent papal addition is found in Pope Francis' personal reflection on effective preaching in Chapter Three of his first encyclical, *Evangelii Gaudium* (November 24, 2013).

In all of these statements, sound homiletic principles are presumed in delivering the gospel message with conviction and credibility. More to the point, however, is the way in which *Nostra Aetate*'s message is variously brought to bear on post-Conciliar homilies: that ordained preaching must present both the Judaism of Jesus and his followers, as well as the faith of Jews today, with accuracy and respect, all the while embracing the four great repudiations of *Nostra Aetate*.³³ Not surprisingly, the principal focus of both the Vatican and USCCB documents is two-fold: (1) the avoidance of prejudiced expressions against Jews and Judaism, and (2) the presentation of the Judaism of Jesus as the essential foundation for God's plan of salvation.

What these documents overlook, however, is an underlying question about all preaching on Jews and Judaism in a Catholic context: How does one read the biblical text so as to avoid prejudice against Jews and to capture as fully as possible the message of the sacred author? Surprisingly, this topic is left unaddressed in the two American documents that have formed the preaching of the ordained since at least 1982, *Fulfilled in Your Hearing* and *Preaching the Mystery of Faith* (2013). While both documents are clear in their call for respecting Jews and Judaism in Catholic liturgical preaching, it is on the level of exegeting the literal sense of any given biblical passage that they bypass this essential question. Instead, the documents choose only to detail the needs of the listening community and to focus on the methods and techniques of homiletic preparation. As a result, if the *Nostra Aetate* question about avoiding anti-Judaism is to be used as an effective tool for liturgical reform, then we must turn elsewhere to gain some sense of how a preacher or teacher of a Lectionary text may approach their task with commensurate exegetical skills.

The answer comes to us in a seminal talk given by Pope John Paul II on October 31, 1997, entitled *The Roots of Anti-Judaism in the Catholic Church*.³⁴ His address was delivered at the conclusion of a challenging Vatican conference entitled *Radici dell'antigiudaismo in Ambiente Christiano* ("The Roots of Anti-Judaism in Christian Circles"), convened to examine the state of anti-Judaism as a religious belief that discounted the value of Judaism as a religion, versus antisemitism, which classified Jews as an inferior and threatening racial sub-group.

In his closing address to the international scholars assembled in Rome for this occasion, the pontiff lays out for the first time ever in papal discourse a criticism of the patristic anti-Judaism that had controlled so much of the reading of Scripture for centuries. He is cautious in his expression, but clear:

> The goal of your symposium is the correct theological interpretation of the relations of the church of Christ with the Jewish people, for which

the Conciliar declaration *Nostra Aetate* has laid the foundation and about which I have had occasion to speak a number of times in the exercise of my ministry. Indeed, in the Christian world – I am not saying on the part of the church as such (*je ne dis pas de la part de l'Eglise en tant que telle*) – erroneous and unjust interpretations of the New Testament relative to the Jewish people and their presumed guilt circulated for too long (*des interpretations erronees et injustes du Nouveau Testament relatives au peuple juif et a sa pretendue culpabilite ont trop longtemps circule, engendrant des sentiments d'hostilite a l'egard de ce peuple*), engendering sentiments of hostility toward this people. That contributed to a lulling of many consciences (*a assoupir bien des consciences*) so that – when Europe was swept by the wave of persecutions inspired by a pagan anti-Semitism that in its essence was equally anti-Christian – alongside those Christians who did everything to save those who were persecuted, even to the point of risking their own lives, the spiritual resistance of many was not what humanity rightly expected of Christ's disciples. Your thoughtful attention to the past, in view of achieving a purification of memory, is particularly opportune for showing clearly that anti-Semitism is without any justification and is absolutely condemnable.[35]

Behind the *papalese* of his expression here, John Paul is accusing certain Fathers of the Church of exegetical bias in reading New Testament texts through the lens of supposed Jewish guilt for the death of Jesus. Perhaps the most explosive of these writings is Augustine's famous *Contra Faustum* (c. 400 C.E.), in which he compares the relationship of Jews to Christians with that of Cain to Abel (PL *Contra Faustum* 12.9: 259). More such writing would follow in the homilies and commentaries of the other Fathers, eventually creating a kind of anti-Jewish hermeneutic in the patristic world, though by no means making it an exclusive one.[36]

John Paul's next step – to identify the morally numbing effect of such readings on the consciences of their listeners – and then to relate it as partial cause and effect for the inaction of Catholics in the face of the Holocaust in Europe is breathtaking. In short, John Paul is claiming that the anti-Judaism of a Justin Martyr- or Augustinian-style exegesis reduces the moral responsiveness of Catholic hearers, who are convinced that Jews in some way deserve their deaths at the hands of the Nazis as God's punishment for their first killing Christ.[37]

The solution, of course, to John Paul's indictment of this form of biased patristic exegesis is to learn to read the Bible in its Jewish context and to do so as a part of establishing the literal sense of any Scriptural passage. For just as Pius XII's 1952 *Divino Afflante Spiritu* opened up the literal sense of a text to include both its philology and literary form, so, too, does John Paul's criticism and later commentary expand the literal sense to retrieving as best as possible the Jewish context in which Scripture was written, including its cultural, social, religious, and political elements. When a Gospel text, for example, is separated from its Jewish context and read otherwise merely in a Hellenistic or even Roman context, two effects are likely: (1) the Judaism in the text is erased or minimized, and (2) Jesus is inevitably separated from his Jewish identity. For John Paul, this distancing of Jesus from his Jewishness could only have been a step away from the centuries-long process of "otherization" of Jews by Christians who as a result cannot see the relation between Jesus and his people today.[38]

If the message of *Nostra Aetate* is to influence the content of preaching in the Catholic Church, this important methodological adjustment must be integrated into biblical studies along with homiletic instruction. It is no longer sufficient for the preacher merely to avoid the negative, but instead, he must break open the Word fully in its original Jewish context, ready for adaptation by the modern believer.[39]

Extending *Nostra Aetate* into the Church's Ecumenical Relations

Every Pope from Paul VI to Francis has repeatedly stated that the reform of the Church in our time is guided by the work of the Second Vatican Council. No other body of Church deliberations – even Roman synods – compares with the authority or weightiness accorded to Conciliar decisions. One area in which most of the Conciliar mandates have been well-implemented is that of ecumenical and interreligious affairs. Whereas before the Council these sorts of relations were minimal at best, in the post-Conciliar period they have flourished.[40]

However, it might be asked whether the implementation of *Nostra Aetate* does not also extend to dialogues in both of these critical areas. Consequently, we might ask, "Shouldn't ecumenical conversations, especially with Eastern churches and the Orthodox communion, undertake a discussion of the *Nostra Aetate* question about the way in which Jews and Judaism are portrayed in the divine liturgy?" The presence of religious anti-Judaism in some Eastern Catholic and Orthodox liturgies, most especially during celebrations of Holy Week and the Easter Season, is undeniable. Well-established by scholars in every instance, overt anti-Jewish expression can be found in many Eastern Rite liturgies with some exception, as in the case of the Maronite Church, which has reformed its expression in light of *Nostra Aetate*. Examples in the Byzantine,[41] Syriac,[42] Ethiopian, Ukranian,[43] and Russian Rites,[44] for example, would surely trigger the cautions of *Nostra Aetate*, hopefully leading to a deeper exchange between the Churches while avoiding a counterproductive intrusion into autonomous internal affairs. The first step in such an exchange would be to raise the *Nostra Aetate* questions within existing dialogue structures where they can bear the weight of such added projects. Some attempt at public discussion between Eastern Churches and Orthodox communities with various Jewish groups has already been made in this regard.[45]

The same issue of how Jews are understood and treated also surfaces in Catholic-Protestant dialogue.[46] A famous instance in which such understandings played a role can be found in the 2001 joint statement of the Southern Baptist Convention and the Bishops Committee on Ecumenical and Interreligious Affairs.[47] There, the dialogue concluded without any agreement to continue, given the background seriousness of disagreement about the salvation of those who do not believe in Christ. Subsequently, Vatican-Baptist colloquia have successfully met to consider issues in sacramentality, ecclesiology, Mariology, and baptism.[48] Could the pontificate of Francis be the opportunity to recommence such earlier local dialogues where feasible and to revisit the *Nostra Aetate* questions about Jews and Judaism in the course of an established agenda, at least *en passant*?

There is, however, nowhere in U.S. Catholic-Protestant dialogue where the influence of *Nostra Aetate* is more keenly at play than in the present controversy over boycott, divestment, and sanctions (BDS) against Israel as a form of protest against Israeli policies related to the Palestinian conflict. The USCCB on this issue continues to attempt to balance the rights of Israel with those of the Palestinian minority but remains bound by the essential religious commitments of *Nostra Aetate*.[49] USCCB dialogues with the Presbyterian Church USA and other major proponents of BDS policies are greatly impacted by this influence.[50]

Conclusion

Before starting his final trip to Israel in celebration of the millennial year 2000, John Paul II led a series of penitential bidding prayers at Mass in St. Peter's Basilica.[51] That occasion was, in fact, the first Sunday of Lent in the liturgical year of 1999, and then-Cardinal Ratzinger (soon to succeed John Paul II as Benedict XVI) shared with him in the public offering of these prayers,[52] partially intending to bring John Paul's 1986 dynamic apologies to the Jewish community into the Roman Rite itself.

It has been widely recognized that without John Paul's linking of *Nostra Aetate* to heartfelt public apologies for acts of anti-Judaism and antisemitism done by Catholics, Jews would not be able to see in the Church's conversion a true *tshuvah*, or repentance, on Jewish terms. This was never visually more poignant than when the Pope, so clearly devastated by Parkinson's disease, took his final, unsteady walk across the open expanse of floor near Yad Vashem's eternal flame to greet a line of Holocaust survivors one by one.[53] He had refused in that moment to remain at his chair, but insisted on going to them, no matter the effort. The Pope's touching struggle to honor the dignity of each survivor was itself an apology in motion.

Today, as we observe the 50th anniversary of *Nostra Aetate*'s promulgation, Jewish voices are questioning their own response to the changes made by the Catholic Church in the first half-century since the *Shoah*.[54] Many ask about the feasibility of dialogue, searching for an authentic Jewish approach beyond *Dabru Emet* (2002)[55] and the even earlier strictures suggested by Rav Joseph Soloveitchik in his now-famous 1964 essay, *Confrontation*,[56] that now appears as a startling bookend to *Nostra Aetate*. Could it be, however, that John Paul's dramatic simplicity at Yad Vashem has answered this question for Jews and Christians alike? For by his example, there can be only one genuine starting point for dialogue: that of *tshuvah* humbly offered and likewise received.

Let the dialogue begin.

Questions for Discussion

1. *What are some of the challenges that still face Christians – Roman Catholic, Protestant, and Orthodox – today, so many years after the Holocaust, Vatican II, and years of dialogue between and among them?*

2. *How are Christian concepts and ideas about* tshuvah *("repentance") similar to and different from Jewish concepts and ideas? How can we Christians and Jews find a way to "bridge the gap" between our views about* tshuvah? *Explain.*

3. *Consider the visits of three (3) popes to Israel (Pope John Paul II, Pope Benedict XVI, and Pope Francis). How did each of their visits contribute to or impede dialogue and understanding between Jews and Catholics and Christians in general? Be concrete and specific in your response.*

4. *What "unfinished business" did each of their visits to Israel leave for future generations of Christians and Jews?*

Further Reading

Banki, Judith H., and John T. Pawlikowski, O.S.M. (Eds.). *Ethics in the Shadow of the Holocaust: Christian and Jewish Perspectives* (Chicago, IL: Sheed and Ward, 2001).

Boys, Mary C., and Sara S. Lee, *Christians & Jews in Dialogue: Learning in the Presence of the Other* (Woodstock, VT: Skylight Paths Publishing, 2006).

Connelly, John. *From Enemy to Brother: The Revolution in Catholic Teaching on the Jews, 1933-1965* (Cambridge, MA: Harvard University Press, 2012).

Cunningham, Phillip. *Seeking Shalom: The Journey to Right Relationship between Catholics and Jews* (Grand Rapids: Eerdmans, 2015).

Levine, Amy-Jill. *The Misunderstood Jew: The Church and the Scandal of the Jewish Jesus* (New York: Harper Collins, 2006).

Film and Video Resources

Abraham Joshua Heschel's Vision of a New Jewish-Christian Relationship and Its Continuing Importance for Today (81 mins). Produced by Institute for Jewish-Catholic Relations. Available at https://www.kaltura.com/index.php/extwidget/preview/partner_id/763372/uiconf_id/14692631/entry_id/1_g4swd4lo/embed/auto?

The Church and the Jews: Fifty Years Since Vatican II (85 mins). Produced by Philip Cunningham and David Berger at the University of Scranton. Available at https://www.youtube.com/watch?v=XTGb9WH6Ag4&feature=youtu.be.

Mind the Gap: Bridging One Dozen Lacunae in Jewish-Catholic Dialogue (58 mins). Produced by the Boston College Center for Christian-Jewish Learning. Available at http://frontrow.bc.edu/program/cook/.

Notes

1. For an overview of the history of the blood libel together with a listing of the trial documents in the case of Simon of Trent, see Richard Gottheill, Hermann L. Strack, and Joseph Jacobs, "Blood Accusation," reprinted online from the 1906 *Jewish Encyclopedia* at http://www.jewishencyclopedia.com/articles/3408-blood-accusation. In the same reprint, see Joseph Jacobs and Aaron Tanzer, "Simon (Simdel, Simoncino) of Trent," at http://www.jewishencyclopedia.com/articles/13752-simon-simedl-simoncino-of-trent. Perhaps the clearest history for its step-by-step account of the forensic evidence in the case of Simon of Trent remains R. Po-Chia Hsia's *Trent 1475: A Ritual Murder* (New Haven: Yale University Press, 1996).
2. Throughout this paper, the text of *Nostra Aetate* cited is taken from the *Acta Apostolica Sedis*, formally cited as *Concilium* Vaticanum II, *Decretum de Ecclesiae Habitudine ad Religiones non-Christianas*, Nostra Aetate AAS 58 (1966) 740-744. Readers are advised, however, that the Holy See occasionally emends its texts and their vernacular translations on its official website, available at http://www.vatican.va/archive/hist_councils/ii_vatican_council/documents/vat-ii_decl_19651028_nostra-aetate_en.html. See Note 8 below.
3. For a pro-Lefebvre account of the breakaway movement, see the documentary *Monseigneur Lefebvre, un évêque dans la tempête*, originally released as *Marcel Lefebvre – Archbishop in Stormy Times* in the U.S. and U.K. This is a 2012 production by French director Jacques-Régis du Cray, primarily based on Bernard Tissier de Mallerais' *The Biography* (Kansas City, MO: Angelus Press, 2004).
4. See http://sspx.org/en/node/1342 accessed on 05.30.16; cf. also John Vennari, *Judaism and the Church: Before and After Vatican II*, available at http://sspx.org/en/node/1342, and especially his article at the same website, "Has Made Obsolete the Former One," for its supercessionist position relative to Judaism. Of note is an unsupported claim that modern Judaism is based "on a rejection of the Messiah."
5. See Prosper of Aquitaine's famous description of the meaning of this phrase in his *De vocatione omnium gentium*, 1, 12 (PL 51, 664C): *obsecrationum quoque sacerdotalium sacramenta respiciamus, quae ab apostolis tradita, in toto mundo atque in omni catholica Ecclesia uniformiter celebrantur, ut legem credendi lex statuat supplicandi* ("Let us also look upon the sacraments of priests' prayers, which were handed down from the Apostles and are celebrated uniformly in every Catholic Church throughout the world, so that the law of praying may uphold the law of believing"; translation mine).
6. The Good Friday prayer for the Jews provides an excellent example of the change from pre- to post-Conciliar liturgical expression based on *Nostra Aetate*. The *Missale Romanum* (1960) offers this text: *Oremus et pro Iudaeis: ut Deus et Dominus noster auferat velamen de cordibus eorum; ut et ipsi agnoscant Iesum Christum Dominum nostrum. Oremus. Flectamus genua. Levate. Omnipotens sempiterne Deus, qui Iudaeos etiam a tua misericordia non repellis: exaudi preces nostras, quas pro illius populi obcaecatione deferimus; ut, agnita veritatis tuae luce, quae Christus est, a suis tenebris eruantur* ("Let us pray for the Jews, that our Lord and God may lift the veil from their hearts that they may acknowledge our Lord Jesus Christ. Let us pray. Let us kneel. Let us stand. Almighty, ever-living God, who do not reject even the Jews from your mercy, hear our prayers which we

offer for this people's blindness, that when informed by the light of your truth who is Jesus Christ, they may be delivered from their darkness"; translation mine). The third typical edition of the post-Conciliar *Missale Romanum* (2000) shows a dramatic difference: *Oremus et pro Iudaeis, ut, ad quos prius locutus est Dominus Deus noster, eis tribuat in sui nominis amore et in si foederis fidelitate proficere. Omnipotens sempiterne Deus, qui promissiones tuas Abrahae eiusque semini contulisti, Ecclesiae tuae preces clementer exaudi, ut populus acquisitionis prioris ad redemptionis mereatur plenitudinem pervenire.* The 2011 English translation of this prayer, as found in *The Roman Missal as Approved for Use in the Dioceses of the United States of America* (Chicago: Liturgy Training Publications, 2011), p. 323, reads as follows: Let us also pray for the Jewish people, to whom the Lord our God spoke first, that he may grant them to advance in love of his name and in faithfulness to his covenant. Almighty ever-living God, who bestowed your promises on Abraham and his descendants, graciously hear the prayers of your Church, that the people you first made your own may attain the fullness of redemption." As can be plainly seen, all the negative language used to characterize Jews, even if adopted from biblical sources, has been replaced in the reformed text by positive expressions that reflect the non-punitive understanding of Jewish history found in *Nostra Aetate*, no. 4.

7. See Benedict XVI, Introductory Letter accompanying *Summorum Pontificum* at http://w2.vatican.va/content/benedict-xvi/en/letters/2007/documents/hf_ben-xvi_let_20070707_lettera-vescovi.html.

8. Throughout this study, the English translation of *Nostra Aetate* is taken from the Vatican's Website text, now considered an official source for both the original Latin and subsequent vernacular translations subject to occasional editing, as found at http://www.vatican.va/archive/hist_councils/ii_vatican_council/documents/vat-ii_decl_19651028_nostra-aetate_en.html. Emendations to Conciliar texts are customarily reported in the *Acta Apostolica Sedis* as they are made.

9. See, for example, John Paul II's January 25, 1998, remarks to the Bishops of Cuba, often thematically repeated in his greetings to episcopal conferences: "I also wish to address a particular greeting to the Jewish community represented here. Your presence is an eloquent expression of the fraternal dialogue aimed at a better understanding between Jews and Catholics, and which, promoted by the Second Vatican Council, continues to be ever more widespread. With you we share a common spiritual patrimony, firmly rooted in the Sacred Scriptures. May God, the Creator and Savior, sustain our efforts to walk together and, encouraged by the divine word, may we grow in worship and fervent love of him" (Available at http://w2.vatican.va/content/john-paul-ii/en/speeches/1998/january/documents/hf_jp-ii_spe_19980125_lahavana-confessioni.pdf). Similarly, Benedict XVI in his remarks at the synagogue of Cologne on August 19, 2005, referred to *Nostra Aetate* as recalling " the common roots and the immensely rich spiritual heritage that Jews and Christians share," but he did not explain the term or its implications (see original Vatican text at https://w2.vatican.va/content/benedict-xvi/en/speeches/2005/august/documents/hf_ben-xvi_spe_20050819_cologne-synagogue.html, accessed as of 05.30.16). Francis, too, at the time of his January 2016 visit to the synagogue in Rome invoked this same concept, adding a few thoughts of his own to its sense, but remained shy of any full explanation of its meaning. See original Vatican text at https://w2.vatican.va/content/francesco/en/speeches/2016/january/documents/papa-francesco_20160117_sinagoga.html.

10. Cf. the language of *Nostra Aetate*, no. 4, echoing this same insight: "As the sacred synod searches into the mystery of the Church, it remembers the bond that spiritually ties the people of the New Covenant to Abraham's stock."

11. See Henri de Lubac, *Motherhood of the Entire Church* (San Francisco: Ignatius Press, 1983), and Joseph Ratzinger's *The Ecclesiology of Vatican II* in *L'Osservatore Romano* (Weekly Edition in English) (January 23, 2002), p. 5.

12. Hans Urs Von Balthasaar, *Herrlichkeit: Eine theologische Asthetick, I: Schau der Gestalt*, trans. Erasmo Leiva-Merikakis (Ensiedeln: Johannes Verlag, 1961), published in English as *The Glory of the Lord: A Theological Aesthetics* (San Francisco: Ignatius Press, 1982). References here are taken from this English translation.

13. Von Balthasaar, pp. 350-433. Cf. also Von Balthasaar, "Who is the Church?," in *Explorations in Theology/Vol. 2: Spouse of the Word*, trans. John Saward (San Francisco: Ignatius Press, 1991), pp. 143-191.

14. See Walter Kapser's remarks on the occasion of the 40th anniversary of *Nostra Aetate* in Rome, October 27, 2005, where he states that the Declaration constitutes only "the beginning of a beginning" and no more, at https://www.bc.edu/content/dam/files/research_sites/cjl/texts/cjrelations/resources/articles/Kasper_27Oct05.htm.

15. See David Vincent Meconi's discussion of this term in his review of Jason Byassee's *Praise Seeking Understanding: Reading the Psalms with Augustine* (Grand Rapids: MI: Eerdmans, 2007) in the *Journal of Early Christian Studies*, 17(1), pp. 160-161.

16. Pius V, *Quo Primum*. July 14, 1570. See Philip Cunningham's reconstruction of the revision of this

prayer by Paul VI in light of *Nostra Aetate* at http://www.saintleo.edu/media/556677/july_28__2007__dr._phillip_cunningham_-_the_controversey_surrounding_the_tridentine_mass_and_its_good_friday_service_language.pdf.

17. Annibale Bugnini, *The Reform of the Liturgy: 1948-1975*, trans. Matthew J. O'Connell (Collegeville: The Liturgical Press, 1990), p. 119. Bugnini then goes on to acknowledge that the Good Friday prayer had to be "completely rewritten" but gives no indication of its final form or the principles of its re-composition.

18. See Cunningham: http://www.saintleo.edu/media/556677/july_28__2007__dr._phillip_cunningham_-_the_controversey_surrounding_the_tridentine_mass_and_its_good_friday_service_language.pdf.

19. See *Sources Chretiennes*, 123, pp. 95-101 for the entire text, but also cf. Routh Rel Sacra 1.122, with one of the fragments that became the epicenter of anti-Jewish language in the liturgy, "God has suffered from the right hand of Israel," subsequently taken to mean that the divine Jesus was killed by the Jewish people.

20. See the revised text of Melito's homily for use in the Office of Readings for Holy Thursday in *The Liturgy of the Hours According to the Roman Rite, Vol. 2*, translated by the International Commission on English in the Liturgy (New York: Catholic Book Publishing, 1976), pp. 458-59.

21. *Patrologica Graeca* 33, pp. 1047-1050: "*Priore namque repudiate, in secunda, catholica videlicet Ecclesia, Deus, uti Paulus ait, 'posuit primum apostolos, secundo prophetas…'*" English translation as given above is taken from *The Liturgy of the Hours According to the Roman Rite, Vol. 3*, translated by the International Commission on English in the Liturgy (New York: Catholic Book Publishing, 1975), p. 560.

22. *Nostra Aetate*, no. 4: *Licet autem Ecclesia sit novus populus Dei, Iudaei tamen neque ut a Deo reprobati neque ut maledicti exhibeantur, quasi hoc ex Sacris Litteris sequatur* ("Although the Church is the new people of God, the Jews should not be presented as rejected or accursed by God, as if this followed from the Holy Scriptures"; translation mine).

23. For example, the month of July alone in the Armenian liturgical calendar for 2016 has feasts for the following figures, some of whom were Jewish, some pagan, and some whose religious identities were unknown: Adam, Abel, Seth, Enosh, Enoch, Noah, Melchizedek, Abraham, Isaac, Jacob, Joseph, Moses, Aaron, Eleazar, Joshua, Samuel, Samson, Jepthah, Barak, Gideon, and others (July 14). As well, the liturgy commemorates the Ark of the Covenant alongside the Feast of the New Ark on July 2; further information available at http://www.armenianprelacy.org/images/prelacy/PDF/07July2016DBR.pdf. See also Jean Danielou's compelling discussion of the patristic soteriology behind these kinds of feasts as commonly observed among the Eastern Churches in *Holy Pagans of the Old Testament*, trans. Felix Faber (London: Longmans, Green and Co., 1957), esp. pp. 127-135, where he relates all who worship the true God to the universal or "cosmic" liturgy of heaven.

24. *The Roman Missal: Lectionary for Mass for Use in the Dioceses of the United States of America, Vol. 1* (2nd Typical Edition) (New Jersey: Catholic Book Publishing, 1998), p. 24.

25. See original text and official English translation at the Vatican website: http://www.vatican.va/roman_curia/congregations/cfaith/pch_documents/rc_con_cfaith-doc¬20020212¬populo-ebraico_en.html.

26. This remarkable document from the Pontifical Biblical Commission goes on to offer a further warning in no. 87: "The partial reading of texts frequently gives rise to difficulties affecting relations with the Jews. The Old Testament, as we have seen, is not sparing in its reproaches against Israelites, or even in its condemnations. It is very demanding towards them. Rather than casting stones at the Jews, it is better to see them as illustrating the saying of the Lord Jesus: 'To whom much is given, from him much is expected' (Lk 12:48), and this saying applies to us Christians as well. Certain biblical narratives present aspects of disloyalty or cruelty which today would be morally inadmissable, but they must be understood in their historical and literary contexts. The slow historical progress of revelation must be recognized: the divine pedagogy has taken a group of people where it found them and led them patiently in the direction of an ideal union with God and towards a moral integrity which our modern society is still far from attaining. This education must avoid two opposite dangers, on the one hand, of attributing to ancient prescriptions an ongoing validity for Christians (for example, refusing blood transfusions on biblical grounds) and, on the other hand, of rejecting the whole Bible on the pretext of its cruelties. As regards ritual precepts, such as the rules for pure and impure, one has to be conscious of their symbolic and anthropological import, and be aware of their sociological and religious functions. In the New Testament, the reproaches addressed to Jews are not as frequent or as virulent as the accusations against Jews in the Law and the Prophets. Therefore, they no longer serve as a basis for anti-Jewish sentiment. To use them for this purpose is contrary to the whole tenor of the New Testament. Real anti-Jewish feeling, that is, an attitude of contempt, hostility and persecution of the Jews as Jews, is not found in any New Testament text and is incompatible with its teaching. What is found are reproaches addressed to certain categories of Jews for religious reasons, as well as polemical texts to defend the Christian apostolate against Jews who oppose

it. But it must be admitted that many of these passages are capable of providing a pretext for anti-Jewish sentiment and have in fact been used in this way. To avoid mistakes of this kind, it must be kept in mind that the New Testament polemical texts, even those expressed in general terms, have to do with concrete historical contexts and are never meant to be applied to Jews of all times and places merely because they are Jews. The tendency to speak in general terms, to accentuate the adversaries' negative side, and to pass over the positive in silence, failure to consider their motivations and their ultimate good faith, these are characteristics of all polemical language throughout antiquity, and are no less evident in Judaism and primitive Christianity against all kinds of dissidents."

27. Note below Ratzinger's stunning linkage of four elements: (1) the influence of the *Shoah* on the reading of the Scriptures by Christians in all contexts, (2) the legitimacy of the use of a fulfillment hermeneutic in the Christian experience of biblical reading, (3) a reflection on how points one and two contribute to and form dialogue between Catholics and Jews, and perhaps most insightfully, (4) how such dialogue shapes the inner consciousness of Christians as Christians. Does Ratzinger here make a contribution to the development of a post-*Nostra Aetate* sense of *anima ecclesiastica*, as alluded to in Section One of this paper? In the Preface, Ratzinger writes: "In its work, the Biblical Commission could not ignore the contemporary context, where the shock of the *Shoah* has put the whole question under a new light. Two main problems are posed: Can Christians, after all that has happened, still claim in good conscience to be the legitimate heirs of Israel's Bible? Have they the right to propose a Christian interpretation of this Bible, or should they not instead, respectfully and humbly, renounce any claim that, in the light of what has happened, must look like a usurpation? The second question follows from the first: In its presentation of the Jews and the Jewish people, has not the New Testament itself contributed to creating a hostility towards the Jewish people that provided a support for the ideology of those who wished to destroy Israel? The Commission set about addressing those two questions. It is clear that a Christian rejection of the Old Testament would not only put an end to Christianity itself as indicated above, but, in addition, would prevent the fostering of positive relations between Christians and Jews, precisely because they would lack common ground. In the light of what has happened, what ought to emerge now is a new respect for the Jewish interpretation of the Old Testament. On this subject, the Document says two things. First it declares that 'the Jewish reading of the Bible is a possible one, in continuity with the Jewish Scriptures of the Second Temple period, a reading analogous to the Christian reading, which developed in parallel fashion' (no. 22). It adds that Christians can learn a great deal from a Jewish exegesis practiced for more than 2000 years; in return, Christians may hope that Jews can profit from Christian exegetical research (*ibid.*). I think this analysis will prove useful for the pursuit of Judeo-Christian dialogue, as well as for the interior formation of Christian consciousness."

28. See Walter Kasper, *The Discussion of the Recent Modifications of the Prayer for the Jews for Good Friday*, originally published in *L'Osservatore Romano*, April 10, 2008, and reproduced in its entirety here: http://chiesa.espresso.repubblica.it/articolo/197381?eng=y.

29. Message to the President of the Holy See's Commission for Religious Relations with Jews on the Occasion of the 40th Anniversary of the Declaration *Nostra Aetate*, available at http://www.ccjr.us/dialogika-resources/documents-and-statements/roman-catholic/pope-benedict-xvi/357-b16-05oct26.

30. See Benedict XVI's *Letter to the Bishops on the Occasion of the Publication of the Apostolic Letter Motu Proprio Data Summorum Pontificum* at http://w2.vatican.va/content/benedict-xvi/en/letters/2007/documents/hf_ben-xvi_let_20070707_lettera-vescovi.html. There, Benedict states, "For that matter, the two Forms of the usage of the Roman Rite can be mutually enriching: new Saints and some of the new Prefaces can and should be inserted in the old Missal."

31. "Apostolic Letter on the Use of the Preconciliar Forms," in *Newsletter*, Committee on the Liturgy of the United States Conference of Catholic Bishops, Volume XLIII, May/June 2007.

32. Here follows a list of both the principal Vatican documents that address the issue of preaching about Jews and Judaism and the statements of the United States Conference of Catholic Bishops: A. Vatican Documents: i. *Guidelines and Suggestions for Implementing the Conciliar Declaration* Nostra Aetate, *no. 4* (December 1974); ii. *Notes on the Correct Way to Present Jews and Judaism in Preaching and Catechesis in the Roman Catholic Church* (June 1985); iii. *We Remember: A Reflection on the Shoah* (March 1998); iv. *The Jewish People and Their Sacred Scriptures* (May 2001); B. USCCB Documents: i. *Catholic Teaching on the Shoah: Implementing the Holy See's* We Remember (March 2001); ii. *God's Mercy Endures Forever* (September 1998); iii. *Criteria for the Evaluation of Dramatizations of the Passion* (March 1988); iv. *Guidelines for Catholic-Jewish Relations* (April 1985); v. *Within Context: Guidelines for the Catechetical Presentation of Jews and Judaism in the New Testament* (May 1986); vi. *Preaching the Mystery of Faith* (June 2013).

33. In summary fashion, they are provided here from *Nostra Aetate*, no. 4: (1) Jews are not collectively

responsible for the death of Jesus – not in his time, and not today; (2) God's covenant with the Jews remains valid and is not broken or abrogated by the death of Jesus; (3) God does not treat the Jews as accursed or abandoned in supposed punishment for any act; and (4) antisemitism has no place in any Christian life.

34. Vatican website English translation available at http://w2.vatican.va/content/john-paul-ii/en/speeches/1997/october/documents/hf_jp-ii_spe_19971031_com-teologica.html. The original French text can be found in *Radici dell'antigiudaismo in ambiente christiano* (Citta del Vaticano: Libereria Editrice Vaticana, 2000), pp. 15-18.
35. Ibid.
36. For a full account of the "anti-Judaeos" literature of the patristic period with an authoritative bibliography of original sources, see Bernhard Blumenkranz's magisterial study, *Les Auteurs Chretiens Latins du Moyen Age sur les juifs et le judaisme* (Paris: Mouton & Co., 1963).
37. The Nazi use of the anti-Judaeos homilies of John Chrysostom is a case in point. See Walter Laqueur's study of Chrysostom's influence on Nazi rhetoric in his *The Changing Face of Anti-Semitism: From Ancient Times to the Present Day* (Oxford: Oxford University Press, 2006), pp. 47-48.
38. John Paul insisted that destroying the connection between Jesus and Judaism would prove deadly. He remarks in his October 31, 1997, address, *The Roots of Anti-Judaism*, that "[T]hose who regard the fact that Jesus was a Jew and that his milieu was the Jewish world as mere cultural accidents, for which one could substitute another religious tradition from which the Lord's person could be separated without losing its identity, not only ignore the meaning of salvation history, but more radically challenge the very truth of the Incarnation and make a genuine concept of enculturation impossible. 4. On the basis of what has just been said, we can draw some conclusions for guiding the attitude of Christians and the work of theologians. The Church firmly condemns all forms of genocide, as well as the racist theories that have inspired them and have claimed to justify them. One may recall Pius XI's Encyclical *Mit brennender Sorge* (1937) and Pius XII's *Summi Pontificatus* (1939); the latter cited the law of human solidarity and of charity towards every individual, regardless of the people to which he belongs. Racism is thus a negation of the deepest identity of the human being, who is a person created in the image and likeness of God. To the moral evil of any genocide the *Shoah* adds the evil of a hatred that attacks God's saving plan for history"; available at http://w2.vatican.va/content/john-paul-ii/en/speeches/1997/october/documents/hf_jp-ii_spe_19971031_com-teologica.html.
39. As an example of this kind of innovative exegesis that changes preaching about the Sunday gospels, see Daniel Harrington, *The Synoptic Gospels Set Free: Preaching without Anti-Judaism* (New York: Paulist Press, 2008).
40. For a brief synopsis of the ecumenical movement and its prodigious growth within Roman Catholicism, see John Crossin, *The Ecumenical Movement: A School for Virtue*, available at http://www.usccb.org/beliefs-and-teachings/ecumenical-and-interreligious/vatican-ii-and-the-ecumenical-movement.cfm, and Brian Farrell, *Ecumenism Today: The Situation in the Catholic Church*, available at http://www.vatican.va/roman_curia/pontifical_councils/chrstuni/documents/rc_pc_chrstuni_doc_20041121_farrell-ecumenismo_en.html.
41. See Bert Groen, "Anti-Judaism in the Present-Day Byzantine Liturgy," in *Journal of Eastern Christian Studies*, 60, 2008, pp. 369–87.
42. See Christine Shepardson, *Anti-Judaism and Christian Orthodoxy: Ephrem's Hymns in Fourth Century Syria* (Washington, DC: The Catholic University of America, 2008); and Karl Gerlach, *The Antenicene Pascha* (Leuven: Peters, 1998), for the origins of anti-Jewish concepts and language in these liturgical families.
43. See added statement by Bishop Paul Peter Jesep on antisemitism at http://www.brama.com/news/press/2007/02/070212bishoppaulpeterjesep_anti-semitism.html.
44. See *Theology after Auschwitz and its Correlation with Theology after the Gulag: Consequences and Conclusions/Proceedings of the Second International Conference, St. Petersburg, Russia, Jan. 26-28, 1998* (St. Petersburg School of Religion and Philosophy, 1998).
45. See the statement of Bishop Paul Peter Jesep, U.S. Director of Public Affairs for the Ukrainian Autocephalous Orthodox Church Diaspora, at http://archive.adl.org/presrele/asint_13/5069_31.html#.V00R4iMrK08.
46. For an overview of the ecumenical impact of *Nostra Aetate* on Catholic-Jewish relations, see Neville Lamadan and Alberto Melloni (Eds), *Nostra Aetate: Origins, Promulgation, Impact on Jewish-Catholic Relations* (Berlin: Lit Verlag, 2007), especially M. Velati's *The Debate on* De Judaeis *and Ecumenical Dialogue* (pp. 145-162) and Petra Heldt's *Protestant Perspectives after 40 Years: A Critical Assessment of* Nostra Aetate (pp. 163-175), both in the same collection.
47. http://www.usccb.org/news/2001/01-180.cfm.

48. The Vatican accounts of these dialogues detail topics and theological arguments presented at each session: http://www.vatican.va/roman_curia/pontifical_councils/chrstuni/Bapstist%20alliance/rc_pc_chrstuni_doc_20101213_report-2006-2010_en.html and http://www.vatican.va/roman_curia/pontifical_councils/chrstuni/Bapstist%20alliance/rc_pc_chrstuni_doc_20130401_commentary-baima_en.html.
49. The USCCB attempts to balance its support of all parties in the conflicts between Israel and the Palestinian authority. See its history of complex and nuanced statements at http://www.usccb.org/issues-and-action/human-life-and-dignity/global-issues/middle-east/israel-palestine.
50. Cf. USCCB's *Guidelines for Catholic Jewish Relations* (1985 Revision) at http://www.jcrelations.net/Dabru_Emet_-_A_Jewish_Statement_on_Christians_and_Christianity.2395.0.html; for a corresponding Jewish view on the same topic, see David Rosen's *Nostra Aetate, Forty Years After Vatican II: Present & Future Perspectives* at http://www.vatican.va/roman_curia/pontifical_councils/chrstuni/relations-jews-docs/rc_pc_chrstuni_doc_20051027_rabbi-rosen_en.html. See also the *Conventio Inter Apostolicam Sedem atque Israelis Statum*, or *Fundamental Agreement between the Holy See and the State of Israel* (1993), esp. nos. 1 and 2.
51. See both John Paul's homily and intercessions for the Mass of the Day of Pardon in St. Peter's Basilica, March 12, 2000, at http://www.ccjr.us/dialogika-resources/documents-and-statements/roman-catholic/pope-john-paul-ii/333-jp2-00mar12. It should be noted that the prayer text in the fourth intercession, *Confession of Sins against the People of Israel*, contained the words of the apology that the Pope would leave in the Kotel during his visit there just a few days later.
52. Ibid.
53. See this compelling moment captured on film at https://www.youtube.com/watch?v=CatGtrfqjJE.
54. Compare two recent statements by Jewish groups relative to the 50th anniversary of *Nostra Aetate* to discover Jewish self-reflections in response: (1) the *Declaration for the Upcoming Jubilee of Brotherhood: A New Jewish View of Jewish-Christian Relations*, signed in Paris on November 23, 2015, at the College des Bernardins by the Chief Rabbi of France, Haim Korsia, and a group of representatives from the Jewish communities of France; and (2) *To Do the Will of Our Father in Heaven: Toward a Partnership between Jews and Christians*, issued December 3, 2015, by American, Israeli, and European Rabbis. Both of these texts may be found at http://www.ccjr.us/dialogika-resources/educational-and-liturgical-materials/curricula/1233-na50.
55. http://www.jcrelations.net/Dabru_Emet_-_A_Jewish_Statement_on_Christians_and_Christianity.2395.0.html.
56. Rabbi Joseph B. Soloveitchik, "Confrontation," in *Tradition*, 6(2), 1964, 5ff. The online version of this text may be found at http://traditionarchive.org/news/originals/Volume%206/No.%202/Confrontation.pdf.

Nostra Aetate and the Failures of Ethics

John K. Roth

The Edward J. Sexton Professor Emeritus of Philosophy and the Founding Director of the Center for the Study of the Holocaust, Genocide, and Human Rights (now the Mgrublian Center for Human Rights), Claremont McKenna College, Claremont, CA

> "Men expect from the various religions answers to the unsolved riddles of the human condition, which today, even as in former times, deeply stir the hearts of men: … whence do we come, and where are we going?"
> Nostre Aetate, no 4

Ethics is civilization's keystone. Defined by the intention to encourage human action that fits sound understanding about what is right and wrong, just and unjust, good and evil, virtuous and corrupt, ethics at its best emphasizes careful deliberation about the difference between right and wrong, encouragement not to be indifferent toward that difference, cultivation of virtuous character, and action that defends what is right and resists what is wrong. Confronting the Holocaust, genocide, and other mass atrocities for more than 40 years – and now reflecting on *Nostra Aetate* 50 years after its promulgation – I have become increasingly aware that I have been following a thread that weaves its way through failure. Inescapable and pervasive, failure riddles existence. Following that thread has particularly compelled me to contend with the failures of ethics. Exposing fault lines in nature and flaws in reality itself, those failures abound in the multiple shortfalls and shortcomings of thought, character, decision, and action that tempt us human beings to betray what is good, right, virtuous, and just, and incite us to inflict incalculable harm.[1]

Good Days for Ethics

With those themes forming the context for reflection on my topic, "*Nostra Aetate* and the Failures of Ethics," consider that after World War II and the Holocaust, good days for ethics occurred on December 9 and 10, 1948, when the General Assembly of the United Nations adopted the Convention on the Prevention and Punishment of the Crime of Genocide and the Universal Declaration of Human Rights. The Convention criminalized specific "acts committed with intent to destroy, in whole or in part, a national, ethnical, racial or religious group, as such," which the contracting parties would "undertake to prevent and punish." Proclaiming that "recognition of the inherent dignity and of the equal and inalienable rights of all members of the human family is the foundation of freedom, justice and peace in the world," the Declaration aimed to become a standard for all peoples and nations, securing "universal and effective" respect for "the right to life, liberty and security of person" and rejection of slavery, torture, and other forms of "cruel, inhuman or degrading treatment or punishment."[2] Two good days for ethics in December 1948 called for more of the same. Although such days have been too few and far between, another of them took place on October 28, 1965, with Pope Paul VI's proclamation of *Nostra Aetate*, the "Declaration on the Relation of the Church to Non-Christian Religions" that emerged from the Second Vatican Council (1962–65).

It is an understatement to say that the 50th anniversary of *Nostra Aetate* has created a stir. One has only to Google the phrase "*Nostra Aetate* fiftieth anniversary" to receive a ginormous number of "hits," many of them noting celebrations and conferences focused on this document, which contains fewer than 1,800 words, only about 600 of them devoted explicitly to Judaism and Jews. Nowhere does *Nostra Aetate* mention the Holocaust, the event from which it is inseparable, let alone acknowledge that Christians, including the Roman Catholic Church, failed to do all that could and should have been done to prevent genocide against the Jewish people and untold violations of human rights unleashed by World War II and the Holocaust. Indeed, *Nostra Aetate* apparently alludes to mid-twentieth century events as if to deny their relevance for its revision of teaching about Judaism and Jews. What I have in mind is the phrase that "the Church, mindful of the patrimony she shares with the Jews and moved *not by political reasons but by the Gospel's spiritual love*, decries hatred, persecutions, displays of anti-Semitism, directed against Jews at any time and by anyone" [emphasis added]. The Catholic scholar Philip A. Cunningham explains that

> the phrase 'not by political reasons' was included because of opposition to the declaration stemming from the Arab–Israeli conflict, as it was then called. Some Council fathers argued that any positive statement about Judaism would be seen as favoring the State of Israel and might bring retaliation upon the Christian minorities living in predominantly

Muslim countries. Thus, *Nostra Aetate* sought to separate its theological inspiration from any political considerations.[3]

I think Cunningham's assessment is correct, but the question remains whether, and with what degree of integrity, the "theological inspiration" driving *Nostra Aetate* can actually be separated from the historical reality and political implications of the Holocaust. A significant failure of ethics, the document's silence about the Holocaust, the very event that provoked and necessitated *Nostra Aetate*, speaks volumes.

Two later documents that interpreted and implemented *Nostra Aetate* are scarcely improvements in that regard. The Vatican's 1974 "Guidelines and Suggestions for Implementing the Conciliar Declaration *Nostra Aetate*" noted, without any elaboration, only that *Nostra Aetate* "finds its historical setting in circumstances deeply affected by the memory of the persecution and massacre of Jews which took place in Europe just before and during the Second World War." No better on historical accountability was the 1985 sequel, "Notes on the Correct Way to Present Jews and Judaism in Preaching and Catechesis in the Roman Catholic Church." That document's obscure and only reference – as bland as it was vague – to the Holocaust was that sound Catholic teaching should "help in understanding the meaning for the Jews of the extermination during the years 1939-1945, and its consequences." Not until the 1998 testimony of "We Remember: A Reflection on the Shoah," written by the Commission for Religious Relations with the Jews, did the Vatican officially move, though still inadequately, toward "getting it right" as far as Christian and Catholic responsibility for the Holocaust is concerned.[4]

More recently and following immediately after the 50th anniversary of *Nostra Aetate*, the Vatican's Commission for Religious Relations with the Jews presented an important document on December 10, 2015. Taking its title from Romans 11:29, this "Reflection on Theological Questions Pertaining to Catholic–Jewish Relations on the Occasion of the 50th Anniversary of '*Nostra Aetate*' (No. 4)" is called "The Gifts and the Calling of God Are Irrevocable."[5] Some of my comments about this widely discussed document will follow below, but at this point I underscore that its references to the *Shoah* are mostly found in the brief history of *Nostra Aetate*'s impact that begin "The Gifts and the Calling of God Are Irrevocable." In that section, the document notes that "the dark and terrible shadow of the *Shoah* over Europe during the Nazi period led the Church to reflect anew on her bond with the Jewish people," and it mentions "the duty of Christians to remember the human catastrophe of the *Shoah*," with the hope, as expressed by Saint Pope John Paul II, that "the unspeakable iniquity of the *Shoah* will never again be possible" (1, 6). Then, near the end of the document, in a section urging that "the Catholic Church neither conducts nor supports any specific institutional mission work directed towards Jews," Christians are reminded that they "are nonetheless called to bear witness to their faith in Jesus

Christ also to Jews, although they should do so in a humble and sensitive manner, acknowledging that Jews are bearers of God's Word, and particularly in view of the great tragedy of the *Shoah*" (40). Nowhere, however, does "The Gifts and the Calling of God Are Irrevocable" make clear that Christianity itself was a necessary condition for the Holocaust, a failure of ethics about which I will have more to say below.

Meanwhile, despite the failures of ethics lurking in the silence about the genocidal history that made *Nostra Aetate* and its sequels as imperative as they were late in arriving – and evasive about the Holocaust to boot – *Nostra Aetate* is not undeserving of the tributes paid to it 50 years on. "A landmark document," "a watershed moment," "groundbreaking," "revolutionary," "arguably the most important moment in modern Jewish-Christian relations" – these are among the accolades, which include Rabbi David Rosen's suggestion that "there is arguably no transformation in *human history* that parallels *Nostra Aetate*".[6] Even if such praise seems excessive, *Nostra Aetate*'s promulgation on October 28, 1965, still qualifies as a good day for ethics.

Two reasons for that judgment stand out. First, as the historian John Connelly underscores, "the church had never in its history looked upon the Jews in the ways specified in *Nostra Aetate*."[7] While credit for a sea change must be given, doing so should not lead us into temptation to excuse what was normative Christian teaching on the Jews prior to *Nostra Aetate* on the grounds that those norms were embedded in biblical interpretations, historical conventions, and cultural traditions that reduced their propagators and adherents to being creatures of time and place who neither could nor should have known and done better than they did. With all due respect to the importance of avoiding judgment of past behavior by standards that were virtually unthinkable at the time, typical Christian attitudes and actions toward Jews and Judaism prior to *Nostra Aetate* were nevertheless failures of ethics, or nothing could be.[8] What follows from that judgment is the second reason why October 28, 1965, stands as a good day for ethics: *Nostra Aetate* can make Christians, Jews, Muslims, and more revisit what it calls "unsolved riddles of the human condition," including "whence do we come, and where are we going."[9]

No Christianity = No Holocaust

Turning in that direction, note that in some circles, constructive Christian-Jewish dialogue preceded the Holocaust and respectful postwar Christian-Jewish relationships have often been motivated by desires to improve communal cooperation and to extend interreligious understanding that are unrelated to or at least not focused explicitly on the *Shoah*.[10] Nevertheless, no event haunts Christian–Jewish relations more than Nazi Germany's genocide against the Jews, for that mass atrocity cannot be separated from the centuries of anti-Jewish hostility that have been deeply rooted in Christian thought and practice. Neither Christianity nor any other single person, institution, or motivation – from the power of Adolf Hitler and the SS, for example, to the widespread racist antisemitism embraced by millions of ordinary Germans during the Nazi period – was *sufficient* by itself to make the Holocaust happen, but Christianity was a necessary condition for the Holocaust. No Christianity = no Holocaust.[11]

As a Protestant American Christian, I think the Holocaust's most important impact on Christian–Jewish relations has been, first, to make at least some of us Christians deeply aware of the Holocaust itself. With that awareness has come cognizance of both our tradition's complicity in that genocide and our responsibility to challenge and correct what took Christianity in that direction. Hand in hand with those factors, at least some of us Christians try to keep learning about Judaism and Jewish traditions and to seek and welcome friendship that respects Jewish particularity and its differences from Christian ways. We also support the State of Israel's need to find just and lasting peace in a turbulent and dangerous Middle East. Steps in these directions, especially when they involve, as they often do, reciprocity from Jews toward Christians, help confirm that Christian–Jewish relations, rocky though they sometimes remain, are much better than they have been for many centuries. Absent *Nostra Aetate*, that claim could not be made.

As far as the United States is concerned, a specific event exemplifies and undergirds the impact I have described. Virtually every day since its doors first opened in April 1993, the United States Holocaust Memorial Museum (USHMM) in Washington, D.C., helps make Americans aware of the Holocaust and Christianity's involvement in it. According to USHMM data, as of June 2015, approximately 38.6 million people have visited the Museum. An estimated 90 percent of them are not Jewish, which means that a very large, if unspecified, number would be Americans who, in one way or another, identify themselves as Christians. Arguably, no other event in the United States does more to exemplify the Holocaust's impact on Christian-Jewish relations, which must begin, after all, with deepened awareness of the Holocaust itself, than the daily opening of the doors at USHMM.

However, as the twenty-first century further unfolds, including now the 50th anniversary of *Nostra Aetate*, what is the Holocaust's impact on Christian–Jewish relations in the United States and elsewhere likely to be? Will that impact grow or diminish? Will it improve or disrupt those relations? As indicated by the Museum's presence in the heart of the U.S. capital, remembrance and study of the Holocaust have been extensively institutionalized in American life. *Yom Hashoah* observances, for instance, take place annually in American synagogues and on many college and university campuses. Christian communities often participate in these observances or acknowledge the Holocaust in other ways. By now, such practices are so widespread as to approach routine. In some places and primarily among individuals, attention to the Holocaust continues to produce deep wrestling with basic issues that Judaism and Christianity encounter about God, Scripture, the identity of Jesus, forgiveness, and much more. But the sense that the Holocaust creates ongoing upheaval, unfinished business, and even crisis for these traditions and their relations may have crested. Outlooks within and between Judaism and Christianity have been changed by the Holocaust, but it is dubious that the depth and influence of the changes are growing and intensifying. Instead, as the Holocaust recedes further into the past and the survivor generation passes away, urgency about attending to it diminishes, an outlook accompanied and driven by feelings that enough, even too much, attention has been paid to that event – "Holocaust fatigue" – and that there are current disasters that deserve attention instead. In short, in the United States and elsewhere, the Holocaust seems not to jar Jews and Christians so much anymore, but the calm can be deceptive and disrupted as events unfold. Two dilemmas illustrate that point.

The first dilemma pivots around unresolved tensions concerning the papacy and religious pluralism. Access to it can begin with the fact that no Christian is more visible, more emblematic of the Christian tradition, than the person who is the Pope at any given time. Currently, Pope Francis, the fourth post-Holocaust Pope to visit Israel, more than fits that description. Almost from the moment that the College of Cardinals elected the Argentinian Jorge Mario Bergoglio to the papacy on March 13, 2013, he has enjoyed warm relations with Jews worldwide. Notable in this regard is his long-standing friendship with the Argentinian rabbi Abraham Skorka. Written prior to Bergoglio's elevation, their bestselling book together, *On Heaven and Earth*, includes significant dialogue about the Holocaust. Dealing with a sore spot in Catholic-Jewish relations, Bergoglio emphasized that the Vatican archives relating to the Holocaust should be opened to clarify what did – and did not – happen with regard to Church policy toward Jews during World War II. "The objective," said Bergoglio, "has to be the truth."[12]

On April 27, 2014, when Pope Francis declared the sainthood of his predecessors, Pope John XXIII and Pope John Paul II, two pontiffs who responded courageously to the Holocaust and its aftermath, those steps, followed by his May 2014 visit to Israel, also bolstered the improving Catholic–Jewish relations that hearken back to Vatican II and specifically to the October 28, 1965, proclamation by Pope Paul VI of *Nostra Aetate* ("In Our Time"), a "Declaration on the Relation of the Church to Non-Christian Religions."[13] A turning-point document in Christian–Jewish relations, one significantly advanced by U.S. Catholic leaders such as Cardinal Richard Cushing and Cardinal Francis Spellman, *Nostra Aetate* did not explicitly mention the Holocaust, but it did reject key elements of what the French Jewish historian Jules Isaac called the Church's "teaching of contempt" toward Jews and Judaism.[14] Insisting that "the Jews should not be presented as rejected or accursed by God," *Nostra Aetate* decried "hatred, persecutions, displays of anti-Semitism, directed against Jews at any time and by anyone." In addition, it rejected the pernicious deicide charge by proclaiming that the crucifixion of Jesus Christ "cannot be charged against all the Jews, without distinction, then alive, nor against the Jews of today." Furthermore, emphasizing the Jewish origins of Christianity, *Nostra Aetate* affirmed that "God holds the Jews most dear," adding that "the Church awaits that day, known to God alone, on which all peoples will address the Lord in a single voice."[15]

Looking back, *Nostra Aetate*, which arrived 20 years after Nazi Germany had nearly destroyed European Jewish life, may seem scarcely more than too little, too late, but it was groundbreaking for Christians and Jews at the time, and it opened doors for further steps in its direction. In retrospect, it can also be said – tentatively perhaps, but said nonetheless – that if *Nostra Aetate*'s teachings had been in place and taken to heart earlier on, the Holocaust might not have happened. That judgment, however, must remain as tentative as it is speculative, because *Nostra Aetate* did not do enough to call into question the assumption that Christianity is still superior to Judaism, one of the presumptions that led Christianity to become a necessary condition for the Holocaust.

An intriguing variation on that theme surfaced in March 2011, when headlines in the announcement of the publication of the second volume of Pope Benedict XVI's book *Jesus of Nazareth* emphasized Benedict's view that the Jewish people cannot be held responsible for the death of Jesus Christ.[16] Having been stated in *Nostra Aetate* 45 years earlier, this proposition was not new, but in some Jewish quarters it was hailed almost as though it were. Observing that "Holocaust survivors know only too well how the centuries-long charge of 'Christ-killer' against the Jews created a poisonous climate of hate that was the foundation of anti-Semitic persecution whose ultimate expression was realized in the Holocaust," Elan Steinberg of the American Gathering of Holocaust Survivors and Their Descendants added that the Pope's new book "seals it [refutation of the deicide charge] for a new generation of Catholics."[17] Abraham Foxman of the Anti-Defamation League called the book's release "an important and historic moment for Catholic-Jewish relations," one that would take the teaching of *Nostra Aetate* "down to the pews."[18] The statements by Steinberg and Foxman indicated that *Nostra Aetate* and what followed in the decades since 1965 did not lay to rest Jewish suspicion that Christianity still harbors supersessionist inclinations, which are never removed from Christian awareness that Jews do not regard Jesus as the Messiah, let alone as God incarnate.

Meanwhile, Pope Francis has emphasized listening to others, engaging in open and honest dialogue, and serving the poor and needy – qualities that thus far have endeared him even to many who reject religion. But deep down a question lurks: Given his role responsibilities as Pope, how far can Francis take his commitment to pluralism and fallibility? No matter how much he accents dialogue that is civil, open, and sincere; insists that respect must be shown for the equality and dignity of the dialogue partners; and holds that "God makes Himself felt in the heart of each person," at the end of the day, Pope Francis may not be able to avoid the reality that his papal role responsibilities entail thinking and acting upon the conviction that his tradition fundamentally embodies the Truth in ways that trump Judaism.[19]

Evidence pointing in this direction exists in *Dialogue in Truth and Charity: Pastoral Orientations for Interreligious Dialogue*, which was issued in Rome by the Pontifical Council for Interreligious Dialogue on May 19, 2014.[20] Emphasizing the importance of interreligious dialogue, the document encourages Catholics engaged in such discussions to build on its "recommendations" (55). The document, however, does much more than offer optional guidelines; instead it emphasizes "essential elements" that will keep Catholic dialogue partners "properly guided by faith" and ensure that dialogue does not "generate a kind of relativism" (6). Respect for the equality of dialogue partners is essential, but the equality does not mean that the doctrines held by non-Catholic partners are equivalent in truth to those of Catholic authority. Nor are the founders of other religions to be seen as equivalent to Jesus Christ (13-14). Furthermore, although "interreligious dialogue, in itself, does not aim at conversion, dialogue neither takes the place of, nor excludes, *evangelization*" (4-5, 11).

Meanwhile, the purpose of interreligious dialogue goes beyond identifying common values. Its aim is to probe their ultimate foundation and to discern truth, which entails grasping, in the words of Pope Benedict XVI, "the essential relationship between the world and God" (12). The truth about that relationship, it turns out, is found in the Church's "basic theological foundations," which include not only that "God is the creator of all human beings" but also that "the focal point of the universal plan of salvation is Jesus Christ, the Incarnate Word of God, fully divine and fully human. In Him, God entered history, assuming human nature in order to redeem it from within. The mystery of man is clarified only in Him" (14-15).

Commitment to the truth of such "basic theological foundations" appears to be nonnegotiable as far as properly oriented Catholic partners in interreligious dialogue are concerned. Some commentators have suggested that *Dialogue in Truth and Charity* much more reflects the thought of Pope Benedict XVI than the disposition of Pope Francis, but the current pontiff is not likely to disagree, at least not openly, with its direction. If he were to say otherwise and put Christianity and Judaism on truly equal footings with regard to their truth status, the result would be earth-shaking. That step would also be a significant correction for the failures of ethics, which have a long history of breeding in Christianity's claiming – implicitly if not explicitly – that it is more truthful than Judaism, a tradition that continues with *Dialogue in Truth and Charity* despite its embrace of interreligious dialogue, and is by no means absent from the more recent "reflection" that the Vatican's Commission for Religious Relations with the Jews issued on December 15, 2015. Repeatedly, that document, "The Gifts and the Calling of God Are Irrevocable," underscores that "the covenant that God has offered Israel is irrevocable" and that "God has never revoked his covenant with his people Israel" (27, 35). But try as it may to remove every sniff of supersessionism, the document fails to do so because it also emphasizes repeatedly not only that "Christ's work of salvation is universal and involves all mankind," but also that "the New Covenant does not revoke the earlier covenants, but it brings them to fulfillment," and that Jesus' "work of salvation in the New Covenant confirms and perfects the dimensions of the Old" (25, 27). All the while insisting that God's covenant with his people Israel remains intact and irrevocable, the document rejects "the theory that there may be two different paths to salvation, the Jewish path without Christ and the path with the Christ, whom Christians believe is Jesus of Nazareth," basing that rejection on the proposition that such an outlook "would in fact endanger the foundations of Christian faith" (35). Indeed, the Church remains "the definitive and unsurpassable locus of the salvific action of God" (32).

Apparently Jews have their own irrevocable covenant with God, but it requires Christian "truth" to fulfill, perfect, and universalize it.

Whether post-Holocaust Jews and Christians will or should find such formulations acceptable remains to be seen, a hurdle heightened by two further claims in "The Gifts and the Calling of God Are Irrevocable." First, the document claims that the ideas that God's covenant with the Jewish people remains in place and that Christianity's "Jewish roots" entail "enduring continuity with Israel" mean that Judaism and Christianity ought not to be considered primarily as "two fundamentally diverse religions" (14, 15). "Jews and Christians," the document affirms, "have the same mother and can be seen, as it were, as two siblings who – as is the normal course of events for siblings – have developed in different directions" (15). Dialogue between Jews and Christians can and should be seen not as interreligious but as "'intra-religious' or 'intra-familial'" (20) – even though the fundamental and apparently intractable difference between Judaism and Christianity continues to be "how the figure of Jesus is to be evaluated. ... The figure of Jesus ... remains for Jews the 'stumbling block,' the central and neuralgic point in Jewish Catholic dialogue" (14).

In that statement, the term *neuralgic* is as apt as it is unfamiliar, for it connotes acute and even uncontrollable pain, which is not likely to go away anytime soon if and when the Jesus found in "The Gifts and the Calling of God Are Irrevocable" becomes the focal point of Christian-Jewish dialogue. Furthermore, little if any relief for that pain is provided by the appeal to "unfathomable divine mystery" to which the document resorts (36). The occasion for that appeal is an attempt to resolve the tension, if not contradiction, between "the Christian confession that there can be only one path to salvation" and the claim that "it does not in any way follow that the Jews are excluded from God's salvation because they do not believe in Jesus Christ as the Messiah of Israel and the Son of God" (36). The tension could be relaxed, the contradiction removed, if the document did not insist that "Christ is the Saviour for all ... the Redeemer of the Jews in addition to the Gentiles" (37). Its underscoring of those more-than-a-little supersessionist propositions, however, leaves "The

Gifts and the Calling of God Are Irrevocable" with mystifying ground, at best, on which to stand: "That the Jews are participants in God's salvation is theologically unquestionable, but how that can be possible without confessing Christ explicitly, is and remains an unfathomable divine mystery" (36).

The path from *Nostra Aetate* to "The Gifts and the Calling of God Are Irrevocable" reflects and advances much needed post-Holocaust sensibilities, but it also reveals that Christians still have work to do if every vestige of the supersessionism that was a necessary condition for the Holocaust is to be expunged from Christianity. That goal, a significant corrective for major failures of ethics, should not be the forlorn cause that it often seems to be, but such is likely to be the fate in store unless Christian thought and practice immerse themselves more deeply in the Holocaust and its implications than *Nostra Aetate* and its sequels have done. In the meantime, a related landmine in Catholic-Jewish relations adds to the tensions swirling around religious pluralism and the papacy. Indeed, it has implications for Christian–Jewish relations generally.

For decades, few if any Holocaust-related controversies have been more fraught than the ones churned by the conduct of Pope Pius XII during and after the Holocaust, a matter exacerbated by the delay in the opening of the Vatican's archives pertinent to his reign (1939–58). On December 19, 2009, Pope Francis's immediate successor, Benedict XVI, currently Pope emeritus, confirmed the 2007 findings of a Vatican committee that attributed "heroic virtues" to the controversial Holocaust-era pontiff, significantly moving him forward in a vetting process that can culminate in Roman Catholic sainthood.[21] Normally, Pius XII could be beatified when a miracle attributed to his intercession is officially certified, and the recognition of a second miracle would set the stage for canonization. Although Pope Francis advanced John XXIII's canonization without those formalities, he has indicated that he would not do so with regard to Pius XII. The elevation of Pius XII, however, may still be waiting in the wings. Reasons for thinking so can be found in Pope Francis's interview, dated June 13, 2014, in the Spanish-language magazine *La Vanguardia*. Referring to "poor Pius XII," Francis urged that the actions of the wartime Pope need to be seen "in the context of the time. For example, was it better for him not to speak so that more Jews would not be killed or for him to speak?" As far as resistance against the Holocaust is concerned, lamented Francis, "everyone takes it out against the Church and Pius XII." But before World War II, Francis claimed, Pius XII was seen as "the great defender of Jews," and during the war, the pontiff "hid many [Jews] in convents in Rome and in other Italian cities, and also in the residence of Castel Gandolfo."[22]

Just as Pope Francis's historical judgments about Pius XII are debatable, it is not certain, at least as the 50th anniversary of *Nostra Aetate* came and went, what Francis's ultimate position toward Pius XII will be. No one, moreover, can be certain what the reverberations, one way or the other, will be if the Vatican ever declares Pius XII a saint. But his canonization is unlikely to help Christian–Jewish relations in the United States or anywhere else because no matter how many miracles may be attributed to Pius XII, his papacy is so encumbered by Holocaust-related ambiguity that the proclamation of his sainthood will always be awkward. Probably the Catholic Church and Christianity generally can never get beyond damage control where Pius XII is concerned. That problem pertains not only to ambiguities surrounding his wartime papacy but also to his posture about the Holocaust and the Jewish people in the aftermath of World War II.[23] Virtually every Jew and countless Christians, including most Roman Catholics, would breathe a sigh of relief if plans to canonize Pius XII were shelved and put to rest forever.

The Palestinian–Israeli Conflict

Turning to the second major post-*Nostra Aetate* dilemma confronting Christian–Jewish relations, while debates continue about links between the Holocaust and the establishment of the State of Israel in 1948, reverberations of the Holocaust affect the Middle East generally and the Palestinian–Israeli conflict in particular. In turn, Christian–Jewish relations in the United States and elsewhere are deeply affected by the Palestinian–Israeli conflict, which has taken turns for the worse 50 years after *Nostra Aetate*. The Holocaust's part in those developments is considerable, if frequently understated.[24]

Following yet another collapse of Palestinian–Israeli peace talks in late April 2014, Shmuel Rosner persuasively argued that the failure of those negotiations succeeded in showing that while Israelis and Palestinians overwhelming prefer to live without violence, "they also want many other things, some of which they want more passionately than peace." More important than "peace and calm," contended Rosner, are "things like national pride, sacred traditions, symbols and land." Such an analysis is not optimistic as far as peace prospects are concerned, but it has frank realism in its favor. Including the Hamas–Israel war that erupted in early July after the 2014 peace talks broke down, three Israeli teens were murdered by Palestinian extremists, and revenge was taken by Israeli extremists who tortured and murdered a young Palestinian, the complex effects of the Palestinian–Israeli conflict on Christian–Jewish relations are too complicated to permit anything approaching adequate treatment here.[25] It must suffice to say that American Christians are scarcely of one mind about the Palestinian–Israeli struggle. With San Antonio, Texas, pastor John Hagee, founder of Christians United for Israel (CUFI), a pro-Israel group established in 2006, often in the vanguard, Christian Zionists have strongly supported Israeli security initiatives, including Jewish settlements in the West Bank and military intervention in Gaza, and they are much less inclined to have sympathy for Palestinian interests than is the case for American denominations who have close ties to Palestinian Christians.[26] The Presbyterian Church in the USA (PCUSA), whose members number about 1.8 million, provides a rancorous example.

For a decade, the PCUSA debated but rejected, albeit by narrow margins, divestment in companies that supply Israel with equipment and products used to dominate Palestinian territory.[27] In a contentious episode on June 20, 2014, however, the church's General Assembly voted 310 to 303 to sell church holdings in Caterpillar, Hewlett-Packard, and Motorola Solutions – worth about $21 million – because those corporations aid and profit from Israeli policies deemed hostile to Palestinian rights. The PCUSA contended that its action on divestment was not "an alignment with or endorsement of the global BDS (Boycott, Divest, and Sanctions) movement" – its goals range from boycotting Israeli companies and institutions to rolling back Israeli settlements in the West Bank and east Jerusalem. The divestment measure also included reaffirmation of "Israel's right to exist as a sovereign nation within secure and internationally recognized borders in accordance with the United Nations resolutions." But the denomination also established a study task force whose charge includes exploring "whether the General Assembly should continue to call for a two-state solution in Israel Palestine, or take a neutral stance that seeks not to determine for Israelis and Palestinians what the right 'solution' should be." Commenting on the crucial divestment vote immediately after it was taken, Heath Rada, the General Assembly's moderator, claimed that the outcome did not reflect "lack of love for our Jewish brothers and sisters." A few days later, on June 26, 2014, the denomination issued "An Open Letter of the Presbyterian Church (U.S.A.) to Our American Jewish Interfaith Partners." It asserted that "we are committed more than ever to sitting at the table and living in community with you."[28]

Although debate about these measures was eclipsed by the Hamas–Israel war in Gaza, which provoked antisemitic protests and even allegations of genocide that distorted Israel's actions and trivialized the Holocaust, most Jews found the official Presbyterian rhetoric about the divestment vote unconvincing and misleading. Tragic and hostile, sad and shameful, hurtful and devastating, disgraceful and outrageous – those words, also voiced by Presbyterians who disagreed with the church's divestment decision, were frequently pronounced in Jewish reactions, which included predictions of rupture with the PCUSA. Underscoring that the divestment move "is an affront to the Jewish community," Rabbi Gary M. Bretton-Granatoor, a vice president of the World Union for Progressive Judaism, alleged that the PCUSA's recent posture toward Israel indicates that Presbyterians "have not … developed a language of understanding and respect upon which to respectfully engage with Jews on political questions."[29] Jane Eisner, editor of the *Jewish Daily Forward*, put a sharper edge on that outlook when she said that Presbyterian divestment felt antisemitic. "When Jewish treatment of Palestinians is judged worse than the way any other dominant group treats a minority, when it is deemed worthy of unique sanction, when other horrors around the world are ignored," said Eisner, "how can I believe that this isn't about the Jews? And that, my Presbyterian friends, is anti-Semitism."[30] By no means did such views belong to those two commentators alone. Rabbi Noam Marans, director of interreligious relations at the American Jewish Committee, also struck a shared note when he stressed that the PCUSA decision would be "celebrated by those who believe they are one step closer to a Jew-free Middle East."[31]

The Holocaust was not at the center of the PCUSA's 2014 General Assembly. Nevertheless, it still shadowed the church's divestment decision because the PCUSA includes pro-Palestinian outlooks, which sometimes stress that the largely Christian West sought to make amends for the *Shoah* by establishing a Jewish homeland in Palestine. As "Kairos Palestine," a 2009 statement by a group of Christian Palestinians that has been widely circulated by the Israel/Palestine Mission Network (IPMN) of the PCUSA, put this point, "The West sought to make amends for what Jews had endured in the countries of Europe, but it made amends on our account and in our land. They tried to correct an injustice and the result was a new injustice."[32] Controversy about such claims intensified in 2014 when the IPMN issued "Zionism Unsettled: A Congregational Study Guide," which questioned the legitimacy of the State of Israel. As Chris Leighton, executive director of the Institute for Christian & Jewish Studies (ICJS) and an ordained Presbyterian minister, aptly evaluated this problematic document, "it portrays Zionism as inexorably leading to 'ethnic cleansing' and 'cultural genocide.' The condemnation of Zionism in all its forms, is not merely simplistic and misleading; the result of this polemic is the theological delegitimization of a central concern of the Jewish people."[33] With anger about this publication reaching a crescendo in the days following the Presbyterian vote on divestment, the PCUSA announced on June 27, 2014, that "Zionism Unsettled" would no longer be for sale on its website.

Provocative variations on the claims contained in the 2009 and 2014 IPMN documents have been articulated by Mark Braverman, an American Jew, in his hard-hitting book called *Fatal Embrace: Christians, Jews, and the Search for Peace in the Holy Land*. Braverman argues that Christian attempts to atone for the Holocaust and Christianity's complicity in that disaster, appropriate though they are, have also had the unfortunate consequence of reinforcing Jewish exceptionalism and chosen-ness in ways that make many Christians complicit in crimes that Braverman believes the State of Israel is committing against Palestinians. Even well-intentioned Christian–Jewish dialogue, he suggests, has contributed to these unfortunate outcomes, because it can intensify Christian guilt in ways that play into the hands of a problematic pro-Israel orientation. Theologically speaking, for example, Braverman contends that

> attempts to correct for Christian supersessionism by preserving or incorporating God's election of Israel ultimately replace Christian supersessionism with Jewish exceptionalism. And if Christian

> triumphalism as expressed in supersessionism led to the ovens of Auschwitz, then Jewish triumphalism as expressed in political Zionism has led to the ethnic cleansing of Palestine.[34]

Put more bluntly, Braverman suggests that "out of repentance for the Holocaust, 'sensitivity' to the feelings of Jews, and fear of being labeled anti-Semitic," many Christians have "sold out the Palestinian people."[35] Such allegations were at least in the background of the PCUSA's divestment stance in June 2014. They strike many Jews as well as Christians, including many Presbyterians, as inaccurate and outrageous, not least because they are likely to inflame antisemitism, adding to the distressing findings of "ADL Global 100 Index," the 2014 largest-ever global survey about antisemitism conducted by the Anti-Defamation League. It found that 26 percent of those polled – 53,000 people in 102 countries and territories – "harbor deeply anti-Semitic views." The most problematic areas were in the Middle East and North Africa, where 74 percent have antisemitic views. In the Palestinian territories of the West Bank and Gaza, the figure rises to 93 percent, a number that likely rose as a result of the 2014 Hamas–Israel war. Furthermore, the report states, "thirty-five percent of those surveyed had never heard of the Holocaust. Of those who have, roughly one-third believe the Holocaust is either a myth or greatly exaggerated."[36] The report further indicates that smaller percentages of Europeans – 34 percent in Eastern Europe and 24 percent in Western Europe – hold "deeply anti-Semitic views," but arguably those numbers do not sufficiently gauge the blurring of a distinction between opposing Israel and opposing Jews or the degree to which European antisemitism has been spiking – without much priority being given to fighting that trend – and fueling realistic worries about the future of Jewish life on that continent.[37]

Much of the antisemitism documented in the ADL's findings is inflamed by hostility toward Israel and has direct links to Islamist radicals and their followers. But without Christian accountability regarding antisemitism's Christian roots, heritage, and lethal ties to the Holocaust, the content, tone, and implications of contemporary antisemitism cannot be adequately assessed and resisted. Whenever and wherever antisemitism exists, including in a largely post-Christian Europe, Christians should be vigilant and outspoken against it.

Meanwhile, views such as Braverman's have gained traction. While it is too soon to tell how they will affect Christian–Jewish relations in the long run, such thinking adds problematic wrinkles to the place of the Holocaust within those relations. Overcoming Christianity's complicity in the Holocaust, a challenge that can never be fully met, is now complicated even further if it turns out that attention to the Holocaust, understood as Braverman thinks it should be, leads to the conclusion that "the meaning of the Holocaust" requires that an anti-Israel priority is given to "working for justice for Palestine."[38]

Despite these difficulties, and ironically because the Palestinian–Israeli conflict is likely to loom large in the foreseeable future, further complicated as it is becoming as uprisings, rebellions, war, and particularly the atrocities committed by ISIS destabilize the Muslim Middle East, the likelihood is that the Holocaust's impact on Christian–Jewish relations in the United States and elsewhere is waning. That prospect might reduce tensions between Christians and Jews, but the value and outcomes of that dispersal of attention on the Holocaust remain to be seen. To the extent that Christians and Jews underplay, distort, or grow complacent about the Holocaust's implications for their own traditions or allow attention to the Holocaust to be eclipsed by other events, the prospects for avoiding dangerous disruptions in the relationships between Christians and Jews are not improved but may be worsened.

Continuing Reverberations

This analysis, which is itself a modest part of the Holocaust's impact on Christian–Jewish relations in the United States, makes clear that descriptions of and forecasts about the Holocaust's impact on Christian–Jewish relations are as complex and fraught as they may be partially gratifying and cautiously hopeful. After – and, tragically, because of – the Holocaust, relations between Christians and Jews in the United States and elsewhere are arguably about as good as they have ever been. But stresses and strains on those relationships remain and may grow more intense.

Christians have not yet come to terms fully with the Holocaust's implication that Christianity can no longer take itself to be superior to Judaism. If that recognition can deepen, it would allow religious pluralism to grow, which would be a fitting development for American Christianity in particular to advance. Such advancement would require profound changes in Christian thought and practice. And if religious pluralism advances in a post-Holocaust world, those developments will not leave Judaism untouched, either.

Much still depends on whether and how the Holocaust is thoroughly encountered. A positive step in that direction was taken on July 29, 2016, when Pope Francis became the third post-Holocaust pontiff to visit Auschwitz and Birkenau. Pope John Paul II had done so in 1979, Pope Benedict XVI in 2006. Francis met survivors and rescuers, prayed in silence, and wrote a guest book entry that said, "Lord, have mercy on your people. Lord, forgive so much cruelty." Important examples though they are, that papal visit and its humble but still predominantly silent response testify primarily to how much work it will take to engage the Holocaust challenges that Christianity still needs to address. Obstacles to such encounters appear to be growing as the *Shoah* recedes further into the past. In addition, the seemingly intractable Palestinian–Israeli conflict extends its increasingly divisive ways, and upheavals in the Muslim world and the global persistence of terrorism and mass atrocity crimes create present-day urgencies that edge the Holocaust away from center stage and require reevaluation of what the credibility of its "lessons" may be. So how are Christian–Jewish relations trending as the 50th anniversary of *Nostra Aetate* comes and goes? The Holocaust remains a civilization-sized trauma. Its reverberations will continue to affect Christian–Jewish relations in the United States and elsewhere, but how they will play out cannot be foreseen because that depends on teaching and research, policy and practice, discourse and dialogue that have yet to be enacted.

Elie Wiesel, the great Jewish writer and Holocaust survivor, died on July 2, 2016, a few weeks before Pope Francis visited the place of death and despair that Wiesel and his family entered in the summer of 1944. All too soon, each and every survivor will be gone, taking the Holocaust itself into the past more and more. Numerous times in his writings and lectures, Wiesel spoke of a "mysterious Talmudic scholar" who became his teacher for several years in postwar France. Equally brilliant and enigmatic, Shushani, as he was known, received high tribute from Wiesel: "I would not be the man I am, the Jew I am, had not an astonishing, disconcerting vagabond [Shushani] accosted me one day to inform me that I understood nothing."[39] Wiesel learned much more than that from his teacher. One of the most important insights he took from Shushani – it became a key part of Wiesel's ethics – is that "man defines himself by what disturbs him and not by what reassures him. ... God means movement and not explanation."[40] The Holocaust should forever disturb Christians and Jews together. Even if *Nostra Aetate* made no explicit reference to the Holocaust, its promulgation in the wake of that catastrophe keeps adding significantly to Shoah-related disturbances that should reject closure and be ongoing. Those disturbances will scarcely be reassuring, but they can be defining in ways that keep protesting and resisting the failures of ethics that still haunt Christian–Jewish relations.

Questions for Discussion

1. *How important was the Holocaust in changing Catholic teachings about Jews and Judaism? Do* Nostra Aetate *and related documents that followed it reflect that importance?*

2. *Have Christians paid too much attention to the Holocaust, too little attention, or just about the right amount of attention? Explain.*

3. *Should Christians think that Christ is the Redeemer of the Jews in addition to the Gentiles? Why or why not?*

4. *In your view, what would be the ideal relationship among Christians, Jews, and Muslims? What are the main obstacles that stand in the way of that ideal relationship?*

5. *If you could take one step to improve relationships between Christians (Catholics in particular), Jews, and Muslims, what would that step be?*

Further Reading

Berger, Alan L. (Ed.). *Post-Holocaust Jewish-Christian Dialogue: After the Flood, before the Rainbow* (Lanham, MD: Lexington Books, 2015).

Bergoglio, Jorge Mario, and Abraham Skorka. *On Heaven and Earth: Pope Francis on Faith, Family, and the Church in the Twenty-first Century*. Trans. Alejandro Bermudez and Howard Goodman (New York: Image, 2013).

Connelly, John. *From Enemy to Brother: The Revolution in Catholic Teaching on the Jews, 1933–1965* (Cambridge, MA: Harvard University Press, 2012).

Cunningham, Philip A. *Seeking Shalom: The Journey to Right Relationship between Catholics and Jews* (Grand Rapids, MI: Wm. B. Eerdmans Publishing, 2015).

D'Costa, Gavin. *Vatican II: Catholic Doctrines on Jews and Muslims* (Oxford: Oxford University Press, 2014).

Roth, John K. *The Failures of Ethics: Confronting the Holocaust, Genocide, and Other Mass Atrocities* (Oxford: Oxford University Press, 2015).

Valkenberg, Pim, and Anthony Cirelli (Eds.). *Nostra Aetate: Celebrating 50 Years of the Catholic Church's Dialogue with Jews and Muslims* (Washington, DC: Catholic University of America Press, 2016).

Film and Video Resources

Constantine's Sword (93 mins). Directed by Oren Jacoby. Available at Amazon.com.

European Antisemitism from Its Origins to the Holocaust (12 mins). Produced by the US Holocaust Memorial Museum. Available at https://www.ushmm.org/confront-antisemitism/european-antisemitism-from-its-origins-to-the-holocaust.

The Longest Hatred: A Revealing History of Anti-Semitism (150 mins). Produced by Frontline, PBS. Available at Amazon.com.

Vatican II: Inside the Council (ten-part series, 30 mins each). Produced by DeSales Media Group. Available at http://netny.tv/shows/vatican-ii/.

Notes

1. For elaboration on these themes, see John K. Roth, *The Failures of Ethics: Confronting the Holocaust, Genocide, and Other Mass Atrocities* (Oxford: Oxford University Press, 2015). This essay emerges from my reflection in that book.
2. The full texts of the Genocide Convention and the Universal Declaration of Human Rights are available online, respectively, at http://www.oas.org/dil/1948_Convention_on_the_Prevention_and_Punishment_of_the_Crime_of_Genocide.pdf, and http://www.un.org/en/documents/udhr/.
3. Philip A. Cunningham, *Seeking Shalom: The Journey to Right Relationship between Catholics and Jews* (Grand Rapids, MI: Wm. B. Eerdmans Publishing, 2015), p. 222.
4. The texts of these documents, along with many others pertaining to the history and impact of *Nostra Aetate*, are accessible at http://www.ccjr.us/dialogika-resources/educational-and-liturgical-materials/curricula/1233-na50. Focused on the 50th anniversary of *Nostra Aetate*, this excellent Web resource has been developed by Dialogika, an online library that chronicles the evolving conversation and relationship between the Christian and Jewish communities, which is maintained through the collaboration of the Council of Centers on Jewish-Christian Relations (CCJR) and the Institute for Jewish-Catholic Relations of Saint Joseph's University in Philadelphia, PA. The quoted passage from "Guidelines and Suggestions" is from that document's Preamble. The quotation from "Notes" appears near the end of that document, in a section called "Judaism and Christianity in History" (p. 25).
5. The text of the document is accessible at http://www.vatican.va/roman_curia/pontifical_councils/chrstuni/relations-jews-docs/rc_pc_chrstuni_doc_20151210_ebraismo-nostra-aetate_en.html. Citations to the document refer to its numbered paragraphs and appear in parentheses within this essay.
6. See, for example, "Celebrating and Deepening the New Christian–Jewish Relationship: A Statement from the International Council of Christians and Jews for the Golden Jubilee of the Second Vatican Council Declaration, *Nostra Aetate*" (June 30, 2015), accessible at: http://www.ccjr.us/dialogika-resources/educational-and-liturgical-materials/curricula/1233-na50. For the Rosen quotation, see "AJC and Archdiocese of Los Angeles Celebrate 50th Anniversary of *Nostra Aetate*" (June 30, 2015). The celebration, called "A Watershed Moment in Catholic–Jewish Relations: Marking the 50th Anniversary of *Nostra Aetate*," took place on February 17, 2015. The article is accessible at http://www.ajclosangeles.org/site/apps/nlnet/content3.aspx?c=mlI0IfN1JyE&b=8581805&ct=14534101&notoc=1.
7. John Connelly, *From Enemy to Brother: The Revolution in Catholic Teaching on the Jews, 1933–1965* (Cambridge, MA: Harvard University Press, 2012), p. 2.
8. Striking a good balance on this point, John Connelly notes, for example, that some of the understandings informing *Nostra Aetate* "were unthinkable before the Holocaust." Prior to the Holocaust, he further observes, "Christians could not suddenly close their eyes to teachings dating back to the second century according to which Jews were fated to suffer until they turned to Christ." Yet Connelly minces no words: the promulgation of *Nostra Aetate* and its positions on Judaism and the Jewish people in particular "shattered centuries of harmful teaching." See *ibid* 207, 175, 167. Shortcomings and shortfalls — failures — are no less real if tradition, culture, and perhaps especially religion convince us that our ways of thinking and acting are what they ought to be. Experience and history often show us that those ways are not what they ought to have been or should be now and in the future. For Christians, the Holocaust had that effect with a vengeance that has not yet been fully comprehended, let alone reckoned with sufficiently.
9. The text of *Nostra Aetate* is accessible at http://www.ccjr.us/dialogika-resources/educational-and-liturgical-materials/curricula/1233-na50.
10. For this reminder, I am indebted to the historian Victoria Barnett, the staff director for the Committee on Ethics, Religion, and the Holocaust at the United States Holocaust Memorial Museum. Her helpful reading of an earlier version of this essay led to an email exchange in which she correctly noted that in the United States, "there have been Christian–Jewish partnerships and conversations, including self-critical theological ones, since the 1890s at least." Barnett sees two tracks of Christian–Jewish dialogue in the United States. One emerges directly out of Holocaust studies, but another, of longer standing, continues without the Holocaust at its base. By now, of course, many initiatives in the second track, Barnett acknowledges, "do incorporate Holocaust commemoration."
11. For amplification of these themes, see John K. Roth, *Holocaust Politics* (Louisville, KY: Westminster John Knox Press, 2001), esp. pp. 188–196.
12. Jorge Mario Bergoglio and Abraham Skorka, *On Heaven and Earth: Pope Francis on Faith, Family, and the*

THE HOLOCAUST AND *NOSTRA AETATE*: TOWARD A GREATER UNDERSTANDING

Church in the Twenty-first Century, trans. Alejandro Bermudez and Howard Goodman (New York: Image, 2013), p. 183.

13. Pope Paul VI, the first pontiff to visit Israel, met a necessary condition for Roman Catholic sainthood with his beatification in October 2014. The relevant text from *Nostra Aetate* can be found at http://www.ccjr.us/dialogika-resources/educational-and-liturgical-materials/curricula/1233-na50.

14. See Jules Isaac, *The Teaching of Contempt: Christian Roots of Anti-Semitism*, trans. Helen Weaver (New York: Holt, Rinehart and Winston, 1964). Isaac's conversations with Pope John XXIII in June 1960 advanced deliberations and reforms reflected in the actions of the Second Vatican Council and *Nostra Aetate*. On the important parts played by U.S. Catholic leaders in support of *Nostra Aetate*, see James A. Rudin, *Cushing, Spellman, O'Conner: The Surprising Story of How Three American Cardinals Transformed Catholic-Jewish Relations* (Grand Rapids, MI: William B. Eerdmans, 2012).

15. As John T. Pawlikowski points out, *Nostra Aetate* entailed that the Jewish people "cannot be seen as exiled from their original covenant with God." It did not resolve, however, two issues that remain contentious: (1) Can Christians affirm both the universal significance of Jesus as the incarnation of God and the continuing validity of the Jewish covenant with God? (2) Should Christians try to convert Jews? See Pawlikowski's "Fifty Years of Christian–Jewish Dialogue—What Has It Changed?" *Journal of Ecumenical Studies*, 49(1), 2014, pp. 99, 102, 105. This article provides a compact and reliable overview of several key moments and developments in Christian–Jewish relations.

16. Sources as diverse as Fox News, the *New York Times*, and the Catholic News Service stressed this point in their early March 2011 stories about the release of Benedict's book. For more information, see the New York Times (March 3, 2011), p. A5, and the following Web sites: http://www.foxnews.com/world/2011/03/02/pope-exonerates-jews-jesus-death-new-book/; http://www.catholicnews.com/services/englishnews/2011/scholars-see-benefits-for-all-faiths-in-pope-s-second-jesus-book-cns-1100974.cfm.

17. Steinberg's statements can be found at the Fox News site identified in the note above.

18. Foxman's statement can be found at http://www.adl.org/press-center/press-releases/interfaith/adl-says-pope-benedicts-exoneration-of-jews-historical.html.

19. Bergoglio and Skorka, *On Heaven and Earth*, p. 19. Pope Francis's encyclical *Evangelii Gaudium* ("The Joy of the Gospel," November 24, 2013) accents that God's covenant with the Jewish people "has never been revoked," but also states that "the Church cannot refrain from proclaiming Jesus as Lord and Messiah," implying that these are among Christian beliefs "unacceptable to Judaism." This outlook does not resolve issues about the ultimate relationship between the two traditions and their truth claims. The key passages from *Evangelii Gaudium* are in a section called "Relations with Judaism" (paragraphs 247–9). *Evangelii Gaudium* is accessible at http://w2.vatican.va/content/francesco/en/apost_exhortations/documents/papa-francesco_esortazione-ap_20131124_evangelii-gaudium.html#Relations_with_Judaism.

20. This document is available at http://pcinterreligious.org/uploads/pdfs/DIALOGUE_IN_TRUTH_AND_CHARITY_website-1.pdf. Page numbers for quotations from it appear in parentheses in the discussion that follows.

21. Earlier in 2009, Pope Benedict XVI found himself embroiled in another controversy that affected Christian–Jewish relations when he lifted the excommunication of four bishops from the ultra-conservative Society of St. Pius X. Apparently, that action's purpose was to open paths for reconciliation that would heal schism, a dreaded reality in Roman Catholicism. A global firestorm ensued when it became clear that one of the rehabilitated bishops, Richard Williamson, had been a Holocaust denier. The Vatican's damage control kept the crisis from spiraling out of control, but Benedict XVI's misstep did nothing to improve Christian–Jewish relations. For insightful commentary by Christians and Jews – many of them Americans – on the Williamson affair, see Carol Rittner and Stephen D. Smith (Eds.), *No Going Back: Letters to Pope Benedict XVI on the Holocaust, Jewish-Christian Relations & Israel* (London: Quill Press, 2009).

22. The full text of this interview is available at http://www.catholicnewsagency.com/news/pope-francis-interview-with-la-vanguardia---full-text-45430/.

23. On these points, two books by Michael Phayer are significant. See *The Catholic Church and the Holocaust, 1930-1965* (Bloomington: Indiana University Press, 2000), and *Pius XII, the Holocaust, and the Cold War* (Bloomington: Indiana University Press, 2008). See also Carol Rittner and John K. Roth (Eds.), *Pope Pius XII and the Holocaust* (New York: Continuum, 2002), and Paul O'Shea, *A Cross Too Heavy: Pope Pius XII and the Jews of Europe* (New York: Palgrave Macmillan, 2011). The State of Israel came into existence in 1948 during the reign of Pius XII, but the Vatican did not officially recognize the State of Israel until 1993. The posture of Pius XII contributed to that delay. Significantly, during Pope Francis's visit to Israel in

the spring of 2014, he laid a wreath at the grave of Theodor Herzl, the father of modern Zionism. That act was widely seen as a decisive repudiation of the position taken by Pope Pius X when he granted Herzl an audience on January 26, 1904. Herzl's diary account of the meeting, which lasted about 25 minutes, documented that the pope rebuffed Herzl's effort to obtain papal support for a Jewish state in Palestine: "The Jews have not recognized our Lord," Herzl quoted the Pope, "therefore we cannot recognize the Jewish people." Herzl's diary entry about this meeting is available at http://www.ccjr.us/dialogika-resources/primary-texts-from-the-history-of-the-relationship/1253-herzl1904.

24. For Christian–Jewish dialogue on these matters, see Leonard Grob and John K. Roth (Eds.), *Anguished Hope: Holocaust Scholars Confront the Palestinian–Israeli Conflict* (Grand Rapids, MI: William B. Eerdmans, 2008).

25. Dated May 9, 2014, Rosner's sobering article, "Kerry's Mideast 'Failure' Was a Success," appeared in the *New York Times* and is available at http://www.nytimes.com/2014/05/10/opinion/rosner-kerrys-mideast-failure-was-a-success.html?action=click&module=Search&region=searchResults&mabReward=relbias%3Ar&url=http%3A%2F%2Fquery.nytimes.com%2Fsearch%2Fsitesearch%2F%3Faction%3Dclick%26region%3DMasthead%26pgtype%3DHomepage%26module%3DSearchSubmit%26contentCollection%3DHomepage%26t%3Dqry321%23%2FShmuel+Rosner.

26. As Melanie Phillips argues, however, evangelical Christians, especially younger ones, are not immune to supersessionism and demonization of the State of Israel. She maintains that, particularly through their involvement in the "Christ at the Checkpoint" conferences run by the Bethlehem Bible College and Holy Land Trust, significant numbers of younger evangelical Christians have accepted an outlook that stresses Palestinian victimology, sees the State of Israel as a brutal oppressor, and jeopardizes solidarity between Christians and Jews. Those perspectives open the door for a resurgence of Christian supersessionism or replacement theology, outlooks that have done immense harm to Jews and to the integrity of Christianity, as well. See her article, "'Jesus Was a Palestinian': The Return of Christian Anti-Semitism," in *Commentary* (June 1, 2014), which is available at http://www.commentarymagazine.com/article/jesus-was-a-palestinian-the-return-of-christian-anti-semitism. In this highly critical account, Phillips musters evidence to show that especially "within the Protestant world," many churches and denominations are "deeply hostile to the State of Israel."

27. For further information about my position on these matters, see John K. Roth, "Duped by Morality? Defusing Minefields in the Israeli–Palestinian Struggle," in *Anguished Hope*, ed. Grob and Roth, pp. 30–49.

28. The full text of the open letter is accessible at https://www.pcusa.org/news/2014/6/26/open-letter-pcusa-us-our-american-jewish-partners/.

29. Gary M. Bretton-Granatoor, "The Presbyterians' Judaism Problem," *Jewish Telegraphic Agency* (June 27, 2014). The full text of the article is accessible at http://www.jta.org/2014/06/27/news-opinion/opinion/op-ed-the-presbyterians-judaism-problem-1?utm_source=Newsletter+subscribers&utm_campaign=ddaff67904-JTA_Daily_Briefing_6_27_2014&utm_medium=email&utm_term=0_2dce5bc6f8-ddaff67904-25357233.

30. Jane Eisner, "Why Presbyterian Divestment Feels Like Anti-Semitism," *Jewish Daily Forward* (June 25, 2014). The editorial is accessible at: http://forward.com/articles/200724/why-presbyterian-divestment-feels-like-anti-semiti/?p=all.

31. Immediately after the PCUSA divestment vote, international media tracked reactions to it. See, for example, Rebecca Shimoni Stoil, "Presbyterian Church Votes in Favor of Divestment," *The Times of Israel* (June 21, 2014), which features a sampling of Jewish commentary. The article is accessible at http://www.timesofisrael.com/presbyterian-church-votes-in-favor-of-divesting-from-israel/.

32. See *Kairos Palestine: A Moment of Truth* (Louisville, KY: Israel/Palestine Mission Network of the Presbyterian Church (USA), 2010), p. 16 (2.3.2). In addition to "Kairos Palestine," this booklet contains a three-week congregational study plan, which, along with *A Steadfast Hope: The Palestinian Quest for a Just Peace*, a film in DVD format, received considerable attention, some of it highly critical, in Presbyterian circles. The Israel/Palestine Mission Network (IPMN) of the Presbyterian Church (USA) identifies itself as "a grassroots organization established in 2004 with a mandate from the denomination's General Assembly to advocate for Palestinian rights and bring a deeper understanding to their struggle under military occupation. As part of its mandate, the IPMN speaks *to* the church, not *for* the church."

33. Chris Leighton, "An Open Letter to the Presbyterian Church" (February 8, 2014). The letter is accessible at the ICJS website, http://www.icjs.org/featured-articles/open-letter-presbyterian-church-0.

34. Mark Braverman, *Fatal Embrace: Christians, Jews, and the Search for Peace in the Holy Land* (Austin, TX: Synergy Books, 2010), p. 114. Braverman's critique aims at several American Christian post-Holocaust

thinkers in particular, among them James Carroll, R. Kendall Soulen, Paul van Buren, and Clark Williamson. He counts three other American scholars as key allies: Walter Brueggemann and Rosemary Ruether, both Christians, and the Jewish liberation theologian Marc Ellis.
35. Braverman, *Fatal Embrace*, p. 188.
36. See Uriel Heilman, "Survey: More Than a Quarter of the World Hates Jews," *Jewish Telegraphic Agency* (May 13, 2014). The article is accessible at http://www.jta.org/2014/05/13/news-opinion/world/survey-more-than-a-quarter-of-the-world-hates-jews?utm_source=Newsletter+subscribers&utm_campaign=5963f2bb97-JTA_Daily_Briefing_5_13_2014&utm_medium=email&utm_term=0_2dce5bc6f8-5963f2bb97-25357233. See also "Int'l Survey Says Anti-Semitic Attitudes Pervasive," *Associated Press* (May 13, 2014). The article is accessible at http://news.yahoo.com/intl-survey-says-anti-semitic-attitudes-pervasive-182442297.html. Further details are available at the ADL website for the survey, http://global100.adl.org/#map/americas.
37. See, for example, Jonathan Sacks, "Europe's Alarming New Anti-Semitism," *The Wall Street Journal* (October 3, 2014). The article is accessible at http://online.wsj.com/articles/europes-alarming-new-anti-semitism-1412270003.
38. Braverman, *Fatal Embrace*, p. 39.
39. Elie Wiesel, *All Rivers Run to the Sea: Memoirs* (New York: Alfred A. Knopf, 1995), pp. 121, 130. Shushani's students included the philosopher Emmanuel Levinas.
40. Elie Wiesel, *Legends of Our Time* (New York: Schocken Books, 1982), p. 93.

1951. New Canaan. Thomas Jefferson's Oath
Image Courtesy of The Arthur Szyk Society

Fifty Years of Catholic-Jewish Relations: The Continuing Challenges

John T. Pawlikowski, O.S.M.

Professor of Social Ethics and Director of the Catholic-Jewish Studies Program, Catholic Theological Union, Chicago, IL

When we look at the history of what became Vatican II's document *Nostra Aetate*, it is clear that it had multiple parentage. A change in the basic perspective between the Old Testament and the New Testament among some biblical scholars in the first part of the twentieth century and the positive experience of Catholics and Jews working together on social issues such as the dignity and rights of workers in countries like the United States certainly had an impact on the birth of *Nostra Aetate*. Even though the Declaration never specifically mentions the *Shoah*, there is little question that the experience of the Holocaust played a central role in its emergence.

As many are no doubt aware, the proposal for a Conciliar statement on the Catholic Church's relationship with the Jewish people resulted from a historic meeting between St. John XXIII and the French Jewish historian Jules Isaac. Both had significant connections to the *Shoah*. Pope John XXIII, as papal nuncio in Istanbul, arranged for many false baptismal certificates for Jews fleeing the Nazis, thus saving them from the death camps. Jules Isaac lost most of his family in that period of dark and evil. We know, as well, that some of the more important proponents of a statement had been involved with Catholic anti-Nazi resistance movements during World War II.

The Nazi ideology of Jewish annihilation, while ultimately against all religion, drew many of its ideas and images regarding Jews and Judaism from the centuries-long history of antisemitism in Christianity, with its roots going back to the patristic tradition. Classical Christian antisemitism provided a fertile seedbed for the growth of Nazi ideology even though the Nazi prescription for Jews and Judaism went considerably beyond what Christianity had ever envisioned. The Christian "plan," if we may call it that, wanted to make Jews miserable and marginal in human society as a punishment for not accepting Jesus as the expected Jewish Messiah. Though, as the late Fr. Edward Flannery estimated in his classic volume *The Anguish of the Jews*,[1] some one million Jews perished at the hands of Christians over the centuries, the Church wished to keep Jews alive in a state of misery as a warning to people of what happens when one rejects Jesus. The Nazi "plan," on the other hand, aimed at the total annihilation of the Jewish population. Continued existence of the Jews in the Nazi vision constituted a drain on humanity as a whole. Both plans were morally outrageous, but they were somewhat different.

Immediately after the war, a number of prominent Christians began to recognize the destructive nature of the history of Christian antisemitism and how it in fact had aided and abetted the Nazi plan for Jews; they set out to erase such views from Christian consciousness. Some of the more important figures, as John Connelly has shown, were Jewish converts to Christianity, such as John Oesterreicher and Karl Thieme.[2] The people who gathered right after the war in 1947 in the Swiss town of Seelisberg and drafted ten points to combat Christian antisemitism also recognized how the Nazi era had exposed the ugliness of the antisemitic cancer within Christianity.[3] This development also helped lay the foundations for the eventual statement from Vatican II that profoundly undercut the basis for the tradition of Christian contempt for the Jews.

A third causal influence on *Nostra Aetate* came from the experience of Christian leaders in working on social issues with Jews in countries like the United States. While these positive experiences in social collaboration did not immediately lead to changes at the level of basic religious teachings, eventually they helped convince the American bishops at the Second Vatican Council that working with Jews should be encouraged, as it produced good results for the members of both communities. The bishops also recognized that any continuation of prejudicial views of Jews and Judaism would harm the enhanced effort at collaboration. Yet, the studies on Catholic textbooks at St. Louis University in the late 50s and early 60s, summarized in my volume *Catechetics and Prejudice*,[4] which were brought to the Council by official observer Rabbi Marc Tanenbaum, illustrated that a major problem still existed with respect to the representation of Jews and Judaism in the most widely used Catholic teaching materials for primary and secondary grades.

While the document that eventually became the Conciliar *Nostra Aetate* was forced to navigate some difficult waters during Council deliberations, in the end it passed by an overwhelming majority, thanks in significant part to the skillful handling of the process by Cardinal Augustin Bea. Its passage set the framework for a significant revamping in which the Secretariat for Ecumenical and Interreligious Affairs of the U.S. Catholic Bishops' Conference took a lead role under the direction of Fr. Edward Flannery and, later, Dr. Eugene J. Fisher.

But so much for the history of *Nostra Aetate*. It certainly has instilled in Catholic consciousness a new template for expressing the Christian-Jewish relationship historically and in the present day. This is particularly true with respect to Jews and Judaism, but also, at least in general terms, with respect to the Church's understanding of how it ought to view all other religious traditions. In short, *Nostra Aetate* reversed the image of these religious traditions from "enemy" and "threat" to one in which "friendship" and "collaboration" became the prevailing motifs. Overall, these new images have held firm in the last 50 years despite some significant tensions in the relationships over the last half-century. This only shows that the new images have developed strong roots in the Church's consciousness and should be seen as a remarkable transformation of basic religious vision, even though major challenges remain.

I would like to turn our attention to some of those continuing challenges both for Christianity and Judaism. Let me begin with the need for a joint Christian-Jewish effort, one that may well include other religious communities (especially Islam) and concerned people who are unaffiliated with a particular religious community to combat the seeming growth of antisemitism and other forms of hatred rooted in religion in many parts of the world. In Europe, for example, many Jews have genuine fears as to their future on a continent that Hitler tried to transform into *Judenrein*. Might his vision, defeated in the last century, become reality in the twenty-first? I do not wish to present a totally alarmist picture by any means. The Jewish presence in Europe still shows signs of definite resiliency and, generally speaking, political leaders in various countries have stood up against this new threat unlike during the period of the Third Reich. The *Shoah* revealed the power and depth of human hatred as the Nazi-organized machine assaulted basic human dignity, first and foremost against the Jews, but also against the disabled, Roma and Sinti, Poles, and gay people. The images of that assault must remain forever before our eyes. The stories of the victims need to be on our lips as we teach in educational programs and exercise our responsibilities as citizens in contemporary society.

And through the lens of the *Shoah*, we must also become sensitive to other situations of human degradation in various parts of the globe. Here I need to single out Islamophobia and the brutal, virtually genocidal attacks on Christians in Syria, Iraq, and elsewhere, as well as the increasing attacks against Christian institutions in Israel, which in many cases have not been adequately prosecuted and which have intensified fears among Israel's Christian population. Let me be clear in this regard: by no means am I equating ISIS and the "price tag" with related militant groups in Israel.

But the situation facing Christians and Muslims in Israel must be carefully watched. The toleration of hatred anywhere intensifies toleration of hatred everywhere.

As we enter the second half-century of the new understanding of the Church's relationship with Jews, several other important issues remain on the dialogue agenda. Besides supporting the notion of continued links with God on the part of the Jews and thus undercutting the very foundations of the historic deicide charge against them that served as a basis for classical Christian antisemitism, *Nostra Aetate* also emphasized the positive contributions of Second Temple Judaism to Jesus' preaching and ministry. This is in sharp contrast to earlier forms of Christian teaching that depicted Jesus as standing against the Judaism of his time. One now finds an emphasis on the positive links between Jesus and the Jewish tradition during his three years of public ministry in most catechetical material used in North America, as well as in official Vatican documents and in the writings of a growing number of theologians. But the question remains, what impact has the movement towards a "Jewish Jesus" had on the articulation of central beliefs in the Christian tradition such as Christology and ecclesiology? In 1986, speaking at the annual convention of the Catholic Theological Society Annual Meeting in Chicago, Canadian theologian Gregory Baum, who served as an official expert at Vatican II and had a hand in the early drafts of what became *Nostra Aetate*, argued that this statement represented the most radical change in the ordinary magisterium of the Church to emerge from the Council. But little awareness of the radical nature of *Nostra Aetate* in terms of the Church's basic faith perspective has actually penetrated Catholic consciousness during the last 50 years. Hence, in this presentation, I would like to focus on what has happened in Christian theology with the new vision of the Church's relationship with the Jewish people.

Over the years a small cadre of individual Christian scholars and a few institutional leaders, such as Cardinal Walter Kasper and Cardinal Joseph Bernardin, have tried to reformulate basic Christian self-understanding in terms of Christology and ecclesiology. There have also been some attempts by theologians such ats Johannes Metz and Jurgen Moltmann to reflect on the impact of the *Shoah* on Christian theology. I will return to this latter question below.

The effort to apply the vision of *Nostra Aetate* to fundamental Christian faith perspectives took on some steam in the first decade or so after Vatican II, but it has waned somewhat in more recent years and partly absorbed into theological considerations regarding a more expansive interreligious vision. Scholars involved in the effort at constructing a post-supersessionist theology of the Christian-Jewish relationship included Monika Hellwig[6] and Paul van Buren, who produced a trilogy outlining a fundamentally new theological vision of the Church's relationship with the Jewish people in which the term "Israel" was defined as including both Jews and Christians.[7] Others such as Mary Boys,[8] Kendall Soulen,[9] and myself[10] have contributed to this ongoing theological discussion. Each has added valuable perspectives, but no one as yet has produced an interpretation that has caught the attention of a significant segment of the Christian theological community. So, with regard to theology, a new understanding of the Christian-Jewish relationship is still in its infancy. The only major change (and the significance of this change is not to be underestimated) is the perspectival reversal from a classical theology of Jewish covenantal exclusion after the Christ Event to a theology of continued Jewish covenantal inclusion.

A renewed theology of the Church's relationship with the Jewish people, including the Christological and ecclesiological implications of such a renewed theology, will need to begin with a grappling of very significant new developments in biblical studies over the past several decades regarding Christian-Jewish relations during the first several centuries of the Common Era. Beginning in the 1980s, there arose a movement sometimes termed the "Parting of the Ways" scholarship. Early participants in this movement included John Gager, Robin Scroggs, and the late Anthony Saldarini. Back in 1986, Scroggs, then a professor at Chicago Theological Seminary and subsequently at Union Theological Seminary in New York City, summarized the essential components of this new vision. As Scroggs saw the situation in the time of Jesus and soon thereafter, the following realities shaped the relationship between the Church and the synagogue: (1) The movement begun by Jesus and continued after his death in Palestine can best be described as a reform movement with the Jewish community of the time; (2) the Pauline missionary movement, as Paul understood it, was a Jewish mission that focused on the Gentiles as the proper object of a divine call to God's people; (3) and prior to the end of the Jewish war with the Romans in 70 C.E., there was no such reality as "Christianity." Followers of Jesus did not have a self-understanding of themselves as a religion over and against Judaism. A distinct Christian identity began to emerge only after the Jewish-Roman war. Finally, (4) the later portions of the Second Testament all show some signs of movement toward separation, but they also generally retain some contact with the original Jewish matrix.[11]

Anthony Saldarini added to this picture originally presented by Scroggs. In various essays he underlined the continuing presence of the "followers of the Way" within the wide tent that was the Jewish community of the time. Saldarini especially underscored the ongoing nexus between Christian theology and practice in the Eastern sectors of the Church and Judaism, a reality that is often ignored in Western theological discourse.[12]

The initial scholarship on the first several centuries of the Common Era has been advanced by an increasing number of other scholars, both Christian and Jewish.[13] John Meier, for example, argues that from a careful examination of New Testament evidence, Jesus must be seen as presenting himself to the Jewish community of his time as an eschatological prophet and miracle worker in the likeness of Elijah. According to Meier, Jesus was not interested in creating a separatist sect or a holy remnant along the lines of the Qumran sect, but he did envision the development of a special religious community within Israel. The idea that this community "within Israel" would slowly undergo a process of separation from Israel as it pursued a mission to the Gentiles in this present world – the long-term result being that this community would become predominantly Gentile itself – finds no place in Jesus' message of practice.[14] And David Frankfurter has insisted that within the various "clusters" of groups that included Jews and Christian Jews, there existed a "mutual influence persisting through late antiquity. There is evidence for a degree of overlap that, all things considered, threatens every construction of an historically distinct 'Christianity' before at least the mid-second century."[15] Finally, Paula Fredricksen questions the term "parting of the ways." For her, the term is unhelpful because it implies two solid blocks of believers, when in fact the various groups were intertwined for several centuries.[16]

One other implication of "parting of the ways" scholarship has to do with our perspective on Paul and his writing. These writings have had a pervasive influence on much Christian theology, Christology in particular, especially in Protestant churches. Recent scholarship has literally turned much of the traditional understanding of Paul, an understanding that has served as a bedrock for Christological interpretation, on its head. Paul is now seen as standing far more within the context of the Judaism of his day than previous Christologies have imagined. To argue, as many have done over the centuries, that Pauline thought represents the ultimate break between the Church and the synagogue, including at the level of theology, is increasingly being challenged by the emerging new scholarship on Paul.[17]

In addition to the scholarly developments just outlined, there also have been important papal reflections on the theology of the Christian-Jewish relationship. On a number of occasions, St. Pope John Paul II spoke of an inherent bond between Jews and Christians. The following quote is but one example of his emphasis on this theme:

> The Church of Christ discovers her "bond" with Judaism "searching into her mystery" (*Nostra Aetate*, 4). The Jewish religion is not "extrinsic" to us, but in a certain way "intrinsic" to our own religion. With Judaism we have a relationship which we do not have with any other religion.[18]

And in his acclaimed Apostolic Exhortation *Evangelii Gaudium* ("The Joy of the Gospel"), Pope Francis says much the same:

> We hold the Jewish people in special regard because their covenant with God has never been revoked, for "the gifts and the call of God

are irrevocable" (Rom 11:29). The Church, which shares with Jews an important part of the Sacred Scriptures, looks upon the people of the covenant and their faith as one of the sacred roots of her Christian identity (cf. Rom 11:16-18). As Christians, we cannot consider Judaism as a foreign religion; nor do we include Jews among those called to turn from idols and to serve the true God (cf. 1 Thes 1-9).[19]

These theological affirmations by Popes John Paul II and Francis raise for Christians today the question as to whether Judaism, especially its texts and traditions, need to be regarded as "in-house" resources for the expression of Christian belief. Put another way, how much do we need to "re-Judaize" Christianity to bring it into conformity with these papal perspectives? A few theologians such as Johannes Baptist Metz have argued for the necessity of such integration into Christian faith today.[20]

But let me note at this point that these perspectives also pose a challenge for Jewish religious thought. I raised this challenge some years ago in an essay in *Moment* magazine.[21] Can Christianity speak of an inherent bond with Judaism if no such understanding can be found in Jewish theological literature? Bondedness cannot be a one-way street. In a brief response to my essay, the prominent Jewish scholar Irving Greenberg acknowledged the validity of my question but went on to say that few Jews have thought of other religions, including their positive significance for Jewish religious self-understanding. In my mind, this remains an unfulfilled goal in Jewish religious thought. I suspect that the issue of theological bondedness and a mutually explored understanding of the continuing link between Judaism and Christianity must decide whether they are intertwined within a single covenantal framework that makes their relationship quite different from the relationship either has with other religious communities or whether they exist today as two quite separate religions despite their ties in the past. In other words, are the findings of the "parting of the ways" scholarship permanently significant for an understanding of the Jewish-Christian relationship?

While there certainly has been something less than a groundswell of Jewish religious scholars who have been willing to engage this issue from their side, a few are beginning to show some interest in the topic. Scholars such as Daniel Boyarin[22] have argued that what Christian theology refers to as Christology was something already existing in the Jewish thought of the time and not created totally anew for Jesus; rather, it was merely applied to him. While such a bold assertion is restricted to Boyarin, others such as Elliot Wolfson,[23] Benjamin Sommer,[24] and the various contributions to the volume *Teaching the Historical Jesus* edited by Zev Garber[25] represent an important breakthrough in this regard given the virtual taboo on this subject in Jewish circles just a few years ago.

The discussion has taken a new important step recently with the publication of a volume by Shaul Magid entitled *Hasidism Incarnate: Hasidism, Christianity and the Construction of Modern Judaism*.[26] In this new work, Magid presents Hasidism as a perspective on Judaism in which the divine/human boundary was permeable and sometimes even crossed. In examining anew the Hasidic tradition we discover, according to Magid, a resurgence of the very incarnational theology that mainstream forms of Judaism basically rejected, in large part clearly to distinguish the Jewish tradition from Christianity. Within Hasidic writings, God and humanity have been reintegrated. Though Magid's view does not venture as far as that of Boyarin, I see some similarities between them. Both seem to say that what has become Christianity's central theological assertion – Christology – has roots in a broader religious perspective found as well in Jewish thought circles of the first century.

The key sources for Magid's argument about the incarnational nature of Hasidism are the writings of noted rabbis such as Nachman of Bratzlav and Levi Yizhak of Berdichev, to name but a couple. Their portrayal of the *tsaddik*, the ultimate spiritual leader in the Hasidic tradition, as the person who intercedes between God and humanity in fact rekindles incarnational theology within Judaism, even though Magid is careful to assert that Hasidic incarnationalism differs substantially from notions of Christology in the Christian tradition. Note that he uses the term "rekindles." The Hasidic rabbis did not invent incarnationalism. Rather, they brought to the surface a notion that was present in Second Temple Judaism but then buried by Jewish thinkers once Christianity assumed dominance as a religious community in Europe. In that context, Jewish leaders felt impelled to maintain a clear boundary between the church and the synagogue for fear of conversion.

I will not pass judgment on whether incarnationalism is an apt term for explaining key elements of Hasidic thought. Prominent scholars such as Moshe Idel have criticized Magid for employing the term.[27] But his work, together with the other Jewish pioneering scholars in this field, have convinced me of the presence of a sense of divine immanence in Judaism which might well make for a fruitful theological conversation with Christian scholars. An area where Christians and Jews classically were viewed as standing on opposite sides of an impenetrable wall just might be showing a few cracks.

I feel an obligation to recall the setting of this conference – the National Catholic Center for Holocaust Education – and turn our attention to the continuing theological dimensions of the Holocaust. Let me be clear: as Christians we do not focus on the Holocaust for theological understanding. We do so to mourn, to repent, and to take concrete steps to prevent further occurrences of its murderous context. But as we undertake these specific acts, examining the theological dimensions of the Holocaust remains a valid and necessary task both for Christians and Jews. And I believe the Holocaust can be connected with a new theological and moral challenge in our time, namely, retention of creational sustainability in the face of massive climate change.

Anyone who knows my previous writings on the Holocaust is aware of my significant appreciation for the creative thought of Irving Greenberg in this area.[28]

Greenberg hit the nail on the head, as the expression goes, in locating the principal theological implication of the Holocaust in the context of divine-human responsibility for the governance of the world. In his initial writings on this topic, Greenberg seems to turn the traditional understanding of this relationship upside down. He claimed that in the light of the experience of the Holocaust, the human community now has assumed the primary role in global governance with God withdrawing to the sidelines. He took significant heat in Jewish circles, even in liberal Jewish circles, for the dramatic nature of the reversal he was positing. As a result, Greenberg has modified his view to a degree in recent years, though he still maintains that the world community has entered a markedly new era in terms of creational responsibility. God still maintains a central role, one that remains greater than the one for which Greenberg initially argued. But I walk arm-in-arm with Greenberg in emphasizing that Christians and Jews, indeed the entire global family, now bear a level of unprecedented responsibility for the future of all of creation, humanity included.

Irving Greenberg, however, was not the first person to influence me in this way of thinking. As an emerging academician in 1972, I participated in a one-time gathering of learned societies of religion in Los Angeles. That experience left a lasting impact on me as a person as well as on my future scholarship, largely because of the conference's powerful keynote address delivered by Hans Jonas. Jonas, a refugee from Hitler's Germany, was then associated with the New School for Social Research in New York. Ethnically Jewish but secular in terms of belief, Jonas' scholarly contributions focused primarily on developing a philosophically grounded ethic for the technological world of our generation and beyond. He also wrote on the significance of the Nazi Holocaust, though he did not do much to integrate these two areas of his concern. His best-known book, which is in effect a collection of essays composed over a period of years beginning in 1959, remains *The Imperative of Moral Responsibility*.[29] As I sat and listened to Jonas make the presentation which basically serves as the opening section of his major volume, my horizons were expanded and my sense of what is required of me as part of contemporary humanity and the rest of creation was enhanced in a way that had never occurred before or since.

Early on in his keynote address, Jonas uttered a sentence that has become permanently implanted in my consciousness. We are the first generation, he insisted, that is forced to ask the question of whether there will be future generations. Never had I been confronted in such a dramatic fashion about the condition of the creation in which I shared as a human. Never had I understood the depth of responsibility that I and the people of my generation now shared for the survival of planet earth and the life it sustains. I came to realize that many of the justice issues with which I had already been engaged, such as racism, economic justice, and human rights, while still critical in their own way, nonetheless relinquished their primacy in the face of the challenge of creational sustainability.

I continued to reflect on Jonas' message as I began a more intense examination of the moral challenges of the Holocaust.[30] It quickly became apparent that his perspective relates quite directly to the Holocaust experience and its continuing moral significance. For the Holocaust did reveal that the human community, through technology in particular, had moved into a new realm of human capacity, a realm in which the choice between massive destruction and human preservation moved front and center. The Nazi ideologues constructed a system in which the human community could destroy in a highly organized, systematic manner. And divine intervention was not going to undermine this system. Only a concerted, organized assumption of responsibility could stop the destructive machine of the Nazis.

So both an analysis of the Nazi Holocaust and our new awareness that creational sustainability has become the issue of our day lead to the same conclusion. Humankind must be prepared to assume responsibility for protecting humanity and the rest of creation from mass destruction, whether through genocidal attacks or widespread pollution of our atmosphere and water. Never before has a generation faced such a stark challenge. I still believe a loving God can help us accept and sustain such responsibility. But we must take the first step. Pope Francis has certainly urged that step upon us in his encyclical *Laudato Si*. It is imperative that educators and pastors begin to inculcate this heightened demand for moral responsibility in the students and congregations we serve. That is the way we can continue to honor the memory of the victims of the Nazis; that is the way we can create a new sense of bonding among Christians, Jews, Muslims, and other faith communities. May we be up to accepting this new challenge of human responsibility.

Questions for Discussion

1. *How is the experience of the Holocaust relevant for ethical decision-making today?*

2. *What are some implications of our new understanding of the gradual separation between Jews and Christians in the first several centuries of the Common Era?*

3. *How do we combat the rise of antisemitism as well as the increase in hatred in certain sectors of Israeli society?*

4. *How would you state positively the Jewish-Christian relationship in light of Vatican II's* Nostra Aetate *and the scholarship it has generated?*

Further Reading

Berger, Alan L. (Ed.). *Post-Holocaust Jewish-Christian Dialogue: After the Flood, before the Rainbow* (Lanham, MD: Lexington Books, 2015).
Boys, Mary C. *Redeeming Our Sacred Story: The Death of Jesus and Relations between Jews and Christians* (New York: Paulist Press, 2013).
---------*Has God Only One Blessing? Judaism as a Source of Christian Self-Understanding* (New York: Paulist Press, 2000).
Garber, Zev (Ed.). *Teaching the Historical Jesus: Issues and Exegesis* (New York and London: Routledge, 2015).
Pawlikowski, John T. *Restating the Catholic Church's Relationship with the Jewish People: The Challenge of Super-Sessionary Theology* (Lewiston, NY: Edward Mellen Press, 2013).
---------*Christ in the Light of Christian-Jewish Dialogue* (Eugene, OR: Wipf & Stock, 2011).

Film and Video Resources

Nostra Aetate 50th Anniversary (7:30 mins). Produced by Religion & Ethics NewsWeekly. Available at https://www.youtube.com/watch?v=_LCYRRR7Lfc.
Tel Aviv Remembers 50 Years of Nostra Aetate (4 mins). Produced by Christian Media Center. Available at http://cmc-terrasanta.com/en/video/ecumenism-3/9865.html.
Timothy Cardinal Dolan: 50 Years of Nostra Aetate (78 mins). Produced by Jewish Theological Seminary. Available at https://www.youtube.com/watch?v=oWXrM_hzGrk.

Notes

1. Edward Flannery, *The Anguish of the Jews: A Catholic Priest Writes of 23 Centuries of Anti-Semitism* (New York: Macmillan, 1965).
2. Cf. John Connelly, *From Enemy to Brother: The Revolution in Catholic Teaching on the Jews, 1931-1965* (Cambridge, MA: Harvard University Press, 2012).
3. Ibid, pp. 176-180.
4. John T. Pawlikowski, OSM, *Catechetics & Prejudice: How Catholic Teaching Materials View Jews, Protestants and Racial Minorities* (New York: Paulist, 1973).
5. Gregory Baum, "The Social Context of American Catholic Theology," *Proceedings of the Catholic Theological Society of America*, 41, 1986, p. 8/.
6. Monika Hellwig, "Christian Theology and the Covenant of Israel," *Journal of Ecumenical Studies*, 7, Winter 1970, pp. 37-51; "From the Jesus Story to the Christ of Dogma," in *Antisemitism and the Foundations of Christianity*, ed. Alan T. Davies (New York: Paulist, 1979).
7. Paul M. van Buren, *A Christian Theology of the Jewish People: A Theology of the Jewish-Christian Reality, Part 2* (New York: Seabury, 1983).

8. Mary C. Boys, *Has God Only One Blessing? Judaism as a Source of Christian Self-Understanding* (New York: Paulist, 2000); *Redeeming Our Sacred Story: The Death of Jesus and Relations Between Jews and Christians* (New York: Paulist, 2013).
9. R. Kendall Soulen, *The God of Israel and Christian Theology* (Minneapolis: Fortress, 1996).
10. John T. Pawlikowski, *Christ in the Light of Christian-Jewish Dialogue* (Eugene, OR: Wipf & Stock, 2011); *Restating the Catholic Church's Relationship with the Jewish People: The Challenge of Super-Sessionary Theology* (Lewiston, NY: Edward Mellen Press, 2013).
11. Robin Scroggs, "The Judaizing of the New Testament," *Chicago Theological Seminary Register*, 75, Winter 1986, pp. 36-45.
12. Anthony J. Saldarini, "Jews and Christians in the First Two Centuries: The Changing Paradigm," *Shofar*, 10, 1992, pp. 12-43; "Christian Anti-Judaism: The First Century Speaks to the Twenty-First Century," *The Joseph Cardinal Bernardin Jerusalem Lecture, 1999*. (Chicago: Archdiocese of Chicago, the American Jewish Committee, Spertus Institute of Jewish Studies, and the Jewish United Fund/Jewish Community Relations Council, 1999).
13. Adam H. Becker and Annette Yoshiro Reed (Eds.), *The Ways That Never Parted: Jews and Christians in Late Antiquity and the Early Middle Ages/Texts and Studies in Judaism, #95* (Turbingen: Mohr Siebeck, 2003). Also see Matt Jackson-McCabe (Ed.), *Jewish Christianity Reconsidered: Rethinking Ancient Groups and Texts* (Minneapolis: Augsburg/Fortress Press, 2007); Dabian Udoh (Ed.), *Redefining First-Century Jewish and Christian Identities: Essays in Honor of Ed Parish Sanders* (Notre Dame Press, 2008); Herschel Shanks (Ed.), *Partings: How Judaism and Christianity Became Two* (Washington, DC: Biblical Archeology Society, 2013); and Zev Garber (Ed.), *Teaching the Historical Jesus: Issues and Exegesis* (New York and London: Routledge, 2015).
14. John P. Meier, *A Marginal Jew: Rethinking the Historical Jesus/Vol.3, Companions and Competitors* (New York: Doubleday, 2001), p. 251.
15. David Frankfurter, "Beyond Jewish-Christianity: Continuing Religious Subcultures of the Second and Third Centuries and Their Documents," in Becker and Reed (Eds.), *The Ways That Never Parted*, p. 132.
16. Paula Fredriksen, "What Parting of the Ways? Jews, Gentiles and the Ancient Mediterranean City," in Becker and Reed (Eds.), *The Ways That Never Parted*, pp. 35-64.
17. On new perspectives on Paul and Judaism, cf. various essays in Reimund Bieringer and Didier Pollefeyt (Eds.), *Paul and Judaism: Crosscurrents in Pauline Exegesis and the Study of Jewish-Christian Relations* (London/New York: T&T Clark International, 2012).
18. Cf. Eugene J. Fisher and Leon Klenicki (Eds.), *Spiritual Pilgrimage: Texts on Jews and Judaism, 1979-1995: Pope John Paul II* (New York: Crossroad & ADL, 1995).
19. Pope Francis, *The Joy of the Gospel: Evangelii Gaudium* (Washington, DC: United States Conference of Catholic Bishops, 2013), pp. 199-120.
20. Johannes Baptist Metz, "Facing the Jews: Christian Theology after Auschwitz," in Elisabeth Schussler-Fiorenza and David Tracy (Eds.), *The Holocaust as Interpretation/Concilium 175* (Edinburgh: T&T Clark, 1984), p. 27.
21. John Pawlikowski, "Rethinking Christianity: A Challenge to Jewish Attitudes," *Moment*, 15(3), August 1990, pp. 36-39. A Response by Irving Greenberg, "Jews have thought little about the dignity of other faiths," p. 39.
22. Daniel Boyarin, *The Jewish Gospels: The Story of the Jewish Christ* (New York: The New Press, 2012).
23. Elliot Wolfson, "Gazing Beneath the Veil: Apocalyptic Envisioning the End," in John Pawlikowski and Hayim G. Perelmuter (Eds.), *Reinterpreting Revelation and Tradition: Jews and Christians in Conversation* (Franklin, WI: Sheed & Ward, 1997), pp. 77-103.
24. Benjamin D. Sommer, *The Bodies of God and the World of Ancient Israel* (Cambridge, UK and New York: Cambridge University Press, 2009).
25. Garber (Ed.), Teaching the Historical Jesus.
26. Shaul Magid, *Hasidism Incarnate: Hasidism, Christianity and the Construction of Modern Judaism* (Palo Alto, CA: Stanford University Press, 2015).
27. Moshe Idel, Ben: *Sonship and Jewish Mysticism* (New York: Continuum, 2002).
28. Irving Greenberg, *For the Sake of Heaven and Earth: The New Encounter Between Judaism and Christianity* (Philadelphia: Jewish Publication Society, 2004).
29. Hans Jonas, *The Imperative of Moral Responsibility* (Chicago: University of Chicago Press, 1984).
30. John Thaddeus Pawlikowski, "The Significance of the Christian-Jewish Dialogue and Holocaust Studies for Catholic Ethics," *Political Theology*, 13(4), 2012, pp. 444-457.

Teaching, Preaching, and Witnessing: Three Women Who Made a Difference

Carol Rittner, R.S.M.

Editor, The Holocaust and *Nostra Aetate*: Toward a Greater Understanding; *Distinguished Professor of Holocaust & Genocide Studies Emerita and Dr. Marsha Raticoff Grossman Professor of Holocaust Studies Emerita, Stockton University, Galloway, NJ*

In his eloquent and erudite book, *What Happened at Vatican II*, John O'Malley, SJ, gives a thorough and detailed history of the Council, situating it in the longer history of the Church and previous councils. O'Malley shows how Vatican II allowed the Catholic Church to modernize while remaining true to its traditions and convictions. *What Happened at Vatican II* is not just an analysis of the 16 Conciliar documents. Rather, it is a book that concentrates on the debates that bubbled beneath the surface and around the deceptive serenity of those documents. Personalities come to the fore in the contest between the minority of bishops who resisted change and the majority who favored it as desirable and necessary. But all of those personalities were male. They were, as the saying goes, "men of the Church": bishops and archbishops, cardinals and Popes (notably, Popes John XXIII and Paul VI, with Pius XII hovering in the background), as well as more than 400 "well-trained, articulate, and committed *periti*," all men, of course. These "priest specialists in Canon Law, Scripture, Church-state-relations, theology, or liturgy" were advisors to the Council Fathers. They "worked as consultants on ... Council committees that prepared draft documents,"[1] including, of course, *Nostra Aetate*, the Vatican II Declaration on the Relation of the Church to Non-Christian Religions. And they were influential. Many of us are familiar with some of these men: Karl Rahner, Yves Congar, Marie-Dominique Chenu, John Courtney Murray, Gregory Baum, Hans Kung, Edward Schillebeeckx, and, of course, Joseph Ratzinger, also known as Pope Emeritus Benedict XVI, to name but a few of these key advisors.

These "men of the Church" made an enormous contribution to the Catholic Church and to "the extraordinary evolution that has taken place in the Catholic Church's official teaching,"[2] and they deserve great credit for influencing our thinking and pastoral practice. But I want to draw attention to three women, none of whom were present at Vatican II, but each of whom in her own way also contributed to "the extraordinary evolution that has taken place in the Catholic Church's official teaching" during and after Vatican II, particularly as that teaching pertains to Jews and Judaism.

Dr. Gertrud Luckner, Mrs. Claire Huchet Bishop, and Sister Rose Thering, OP encouraged, urged, one could even say "demanded" that the Roman Catholic Church rethink and reformulate in a positive way its relationship to Jews and Judaism. For these three women, the *Shoah*, the Holocaust of the Jews during World War II, was the ominous "sign of the times," to use the phrase made famous by Pope John XXIII, that motivated them to do what they did when it came to trying to change how Roman Catholic Christians thought about and related to living Jews and Judaism.

Gertrud Luckner

I met Dr. Gertrud Luckner almost 30 years ago. She was one of the speakers Elie Wiesel and I invited to a conference on non-Jewish victims of the Nazis we organized and that was held at the U.S. State Department in Washington, D.C., under the auspices of the then-U.S. Holocaust Memorial Council (USHMC). By the time I met Dr. Luckner, she was already frail, and I remember that she rambled quite a bit in her presentation. I had the unenviable task of having to politely but firmly help her conclude her comments and move off the stage so others could speak. Of course, I was mortified to do so, but I could not think of any other way to help her stop rambling and allow the program to move forward. Even in her dotage, however, observing her passion, it was clear that what drove Gertrud Luckner to do what she did during the Nazi era, World War II, and the Holocaust, and continued to do in the years following the end of the war, was her commitment to doing what she could to change the negative attitudes Christians had about Jews and Judaism. One cannot discount her influence, even from the margins, on the Catholic Church and its rethinking of its religious attitudes toward Jews and Judaism after the Holocaust. But who was Gertrud Luckner?

It seems almost a cliché to call her extraordinary, but that is what she was – *extraordinary*. When most ordinary people in Nazi-dominated Germany were turning their backs on their Jewish neighbors and colleagues, Gertrud Luckner was looking for ways to help them. When most ordinary Germans were closing their eyes so as not to notice that Jews were being forced out of Nazi Germany, Gertrud Luckner was looking for ways to connect them with her contacts in England and elsewhere so they might find a place of refuge. When most ordinary citizens in Nazi Germany were refusing to extend a helping hand to infirm and elderly Jews who had no one to look after them, Gertrud Luckner was conspiring with her friend Rabbi Leo Baeck in Berlin to visit them and bring food and medicine to them so they would not feel alone and abandoned. And when the Nazis were beginning to arrest and deport the Jews of Germany to concentration camps in Poland, Gertrud Luckner, a slightly built, intelligent, and fearless woman, was risking her life to help hide and save Jewish men, women, and children.

Who was this Catholic woman who refused to be infected with the theological anti-Judaism coursing through her Roman Catholic Christian religious tradition, who resisted the racist antisemitism animating her society? Who was this woman who refused to be daunted by the Nazis and the Holocaust? And who was this German woman of courage who, after 1945, refused to give in to the physical and psychological effects she endured following years of Nazi harassment, torment, and imprisonment during the war and the Holocaust?

Gertrud Luckner was born to German parents in Liverpool, England, on September 26, 1900. They returned to Germany when Gertrud was six years old. She had no brothers or sisters and once said, "My family was [only] a small part of my life."[3] World War I, however, was not a small part of her life. It impacted her greatly, and while she missed out on some regular schooling because of the war, she developed an early and abiding interest in social welfare and international solidarity. She went to university and "received [her] degree from Frankfurt am Main in 1920, in the political science department."[4] She also studied economics with a specialization in social welfare at the Quaker college for religion and social work in Birmingham, England. She returned to Germany in 1931 and was shocked by the popular support for Hitler and the Nazis.[5] She obtained her doctorate from the University of Freiburg in 1938, just as Hitler and the Nazis were consolidating their power, stepping up their harassment and persecution of Jews in Germany, and preparing for all-out war in Europe.

Luckner worked with the German Catholic Caritas organization in Freiburg. She was active in the German Resistance to Nazism and was also a member of the banned German Catholic Peace Movement (*Friedensbund deutscher Katholiken*). Even before the Nazis came to power in Germany (1933) and before World War II and the Holocaust, Gertrud Luckner was ecumenical in mind and spirit. She was raised a Quaker but became a Catholic after hearing and being impressed by the Italian Catholic priest and politician Father Luigi Sturzo (1871-1959).[6] For her, religion was about compassion and reaching out from one person to another.[7] What mattered to her were human beings and their well-being. Her political views, influenced by her Quaker upbringing and her Catholic social justice views, contributed to her early identification of Hitler's political and international danger.[8]

After the outbreak of World War II in 1939, she organized within the Caritas organization, and with the blessing and active support of Freiburg's Catholic Archbishop Conrad Gröber, a special "Office for Religious War Relief" (*Kirchliche Kriegshilfsstelle*). Although the record of the institutional Christian churches – Catholic and Protestant alike – in Germany during the Nazi era and the Holocaust was less than exemplary, there were individual church people – clergy and laity alike – who tried to help people who were being persecuted by the Nazis. As the war wore on, the Office for Religious War Relief became the instrument through which the Freiburg Catholics helped racially persecuted "non-Aryans," including both Jews and Christians. Gertrud Luckner was the driving force behind this relief effort.

Luckner often worked with Rabbi Leo Baeck, the leader of the Reich Union of Jews in Germany (*Reichsvereinigung der Juden in Deutschland*), to help the Jews. She remained in close contact with him until his arrest and deportation to Theresienstadt in early 1943. Then, on November 5, 1943, as she was on her way by train to Berlin to transfer 5,000 German marks to the last remaining Jews in that city, Luckner was arrested by the Gestapo. For nine weeks she was interrogated by the Gestapo, but she never revealed anything. She was sent to Ravensbrück concentration camp, where she endured 19 harrowing months until she and thousands of other women were liberated by the Soviet army on May 3, 1945.

After the war, Luckner established a center for Catholic-Jewish reconciliation in Freiburg, although the mood in the country in the 1950s did not support such work, nor did the Vatican, but "[h]aving risked her life for Jews and spent the last two years of the war in Ravenbrück concentration camp, Luckner found it impossible to abandon the remnant of Jewish humanity that survived the Holocaust."[9] She established the Freiburg circle, a German dialogue group devoted to conciliatory work with Jews, as well as a journal, the *Freiburger Roundbrief*, which because of Luckner's personal credibility attracted Jewish readers and correspondents of international reputation. Her friend Rabbi Baeck survived the war and the Holocaust. He never forgot that Luckner had been risking her life to give Jewish people relief when she was arrested by the Gestapo.

Luckner devoted herself to the work of Christian-Jewish reconciliation, and Rabbi Baeck supported her in her efforts. Perhaps one could say that Gertrud Luckner exemplified "dissent": dissent from the practical antisemitism of her day, dissent from the intellectual anti-Judaism of centuries, and dissent from the mean-spiritedness and small-mindedness of centuries of Christian teaching and preaching about Jews and Judaism that helped to disable baptized Christians from helping their Jewish neighbors and colleagues during the Nazi era, World War II, and the Holocaust.

Perhaps she was not as intellectually influential as others in helping to prepare the seed-ground that contributed to the new thinking in the Roman Catholic Church that eventually led to *Nostra Aetate*, but she was profoundly influential in Germany and beyond in exemplifying the Golden Rule, "Do unto others as you would have them do unto you." Others, both clergy and lay, women and men, may have been more important in helping the Catholic Church rethink its religious and practical relationship with living Jews and Judaism, but none were more dedicated to this task than Gertrud Luckner. She may not have been present at Vatican II, but her influence on the "men of the Church" at Vatican II and thus on *Nostra Aetate* should not be underestimated. On February 15, 1966, Yad Vashem recognized Gertrud Luckner as Righteous Among the Nations, highlighting her efforts to help Jews during the Nazi era, World War II, and the Holocaust.

Claire Huchet Bishop

Another woman who impacted Christian and Jewish Relations was Claire Huchet Bishop. I never personally met her, nor did I ever hear her speak, but I have read some of her work, including *How Catholics Look at Jews*, her important inquiry into Italian, Spanish, and French teaching materials.[10]

Born in Geneva in 1899, she was raised in the French seaport city of Le Havre. Her family was a family of storytellers. Her grandfather was a popular storyteller in his island village off the coast of Brittany. In the winter evenings people would gather around his fire to listen to him. Her mother, too, was a dramatic storyteller, so it was only natural that Claire herself would begin to tell stories, as well. Asked how she got started, she said, "I think I have always done it."[11]

She went off to study at the Sorbonne in Paris but apparently left without obtaining a degree. Asked why she left, Claire replied, "Although I was fairly successful, I disliked intellectual life." That, however, did not bring an end to her interest in literature and stories. She became involved in the opening of the *L'Heure Joyeuse* library in Paris, the first library in France devoted to children's literature. She left Paris after marrying the American concert pianist Frank Bishop. They moved to New York City, where she settled down to a new life as a homemaker. But such a quiet life did not last long. She went to work at the New York City Public Library, where she resumed her favorite occupation as "children's storyteller."

She wrote numerous books for children. The one I know best – and you may know it as well – is *Twenty and Ten*.[12] It is the story of a group of 5th-grade children who hide ten young Jewish refugees from the Nazis. The book later was made into a movie in 1985, *Miracle at Moreaux*, and shown on PBS with Loretta Swit, of M★A★S★H fame, starring as the main character, Sister Gabrielle.[13] *Twenty and Ten* is based on a true story. It is a children's book, but its theme is very adult, very biblical, very challenging: "You shall not stand idly by when someone is in danger." And make no mistake about it: the ten Jewish refugee children in that story were very much in danger, as were all Jewish children in France during World War II and the Holocaust.

When the young man in the story comes to their school and asks them whether they would be willing to take in and hide ten Jewish kids, the children all cry, "Yes! Yes!" Sister Gabriel, however, reminds them, "If we take them we must never let on that they are here. Never. Even if we are questioned. We can never betray them, no matter what the Nazis do to us. Do you understand?"[14]

Whether those children completely understood the possible consequences of what they were about to do is perhaps less important than the fact that they were willing to do it in a time when so many people in Nazi-occupied Europe closed their eyes, turned their backs, and refused to help Jews. The persecution, discrimination, and annihilation of Jews in France, Germany, Austria, Poland, and elsewhere in Nazi-occupied Europe took place on a continent that had been "Christian" for more than 1,500 years. The Holocaust took place in the centers of Christian teaching and preaching in Europe – in Rome and in Augsburg, in Paris and in Athens, Moscow, Cracow, Warsaw, Amsterdam, Prague, and many other cities, towns, and villages – places where Jews were rounded up, deported, even shot under the windows and outside the doors of Christian institutions and within sight of an overwhelmingly "Christian" population.

How could this be? How could it be that people baptized in the name of Jesus Christ could turn their backs on Jesus' own people, the Jewish people, who in the name of "blood and race" were being hunted and murdered throughout Nazi-occupied Europe? These questions – and others – have never ceased to baffle me. And they baffled Claire Huchet Bishop, too, who once described herself as "a French Catholic who [could not] understand from a Christian point of view, crusades, inquisitions, Passion plays, religious wars, pogroms or the Holocaust."[15]

In her obituary in *The New York Times*, Bruce Lambert wrote that it was "the persecution of Jewish friends in France in World War II" that prompted her to become "an advocate in efforts for religious and racial harmony. … She … served as the president of the International Council of Christians and Jews in 1975-77 and of the Jewish-Christian-Fellowship of France from 1968 to 1981."[16]

Her accomplishments were many – she wrote more than 30 books for both children and adults, "including works which won her a number of important literary and spiritual awards and citations."[17] But as Edward Skillin wrote in Commonweal after her death,

> [A]ll these pale before Claire Bishop's valiant and tireless struggle against Christian anti-Semitism. Although she was frail of health, this great cause was the impassioned motivation of her extremely active later years. Anti-Semitic references in French, Spanish, and Italian textbooks were removed as the result of her efforts. Thanks in part to her *How Catholics Look at Jews* (Paulist Press, 1974), so were anti-Semitic passages in Catholic catechisms.[18]

Three years before the publication of *How Catholics Look at Jews*, Claire Bishop helped bring to the attention of the English-speaking world the work of Jules Isaac. Isaac, a French Jewish scholar who lost his wife and daughter and other members of his family during the Holocaust, survived only because he was not home when the Germans and their collaborators came calling. He went into hiding and survived because French Catholics hid him. What Isaac could not understand, either during the war or after, was why the Nazis and their collaborators targeted and killed people simply because they were Jews. From where, he wondered, did this murderous antisemitism spring? What was its origin? Why didn't the Pope in Rome – Pius XII – speak up and condemn the Nazis? He began to do research, even while he was still in hiding from the Nazis.

Working with borrowed books supplied by priests, pastors, and friends – particularly a four-volume commentary on the Gospels by Père Lagrange – he set out to document his intuition: that antisemitism, more precisely anti-Judaism, was a doctrine of contempt founded upon and elaborated from false and mendacious readings of the Gospels. Isaac published his book in 1947, just two years after the end of World War II and the Holocaust.

Entitled *Jesus and Israel*, the book sent shock waves through postwar French Christian communities, Catholic and Protestant alike. Isaac compared texts from the New Testament (Christian Scriptures) with various Catholic and Protestant commentaries on those texts. He showed how many Gospel commentaries presented a completely distorted picture of Jesus' attitude toward Israel and Israel's attitude toward Jesus. He argued that these Commentaries – which for centuries had influenced Christian teaching, preaching, and liturgy – were inaccurate, although widely used by priests, ministers, seminarians, teachers, catechists, and students as the basis for their own teaching and preaching. Such demonization, he argued, contributed to centuries of pogroms in Europe and to what became genocidal hatred of the Jews by Christians. Jews became an outcast people, religiously marginalized, pushed to the periphery of society, cast outside the universe of moral obligation, beyond the boundaries of normal care and concern.

Claire Huchet Bishop read her friend Jules Isaac's book. More than two decades after its publication in France, *Jesus and Israel* was translated into English by Sally Gran and meticulously edited by Bishop, who also provided valuable annotation that extended and underscored Isaac's own footnotes. That book went a long way toward helping Christian scholars, teachers, and clergy open their eyes to an underside of Christian theology and history about which many had been ignorant. It also helped to make known in English a phrase that Jules Isaac used to characterize Christian teaching about Jews and Judaism down through the centuries: "the teaching of contempt."

In June 1960, in the midst of preparing for Vatican II, Pope John XXIII received Jules Isaac in a private audience at the Vatican. Their conversation lasted a mere 25 minutes, but it began one of the most profound renewals of the Catholic Church's 2,000-year history. Toward the end of their meeting, the old Jewish scholar asked Pope John XXIII "whether there was any hope of ridding Christian teaching of the many anti-Jewish myths that had become encrusted on it like barnacles on a ship." John replied with characteristic honesty, "You have every right to more than hope." One could say that *Nostra Aetate* began with that meeting of Jules Isaac and Pope John XXIII, because shortly thereafter, the Pope asked Cardinal Augustin Bea to draft a statement concerning the Jews that could be presented to all those "men of the Church" who in October 1962 would gather in St. Peter's Basilica to begin Vatican II.

How important and influential was Claire Huchet Bishop's work? Here is what Dr. Eugene Fisher had to say when I asked him about her:

> As one who staffed the dialogue between Catholics and Jews for the U.S. Conference of Catholic Bishops for thirty years (from 1977 to 2007), I can say with confidence that Claire Huchet Bishop was one of the great pioneers of Catholic-Jewish relations internationally, and within the United States. Her book, *How Catholics Look at Jews* (Paulist Press, 1974) summarized and analyzed the results of studies of how European Catholic religious education materials presented, and sadly often misrepresented, Jews and Judaism. Given the fact that the perpetrators of the *Shoah* were, in point of fact, virtually all baptized Christians, many of them Catholics, Bishop's study would prove to be fundamental in the implementation of the Second Vatican Council's historic declaration and mandate for changing Church teaching on Jews and Judaism, *Nostra Aetate*. … Claire Huchet Bishop also translated into English the seminal work of Jules Isaac, *Jesus and Israel*. … By making his work available to large numbers of Catholic and Jewish scholars, and indeed, bishops in this country, Claire Huchet Bishop greatly furthered the American dialogue. She was personally a great inspiration to me in my own work in the field over the years and along with a handful of others a major source of the good work that has been accomplished over the years in this country both before and since the Second Vatican Council.[19]

Claire Huchet Bishop's work with Catholics and Jews contributed in a positive way to Catholic-Jewish relations. Whether in formal presentations or during informal conversations before, during, and after Vatican II, Claire Bishop was always trying to influence the thinking of Catholics and Jews. And she did – for the better.

Rose Thering, OP

Which brings me to the third woman to whom I want to draw your attention: Sister

Rose Thering, OP, a woman I did know and met many times in this country and in Israel. She was, as Judith Banki once said, "a feisty nun!"[20] Those of us who knew her – and many of us *did know* Rose – would agree, as we would agree with something else Judy Banki said about her: When Rose died in May 2006, a huge hole was left in the fabric of Jewish-Catholic relations.[21] Many of us probably also would agree with Rabbi Jim Rudin's assessment: Sister Rose, he said, "was a one-woman wrecking crew!" And what she helped to wreck was 2,000 years of "the teaching of contempt" of Jews and Judaism that was built into so much Christian teaching and preaching.

Who was this woman of the Roman Catholic Church, known to many and admired by Jews and Christians alike? Rose Thering was a Roman Catholic Dominican Sister. Her life stood for love of Jews, for fighting prejudice, antisemitism, and Holocaust denial. Born on August 9, 1920, to second-generation German Catholic parents in Plain, Wisconsin, Rose Elizabeth Thering grew up on a dairy farm in an overwhelmingly Catholic part of the country. The Therings were a pious family, praying together three times a day. All 11 children went to Catholic schools. "There were no Jews where I grew up," and if they were spoken about at all, it was in "whispers," she often said; "I only knew them from what we read in our religious text books." And what she read and learned was what so much of the Christian world read and learned: "the Jews killed Christ"; the Jews failed to recognize Jesus as the Messiah; the Jews were stiff-necked and stubborn; the Jews were unfaithful to God and the covenant; the Jews were replaced by Christians as God's "Chosen People."

Over the centuries, such anti-Judaism had been bred deep in the bones of the devout. Over the centuries, the readings of the passion narrative that Rose Thering and her family heard and that Christians of all stripes, including Roman Catholics, heard were from John's Gospel in which "the Jews" cry out, "Crucify him" (John 19:14,15), and from Matthew's, in which they declare, "His blood be on us and on our children" (Mt. 27:25), were all too familiar. For nearly 1,900 years, such readings were standard fare during Lent and Holy Week.

Even at a young age, the message of intolerance toward Jews that Rose Thering learned in her Catholic school and church in Wisconsin unsettled her. Nevertheless, at the age of 16, she joined the Roman Catholic religious order of the Sisters of St. Dominic in Racine, Wisconsin, and following her profession of vows began teaching in Catholic elementary and high schools, where she continued to find anti-Jewish references in the Catholic school texts she was required to use.

Sister Rose graduated from Dominican College in Racine, eventually going on to earn a MA from the College of St. Thomas in Minnesota and a PhD from St. Louis University in Missouri. Her doctoral dissertation was devoted to the Catholic Church's teachings about Jews and other religions. Her research culminated in 1961 with an examination of how Catholic teaching materials dealt with ethnic groups and other faiths, focusing primarily on Jews and Judaism.

Judy Banki, who was working with the American Jewish Committee at about the same time as Rose was completing her doctoral work, was sent off to meet this Sister Rose Thering to see how her research findings could be coordinated with Protestant and Jewish textbook self-studies. Here is what Judy Banki wrote about Rose and her work:

> We were both distressed by the hostility and calumny found in descriptions of Jews and Judaism in the textbooks. The accusations against Jews included bearing guilt for the death of Jesus, and thereby being accursed and rejected by God. The suffering and persecution of the Jews over the centuries – at the hands of Christians – were understood as signs of providential punishment. These libels were described as "the teaching of contempt" by the French historian Jules Isaac. Rose's research provided the crucial basis for the request made to the Second Vatican Council by the [American Jewish Committee] for the church to issue an authoritative repudiation of the religious roots of anti-Semitism. I believe that the evidence of anti-Semitism Rose uncovered helped convince the council fathers of the need for what eventually emerged, after a long and bitter struggle, as *Nostra Aetate*.[22]

Transformed by the implications of her research, Rose became an activist as well as a teacher.[23] At Seton Hall University in New Jersey, where she joined the faculty in 1968, Sister Rose established workshops on Judaism for church leaders and teachers. "I know the power of teachers," she often said. She spent much of her professional life encouraging and developing teachers, helping them be more effective in the classroom. Rose helped write a law mandating the teaching of the Holocaust and genocide in all elementary and high schools in the State of New Jersey, and she led student groups on more than 50 tours of Israel.

Rose felt strongly that religious beliefs fostered by centuries of "the teaching of contempt" for the Jews and Judaism had nurtured the thinking and attitudes among baptized Christians that made the Holocaust possible. She threw herself into Holocaust education, working closely with the late Dr. Paul Winkler (1936-2016) and the New Jersey Commission on Holocaust Education to make sure that students and teachers alike understood that Nazi Germany's targeting of Jews cannot be explained apart from the anti-Jewish images that had been deeply rooted in Christian teaching and preaching through the centuries.

It was *Nostra Aetate* that reversed Church policy and declared of Jesus' death that "what happened in His passion cannot be blamed upon all the Jews then living, without distinction, nor upon the Jews of today."[24] For nearly two millennia, the persistent Christian "belief" that the Jews were responsible for the death of

Jesus had fed and kept alive anti-Jewish prejudice and hatred. The Nazis used racist antisemitism, bolstered by theological anti-Judaism, to justify the "legal" discrimination and persecution of the Jews of Germany in the 1930s, the deportation of Jews from throughout German-occupied Europe to the Nazi death camps in the 1940s, and the use of modern industrial methods to exterminate the Jews in the very heart of Christian Europe during the Holocaust. Only with the defeat of Nazi Germany in May 1945 were those Nazi concentration and death camps finally closed down, even if the underlying ideologies that helped sustain them continued to linger in the Christian churches and civil society. Vatican II repudiated, once and for all, the idea that the Jews killed Jesus as well as the sinister notion that the Jews were rejected, even cursed by God, because the great majority of them refused to accept Jesus as their messiah.

While the history of the Holocaust testifies that Christianity was not a sufficient condition for the Holocaust, it was a necessary condition for that disaster. That statement does not mean that Christianity caused the Holocaust, but it does mean that apart from the anti-Jewish images so common in Christian teaching and preaching for centuries, apart from the anti-Jewish and antisemitic attitudes of Catholic, Protestant, and Eastern Orthodox Christians in Europe – and elsewhere – it is doubtful that so many Germans and other Europeans would have become such "willing executioners," to use Daniel Goldhagen's phrase. Nor would they have been such compliant and complicit bystanders throughout occupied Europe during World War II and the Holocaust. Sister Rose Thering made sure all of us understood that. Although she did not confine herself only to Holocaust education, it was one of her major passions.

Her activism on behalf of Holocaust survivors and oppressed Jews throughout the world led her to Austria to protest the inauguration of Kurt Waldheim, a former Nazi, as its president. In 1987, Rose traveled to the Soviet Union to visit 22 *refusenik* families in a show of solidarity before *glasnost* secured the freedom of Soviet Jews. She stood with others in 1993 in protest of bigotry on the campus of Kean College (now Kean University) in New Jersey, when Khalid Abdul Muhammad was invited to speak there. In spring 1994, when Louis Farrakhan came to Kean to preach, Rose made it clear where she stood. Her letter decrying Muhammad's visit appeared in *The New York Times*. It is a tribute to her conviction of spirit and diplomacy that she later served as a member of the Kean University Board of Trustees from 1994 to 2005.

Mary Boys, SNJM, once summed up the post-Vatican II Catholic teachings on Catholic-Jewish relations as "the six Rs: (1) repudiation of anti-Semitism; (2) refutation of the deicide charge that the Jews killed God by killing his son, Jesus; (3) repentance after the *Shoah* (Holocaust); (4) recognition of Israel; (5) review of the teaching about Jews and Judaism and (6) rethinking efforts to convert Jews."[25] No one more than Sister Rose Thering exemplified that summation of post-Vatican

II Catholic teachings on Catholic-Jewish relations. She was tireless – lecturing, advocating, speaking throughout the state of New Jersey and the United States, even internationally, making bishops and priests, nuns and lay people, students of all ages aware of the tenets of Judaism and Catholicism, doing her best to help eradicate intolerance toward Jews and Judaism.

Rose Thering earned more than 80 humanitarian awards, including the Anti-Defamation League's Cardinal Bea Interfaith Award (2004) – she was the first woman to receive that award. In 1987, Rose was given the prestigious Jerusalem Award. Teddy Kollek, Jerusalem's mayor at the time, presented it to her after she testified before the United States Senate Foreign Relations Committee in support of a bill to move the American embassy from Tel Aviv to Jerusalem. Rose Thering was a passionate supporter of the State of Israel, as those of us acquainted with her knew.

She shared her unique life story with the world in 2004 through *Sister Rose's Passion* (Storyville Films), a 39-minute documentary film that chronicled her life's dedication to reconciling Jews and Christians through education on the evils of antisemitism. Rose "was not easily cowed."[26] She was not impressed by titles, political or religious. In *Sister Rose's Passion*, she reports that a bishop urged her not to publicize the evidence of antisemitism her doctoral research revealed. "Don't hang out our dirty laundry in public," he said. "Well," she said, "I hung it out!"[27]

After winning the Best Documentary Short at the Tribeca Film Festival in New York City in 2004, *Sister Rose's Passion* was nominated in 2005 for an Academy Award. It did not win, but it did reach hundreds of thousands of people, influencing them, educating them about the evil of antisemitism and the importance of better Jewish-Christian relations.

On May 1, 2001, Rose Thering finally received long overdue acknowledgement for the role her research had played at the Second Vatican Council, an award from the International Liaison Committee of the Holy See's Commission on Relations with the Jews and the International Jewish Committee for Interreligious Consultations. Judy Banki said, "It was my privilege to present the award to her ... [Rose was] hailed as a planter of mustard seeds, which have and will continue to produce a harvest of understanding and mutual respect."[28]

Conclusion

Dr. Gertrud Luckner, Mrs. Claire Huchet Bishop, and Sister Rose Thering, OP. Each in her own way made significant contributions to Jewish-Christian relations and understanding. All of them were impacted by the Holocaust. All of them, in one way or another, impacted Vatican II. Each of them was a preacher, if not in a traditional manner sharing their words from pulpits during Roman Catholic Eucharistic Liturgies, then in the spirit of St. Francis of Assisi, using words when necessary, but always witnessing by their lives the Golden Rule of love. Luckner, Bishop, and

Thering preached with their lives *and* with their words. They preached and taught the "six Rs" of "post-Vatican II Catholic teachings on Catholic-Jewish relations." They repudiated antisemitism and refuted the deicide charge that the Jews killed God by killing his son, Jesus. They repented after the *Shoah* (Holocaust) by doing what they could where they were with what they had to defeat the evils of that watershed event. They recognized Israel, supported Israel, in good times and bad. They reviewed and renewed Christian teaching about Jews and Judaism, and they disavowed every effort to convert Jews.[29]

Despite the obstacles they often encountered from the "men of the Church," these three women – Gertrud Luckner, Claire Huchet Bishop, and Rose Thering, OP – gave unrelenting and sustained witness to the remarkable transformation in Christian, specifically Roman Catholic Christian, religious attitudes and practical relationships toward the Jews and Judaism after the Holocaust and, as a result, of Vatican Council II.

We owe them a debt of gratitude, a debt that can be repaid by each of us, by all of us doing what we can, where we are, with what we have to continue and extend their work. Let us remember them, honor them, teach about them, and do what we can to imitate them in the classroom and beyond.

Questions for Discussion

1. *Are there other people – teachers, scholars, clergy, lay, or religious – in the USA who were influential in helping improve Christian-Jewish relations after the Holocaust? Who are they? What did they do; what are they doing? How can we make them and their contributions better known?*

2. *Why do women always seem to be overlooked when it comes to acknowledging their intellectual and scholarly contributions? In a positive way, what can we do about it?*

3. *Who are the women in your parish, congregation, diocese, or synod who are actively involved in promoting Christian-Jewish relations?*

4. *If you had the opportunity to re-write no. 4 of* Nostra Aetate *today, what changes and/or additions would you make to it? Why?*

Further Reading

Block, Gay, and Malka Drucker. *Rescuers: Portraits of Moral Courage in the Holocaust.* (New York: Holmes & Meier Publishers, Inc., 1992).

Gushee, David P. *Righteous Gentiles of the Holocaust: Genocide and Moral Obligation* (2nd ed.) (St. Paul, MN: Paragon House, 2003).

Kessler, Edward. *An Introduction to Jewish-Christian Relations* (Cambridge: Cambridge University Press, 2010).

Lambert, Carol J. *Against Indifference: Four Christian Responses to Jewish Suffering during the Holocaust* (New York: Peter Lang Publishing, Inc., 2015).

O'Malley, John W. *What Happened at Vatican II* (Cambridge, MA: Harvard University Press, 2008).

Rogers, Carole Garibaldi. *Habits of Change: An Oral History of American Nuns* (Oxford: Oxford University Press, 2011).

Rudin, James. *Cushing, Spellman, O'Connor: The Surprising Story of How Three American Cardinals Transformed Catholic-Jewish Relations* (Grand Rapids, MI: William B. Erdmans Publishing, 2012).

Films/Videos

Constantine's Sword (96 mins). Directed by Oren Jacoby. Available from Amazon.com.
The Miracle at Moreaux (58 mins). Directed by Paul Shapiro. Available from Amazon.com.
Sister Rose's Passion (39 mins). Directed by Oren Jacoby. Available from Amazon.com.

Notes

1. Colleen McDannell, *The Spirit of Vatican II: A History of Catholic Reform in America* (New York: Basic Books, 2011), pp. 66-67.
2. Gregory Baum, *Amazing Church: A Catholic Theologian Remembers a Half-Century of Change* (Maryknoll, NY: Orbis Books, 2005), p. 7.
3. "Gertrud Luckner," in *Rescuers: Portraits of Moral Courage in the Holocaust*, eds. Gay Block and Malka Drucker (New York: Holmes & Meier Publishers, Inc., 1992), p. 146.
4. Ibid.
5. Elizabeth Petuchowski, "Gertrud Luckner: Resistance and Assistance. A German Woman Who Defied Nazis and Aided Jews," in *Ministers of Compassion During the Nazi Period* (South Orange, NJ: The Institute of Jewish-Christian Studies, 1999), p. 7.
6. Ibid, p. 8.
7. Ibid, p. 9.
8. Ibid. p. 8.
9. Michael Phayer, *The Catholic Church and the Holocaust, 1930-1965* (Bloomington, IN: Indiana University Press, 2000), p. 185.
10. Claire Huchet Bishop, *How Catholics Look at Jews: Inquiries into Italian, Spanish, and French Teaching Materials* (New York: Paulist Press, 1974).

11. See further, Norah Smaridge, *Famous Modern Storytellers for Young People* (New York, NY: Dodd Mead, 1969).
12. Claire Huchet Bishop, *Twenty and Ten* (New York: Puffin Books, 1978).
13. The DVD *Miracle at Moreaux* is available from Amazon.com.
14. Bishop, *Twenty and Ten*, p. 21.
15. Bishop, *How Catholics Look at Jews*, n.p.
16. Bruce Lambert, "Claire Huchet Bishop, 94, Author of Popular Books for Children," *The New York Times* (March 14, 1993).
17. Edward S. Skillin, "Claire Huchet Bishop," *Commonweal*, April 9, 1993, p. 4.
18. Ibid.
19. Personal email from Dr. Fisher to the author, September 15, 2015.
20. http://www.ushmm.org/research/the-center-for-advanced-holocaust-studies/programs-ethics-religion-the-holocaust/programs/the-interfaith-story-behind-nostra-aetate/the-interfaith-story-behind-nostra-aetate.
21. Judith Banki, "Pivotal Figure: The Woman behind '*Nostra Aetate*," *Commonweal* (June 16, 2006), p. 11.
22. Ibid, p. 12.
23. Banki, "Pivotal Figure," p. 12.
24. *Nostra Aetate*, #4.
25. Anthony J. Cernera and Eugene Korn, "The Latin Liturgy and the Jews," *America*, (October 8, 2007); available at http://americamagazine.org/sites/default/files/issues/cf/pdfs/628_1.pdf.
26. Banki, "Pivotal Figure," p. 11.
27. Ibid.
28. Ibid, p. 12.
29. Cernera and Korn, "The Latin Liturgy and the Jews."

Whither Christian-Jewish Relations in the 21st Century?
A Judaic Perspective

Steven Leonard Jacobs

Associate Professor and Aaron Aronov Endowed Chair of Judaic Studies, Department of Religious Studies, University of Alabama, Tuscaloosa, AL

> "The hardest thing for Jews to remember is that
> not every German is a Nazi and not every Christian is an antisemite."
> Rabbi Harold M. Schulweis (1925-2014)[1]

My topic concerns Christian-Jewish relations in the 21st century, so I would like to begin by sharing with you the course description for an advanced seminar I teach called "Jewish-Christian Relations":

> In this course, we will critically examine the 2,000-year-old relationship between Jews and Christians, both historically and contemporarily, by focusing our microscope on such areas as the following: (1) Hebrew Bible/Old Testament versus New Testament, (2) Rabbinic Judaism versus Jewish/Gentile Christianity, (3) Jewish Messiah versus Christian Jesus,[2] (4) Jewish Mission versus Great Commission, (5) Antisemitism versus Anti-Judaism, (6) Holocaust or Shoah, (7) Land/State of Israel versus Holy Land, (8) Jewish Movements versus Christian

Denominations. Class format will consist of lectures, discussions, reactions to readings, and student presentations.[3]

I use the word "versus" in seven of the eight topics that comprise this course. It is used purposefully to confirm for my students that each topic, individually and collectively, is a source of greater or lesser tension between our various Jewish and our various Christian communities, both then and now.

For my students, each of these topics has proven something of a revelation on both sides of the divide. At the University of Alabama, I have taught non-Jewish students who have never encountered a Jewish student or had a meaningful conversation with one before coming to our university. I have also taught Jewish students who have never seriously discussed these topics with a Christian student in an appropriate non-judgmental academic environment before coming to the University of Alabama.

It is the one class I teach where I consciously violate the canons of our secular state university the first day of class. Each of the 20-25 students in the seminar is required to identify with one religious community: either the religious community with which they are presently identified, or the religious community into which they were born but with which they no longer identify, or the religious community with which they would like to identify (atheism is not an option.) They are then grouped according to community identity (Jewish, Christian – Baptist, Catholic, Methodist, Presbyterian, etc.). Their first task is to discover what the various Christian or Jewish groups *officially* say about the other, share their findings with the class, then based on their findings, suggest the possibilities or impossibilities of dialogue. That's where the real learning begins: most students usually identify with their own present or birth religious community and are fascinated by what those communities *officially* say about other religious communities. At semester break they return to their home communities, arrange a meeting with their home clergy, share the findings from our seminar, ask for input from their clergy, then when they return to campus, share those conversations with the class.

What we often find is the following: Christian denominations are usually divided houses, by which I mean they are split between positive and negative statements about Jews and Judaism, including statements expressing opposition to various Israeli governmental and military policies, particularly in terms of the ongoing conflict between Israelis and Palestinians. Jewish religious communities are no different: there are many positive statements about Christians and Christianity, but also negative ones, usually in regard to the more fundamentalist evangelical religious groups. At the same time, however, these Jewish religious communities welcome support for the State of Israel from the evangelicals about whom they have negative views.

Students also discover that clergy, both Jewish and Christian, rarely are aware of their own official denominational positions about other religious communities, and, at least in Alabama, they discover that their own religious communities have not disseminated or implemented those statements in their congregations.[4] Open, honest, and forthcoming dialogue is not a mainstay of the religious landscapes in many, if not most, of the religious communities where my students live.[5] And in my travels around the United States addressing this particular topic, I have found similar results.

In the US, Vatican II (1962-65) precipitated a true "sea change" in the relationship between our two religious communities, but the dialogical efforts that have been shared with me over the last several years have focused more on Israel and the Middle East/Palestinian conflict than on Jews and Judaism or Christians and Christianity. All of this despite the fact that, at least in the United States, unlike in Europe and the Middle East, Jews and Christians exist in the most harmonious relationship in the history of both communities.

What is unique to the history of these United States is the wall of separation between church/synagogue and state/nation. While this wall of separation has been attacked and critiqued over the years by those who continue to proclaim America as a "Christian nation" – with those of us who are not Christian feeling, at best, like "tolerated" guests and outsiders – the wall of separation continues to hold firm. All religious communities continue to benefit from it, as none dominate the national religious landscape, despite claims to the contrary. I find no evidence to suggest there will be future changes in this country's grand experiment in religious accommodation and/or toleration.[6] That includes the supposed myth of our increasing hostility and inhospitality to members of the Muslim/Islamic community, both native-born and foreign-born.

While Vatican II marked a dramatic change in the relationship of our two communities, one from which both of us have benefited, I want to bring to your attention the fact that *Nostra Aetate* was preceded more than 20 years before by a document which, sadly, is often forgotten. In 1947, in the aftermath of the Second World War and the Holocaust/*Shoah*, in Seeligsburg, Switzerland, the International Council of Christians and Jews affirmed what has come to be known as "The 10 Points of Seeligsburg." Here is a listing of those breakthrough statements:

1. Remember that One God speaks to us all through the Old and the New Testaments.
2. Remember that Jesus was born of a Jewish mother of the seed of David and the people of Israel and that His everlasting love and forgiveness embraces His own people and the whole world.
3. Remember that the first disciples, the apostles and the first martyrs, were Jews.
4. Remember that the fundamental commandment of Christianity, to love God and one's neighbor, proclaimed already in the Old

Testament and confirmed by Jesus, is binding upon both Christians and Jews in all human relationships, without any exception.
5. Avoid distorting or misrepresenting biblical or post-biblical Judaism with the object of extolling Christianity.
6. Avoid using the word "Jews" in the exclusive sense of the enemies of Jesus, and the words "the enemies of Jesus" to designate the whole Jewish people.
7. Avoid presenting the Passion in such a way as to bring the odium of the killing of Jesus upon all Jews or upon Jews alone.[7]
8. Avoid referring to the scriptural curses, or the cry of a raging mob, "His blood be upon us and our children" [Mt 27:25], without remembering that this cry should not count against the infinitely more weighty words of Our Lord, "Father: Forgive them for they know not what they do" [Lk 23:34].[8]
9. Avoid promoting the superstitious notion that the Jewish people are reprobate, accursed, reserved for a destiny of suffering.
10. Avoid speaking of the Jews as if the first members of the Church had not been Jews.[9]

My point is that the stage had already been set for better, more positive relations between Jews and Christians more than two decades before Vatican II. Without going into detail, suffice it to say that World War II and the Holocaust/*Shoah* had an enormous impact on Christians and their reconsideration of their beliefs and attitudes toward Jews and Judaism. The Roman Catholic Church also was impacted by these events, as we know. The bishops, archbishops, and cardinals of the Roman Catholic Church during Vatican II produced 16 documents of importance, among which were documents addressing such topics as Roman Catholic liturgy (*Sanctosanctum Concilium*, 1963); religious life (*Perfectae Caritatis*, 1965); Christian education (*Gravissimum Educationis*, 1965); priestly training (*Optatam Totius*, 1965); religious freedom (*Dignitatis Humanae*, 1965); and ecumenism (*Unitatis Redintegratio*, 1965), all of which one could examine for such influence. But most important and relevant to my topic of Jewish-Christian relations in the 21st century is the document *Nostra Aetate* ("In Our Time"), the "Declaration on the Relation of the Church to Non-Christian Religions," passed by the Council in December 1965 just as Vatican II was drawing to a conclusion. (Dr. Eugene Fisher, former Associate Director of the Secretariat for Ecumenical & Interreligious Affairs of the National Conference of Catholic Bishops, Washington DC, once suggested that we Jews should translate its title, *Nostra Aetate*, as "It's about time!")

What most of us forget, or perhaps never knew, is that Pope John XXIII (Angelo Roncalli, 1881-1963) – the Pope who convened Vatican II – was the papal nuncio (Emissary) in Turkey during World War II. He met and talked to Jews fleeing the horrors of Nazi Germany and the Holocaust/*Shoah* during that same period. In the late 1950s, the work of French-Jewish historian Jules Isaac (1877-1963), himself a Holocaust survivor who lost both his wife and child in the death camps, specifically his 1948 book *Jésus et Israel/Jesus and Israel*, was brought to the Pope's attention. A meeting was arranged between these two men.[10] Jules Isaac urged Pope John XXIII "to do something for the Jews," which began the process that ultimately led to *Nostra Aetate*.

Not all was smooth sailing, however, as the conservatives within the Catholic Church still regarded the Jews with suspicion, as objects of both ridicule and derision and as candidates for conversion.[11] Still, the final vote on *Nostra Aetate* was 2,221 in favor, 88 opposed.[12] However difficult its passage, that stellar document contained two important paragraphs which would ultimately chart a new direction for Catholic-Jewish relations, and as a consequence, for Protestant Christian-Jewish relations, echoes of which resound to this day.[13]

As Mark A. Kellner of *The Washington Times* wrote, "Vatican II ... revamped Catholics' relationship to the Mass, to the Bible, and to people of other faiths, most notably perhaps the Jews, who are no longer held responsible for Christ's death, but rather would come to be seen as 'elder brothers' in the universe of faith." In his essay, Kellner quotes Abraham Foxman, a Holocaust survivor and former National Director of the Anti-Defamation League of B'nai B'rith (ADL):

> Vatican II marked a special movement in the history of the church and its relation to other religions, especially to Judaism. The council repudiated the centuries-old teaching of contempt for Judaism and the Jewish people. This change in theological attitude was the result of profound reckoning of the soul on the part of the leadership of the Church.[14]

A veritable Babel of Jewish voices, religious and secular, followed the passage of *Nostra Aetate*, overwhelmingly supportive – though there were critics as well[15] – who questioned "behind the scenes Jewish involvement" and the necessity of Jewish affirmations in support of a document exonerating Jews from a crime they had never committed. Despite the naysayers, *all* of the Jewish denominational movements – Reform, Conservative, Reconstructionist, and even Orthodox – passed both rabbinic and lay conference resolutions profoundly acknowledging this milestone event.

One important dissident voice, however, was that of the late Orthodox Rabbi Joseph B. Soloveitchik (1903-1993), the *Rosh Yeshiva* (Dean) of the Rabbi Isaac Elchanan Theological Seminary at Yeshiva University in New York City, responsible for ordaining more than 2,000 Orthodox rabbis and known respectfully and affectionately as *Ha-Rav* (The Rabbi). Soloveitchik supported a positive synthesis between Western scholarship and traditional Torah learning in his two most well-known texts, *The Lonely Man of Faith* (1965) and *Halakhic Man* (1983).[15] Though an advocate of involvement with the larger non-Jewish community regarding social and social justice issues, he stopped short of, and in fact rejected, full theological dialogue in a controversial article entitled "Confrontation."[16]

For many Orthodox Jews today, both rabbis and laity, his position remains the standard by which to determine their involvement, to the affirmation of many and the chagrin of some. For Soloveitchik, his response to the possibilities of Jewish-Christian theological dialogues and encounters was framed by what I would characterize as a 2,000-year "bad relationship." Soloveitchik advised those who stood with him within the American Orthodox Jewish communities to partner with non-Jews, Christians, over common issues of social concern, but not to engage in theological encounters.

For far too many within our most traditional communities, sadly, that remains the *sine qua non* of their non-involvement even today, 50 years after *Nostra Aetate*. In 2013, George E. Johnson, former Research Director of the Institute for Jewish Policy Planning and Research, published an essay, "We Have Found the Enemy, and the Enemy is Us: Rethinking Rav Soloveitchik's Views on Orthodox-Non-Orthodox Relations." In that essay, Johnson shows how Rabbi Soloveitchik's ideas about those relations, like Jewish-Christian relations, should be guided by pragmatic rather than religious concerns:

> The Rav sanctioned cooperation among the rabbinical and congregational organizations only to the extent that such cooperation did not require discussions of religious or Halakhic (i.e., Jewish legal) issues. […] What the Rav considered heretical ideas emanating from the non-Orthodox movements (i.e., Reform, Conservative, Reconstructionist) were the principal reasons for not engaging in cooperation with these movements.[17]

To his credit, Johnson acknowledges that our world has dramatically changed since Rav Soloveitchik penned his essay, especially in the arenas of Jewish-Christian relations and Jewish-Jewish relations. The very "at-home-ness" of the American Jewish communities, part and parcel of the American story since the first Sephardic/Spanish settlers arrived in New Amsterdam from Recife, Brazil, in 1654, have largely contributed to religious dialogues and encounters among all manner of persons and groups. And there appears on the horizon no indication – none whatsoever! – there will be any lessening of such contacts.

To be sure, there will be bumps on the roads we Jews and Christians travel: a politician or religious leader may give voice to a remarkably insensitive comment regarding our two communities, or a particular sub-group of one of us may exacerbate tensions momentarily within some dialogical circles. I am thinking, for example, of members of the Westboro Baptist Church of Topeka, Kansas who have made disparaging, even hateful, statements about homosexuals. There also are members of one Hasidic Jewish group – *Neturei Karta* – who traveled to Iran to participate in a Holocaust-denying conference at the invitation of its antisemitic former President Mahmoud Ahmadinejad and relished the photo-op embracing him. Neither of these actions or statements do much to encourage respectful dialogue about issues on which we may disagree. There is also the ongoing and seemingly endless Middle East conflict that can cause tensions between our two religious communities.

We Jews and Christians also know that the momentously important Roman Catholic document, "We Remember: Reflections on the *Shoah*" (1998) was not received well within Jewish circles. In my view, this "lack of appreciation among Jews" for "We Remember" occurred primarily for two reasons: (1) the failure of the Vatican to recognize that among the perpetrators were baptized Christians who considered themselves "good" Christians but who nevertheless participated in the round-up and murder of Jews during the Holocaust/*Shoah*, and (2) the failure of the Roman Catholic Church to accept some level of responsibility for that "bad history" on the part of the Roman Catholic Church itself. Nevertheless, here in the United States, the wall of separation continues to hold; the dialogues continue to take place; Jews and Christians continue to live side by side, work side by side, and educate themselves and their children side by side. Perhaps most importantly, we continue to break bread together in many, many venues.

In 2002, four well-known Jewish academics – the late Tikva Frymer-Kensky of the University of Chicago, David Novak of the University of Toronto, Peter Ochs of the University of Virginia, and the late Michael Signer of the University of Notre Dame – published a remarkable document entitled "*Dabru Emet* ('Speak Truth!'): A Jewish Statement on Christians and Christianity."[18] It elicited literally hundreds of signatures of support from both rabbis and fellow Jewish academics, and a Christian response document as well. Here, in brief, are eight points *Dabru Emet* makes:

1. Jews and Christians worship the same God.
2. Jews and Christians seek authority from the same book – the Bible (what Jews call "Tanakh" and Christians call the "Old Testament").
3. Christians can respect the claim of the Jewish people upon the land of Israel.
4. Jews and Christians accept the moral principles of Torah.
5. Nazism was not a Christian phenomenon. (NB: *The most controversial of its statements!*)
6. The humanly irreconcilable differences between Jews and Christians will not be settled until God redeems the entire world as promised in Scripture.
7. A new relationship between Jews and Christians will not weaken Jewish practice.
8. Jews and Christians must work together for justice and peace.[19]

That same year, 2002, the Christian Scholars Group on Christian-Jewish Relations published their response to "*Dabru Emet*."[20] Entitled "A Sacred Obligation: Rethinking Christian Faith in Relation to Judaism and the Jewish People,"[21] the following are its major points:

1. God's covenant with the Jewish people endures forever.
2. Jesus of Nazareth lived and died as a faithful Jew.
3. Ancient rivalries must not define Christian-Jewish relations today.
4. Judaism is a living faith, enriched by many centuries of development.
5. The Bible both connects and separates Jews and Christians.
6. Affirming God's enduring covenant with the Jewish people has consequences for Christian understandings of salvation.
7. Christians should not target Jews for conversion.
8. Christian worship that teaches contempt for Judaism dishonors God.
9. We affirm the importance of the land of Israel for the life of the Jewish people.
10. Christians should work with Jews for the healing of the world.[22]

Unlike the many, many positive responses from Jewish and Christian religious communities to the 1947 Seeligsburg Declaration or to the Vatican II 1965 document *Nostra Aetate*, I have been unable to find any official affirmative statements by any denominational community, Jewish or Christian, either expressing appreciation for "*Dabru Emet*" or "A Sacred Obligation." Nor have I found any evidence that either of these documents has been incorporated into official denominational resolution processes. One wonders why this is the case.

A "bump in the road" in terms of Jewish-Christian relations was Mel Gibson's movie, "The Passion of the Christ," which in 2004 – and still today – has caused heated discussion, controversy, lively debates, and dialogical encounters throughout this country and abroad about its anti-Jewish and antisemitic perspective on the passion and death of Jesus, who was for Christians, the Christ (Messiah), and for Jews, at best a prophet. A vast literature of books, articles, blog posts, and newspaper and magazine editorials, including two pieces by yours truly, attests to just how controversial the movie was and is.[23] At the time the film was released, there were fears within the Jewish communities of the United States and elsewhere that Gibson's film would spark a veritable avalanche of antisemitic incidents, reminiscent of the worst excesses of the Middle Ages. These fears proved unfounded, though isolated incidents did occur.

Conclusion

Almost 50 years ago, Jewish scholar and theologian Abraham Joshua Heschel (1907-

1972), drawing upon the work of both Moses Maimonides (1135-1204) and Rabbi Jacob Emden (1697-1776), wrote that both Christianity and Islam are communities created "for the sake of Heaven" (his phrase), and together with Judaism, are preparatory for welcoming the worship of G-d "with one accord" (Maimonides' phrase). Heschel did so in a remarkable essay entitled "No Religion is an Island," an obvious wordplay/riff on John Donne's (1572-1631) poem, "No Man is an Island." In that same essay, he wrote:

> Horizons are wide, dangers are greater. ... *No religion is an island*. We are all involved with one another. Spiritual betrayal on the part of one of us affects the faith of all of us. Views adopted in one community have an impact on other communities. Today religious isolationism is a myth. For all the profound differences in perspective and substance, Judaism is sooner or later affected by the intellectual, moral, and spiritual events within the Christian society, and vice versa.[24]

Indeed, we Jews and Christians have traveled a twisting road these past 2,000 years, filled with speed bumps and potholes, but we have continued our journey. Today this road, to a degree perhaps as never before, is more twisted and bumpier, containing potholes even bigger than they were in the past, though I'm not at all sure our historians would agree, especially those whose specialty is the Middle Ages (perhaps a better term than the Dark Ages, though much of it was indeed dark with violence, intolerance, illiteracy, and ignorance). Respect for our two religious traditions mandates not only recognizing both our very real differences and our too-often overlooked commonalities in a dialogue of equals and an activist commitment to human betterment, but to continuing the journey as well. As 2nd-century Rabbi Tarfon would have it,

> The day is long and the work is much. The workers are sluggish but the Master of the house is urgent. It is not incumbent upon us to finish the task, but neither are we free to desist from it altogether.[25]

Discussion Questions

1. *Share your own assessments of the eight (8) topics outlined in the author's REL 347 course, "Jewish-Christian Relations." Are there others that should be included? Why or why not?*

2. *Share your own responses to (a) the Ten Points of Seeligsburg, (b) the Eight Points of* Dabru Emet, *and (c) the Ten Points of "A Sacred*

Obligation" (page 19). Write your own "Statement on Jewish-Christian Relations."

3. *You are the rabbi of the local synagogue or the priest/minister/parson/preacher/pastor/reverend of the local church. The two of you are tasked with constructing a multi-session adult-education curriculum that will bring together representative members of both your congregations in a face-to-face dialogue. Construct such a program and determine the number of sessions. Outline the topics to be covered, your rationale for inclusion, whatever resources are to be used (readings outside of meetings, readings together, video materials, handouts, etc.), and what you hope the participants will take away from both the individual sessions and the overall program.*

Further Reading

Berger, Alan L. (Ed.). *Post-Holocaust Jewish-Christian Dialogue: After the Flood, before the Rainbow* (Lanham, MD: Lexington Books, 2015).

Boys, Mary C. *Redeeming Our Sacred Story: The Death of Jesus and Relations between Jews and Christians* (New York: Paulist Press, 2013).

Cernera, Anthony J. (Ed.). *Examining* Nostra Aetate *After 40 Years: Catholic-Jewish Relations in Our Time* (Fairfield, CT: Sacred Heart University Press, 2007).

Cunningham, Philip A. *Seeking Shalom: The Journey to Right Relationship between Catholics and Jews* (Grand Rapids: William B. Eerdmans, 2015).

Feldman, Egal. *Catholics and Jews in Twentieth-Century America* (Urbana & Chicago: University of Illinois Press, 2001).

Milestones in Modern Jewish-Christian Relations (website with resources). Available at http://www.scarboromissions.ca/interfaith-dialogue/jewish-christian-relations/milestones-in-modern-jewish-christian-relations.

Oesterreicher, John J. *The New Encounter between Christians and Jews* (New York: Philosophical Library, 1986).

Stow, Kenneth. *Jewish Dogs: An Image and Its Interpretation: Continuity in the Catholic-Jewish Encounter* (Stanford, CA: Stanford University Press, 2006).

Wilde, Melissa. J. *Vatican II: A Sociological Analysis of Religious Change* (Princeton and Oxford: Princeton University Press, 2007).

Film and Video Resources

Faith and Doubt at Ground Zero (114 mins). Produced by PBS Frontline. Available at http://www.pbs.org/wgbh/frontline/film/showsfaith/.

Notes

1. Speaking to the Jewish Community of Birmingham, Alabama, January 1975.
2. On this specific question, see my essay, "Teaching Jesus at the University of Alabama," in *Teaching the Historical Jesus: Issues and Exegesis*, ed. Zev Garber (New York and London: Routledge, 2015), pp. 49-58.
3. This semester, the texts for the class include Adam H. Becker and Annette Yoshiko Reed (Eds.), *The Ways that Never Parted: Jews and Christians in Late Antiquity and the Early Middle Ages* (Minneapolis: Fortress Press, 2007); Jacques Berlinerblau, *How to Be Secular: A Call to Arms for Religious Freedom* (Boston and New York: Mariner Books, 2012); David Cheetham, Douglas Pratt, and David Thomas (Eds.), *Understanding Interreligious Relations* (Oxford: Oxford University Press, 2013); and Edward Kessler, *An Introduction to Jewish-Christian Relations* (Cambridge and New York: Cambridge University Press, 2010).
4. For example, on a related matter, see my essay, "The Impact of the *Shoah* on American Jewish-Christian Relations" in *The Impact of the Holocaust in America: The Jewish Role in American Life: An Annual Review*, vol. 6, ed. Zev Garber (Los Angeles: University of Southern California, 2008), pp. 139-157.
5. Ibid.
6. See the important text *American Grace: How Religion Divides and Unites Us*, by Robert D. Putnam, Harvard University, and David E. Campbell, University of Notre Dame (New York and London: Simon & Schuster, 2010). An interesting counter-argument is that of David Sehat of Georgia State University in his book *The Myth of American Religious Freedom* (New York and Oxford: Oxford University Press, 2011).
7. One cannot help but think here of the ongoing conversations regarding the Oberammergau Passion Play in Germany, performed annually, and the revisions that have followed in the wake of the Second World War and the Holocaust/*Shoah*.
8. See further, "Blood on Our Heads: A Jewish Response to Saint Matthew" in *A Shadow of Glory: Reading the New Testament after the Holocaust*, ed. Tod Linafelt (New York, NY: Routledge, 2002), pp. 57-67.
9. http://www.iccj.org/fileadmin/ICCJ/user_upload/Copeland/TwelvePoints.PDF.
10. Isaac was also the author of the important text *The Teaching of Contempt* (New York: McGraw Hill, 1965). Paralleling this text was one of equal importance by the late Roman Catholic priest Edward H. Flannery (1912-1998), *The Anguish of the Jews: Twenty-Three Centuries of Antisemitism* (New York: Paulist Press, 2004; Revised and Expanded Edition).
11. See further, Gavin G. D'Costa, "What Does the Church Teach About Mission to the Jewish People?," pp. 590-613; along with two important responses: "A Jewish Response to Gavin D'Costa" by Edward Kessler, pp. 614-628; and "A Catholic Response to Gavin D'Costa" by John T. Pawlikowski, O.S.M., pp. 629-640; all in *Theological Studies*, 72(3), 2012.
12. The overall vote regarding the Church's attitude to non-Christian religions (including Islam, Buddhism, and Hinduism) was 1,651 in favor; 99 opposed; and 242 in favor with reservations.
13. The following three volumes are an excellent place to start: Anthony J. Cernera (Ed.), *Examining* Nostra Aetate *after 40 Years: Catholic-Jewish Relations in Our Time* (Fairfield, CT: Sacred Heart University, 2007); Franklin Sherman (Ed.), *Bridges: Documents of the Christian-Jewish Dialogue/Vol. One: The Road to Reconciliation* (1945-1985) (New York: Paulist Press, 2011), and *Vol. Two: Building a New Relationship* (1986-2013) (New York: Paulist Press, 2014). See also John Connelly, *From Enemy to Brother: The Revolution in Catholic Teaching on the Jews, 1933-1965* (Cambridge and London: Harvard University Press, 2012).
14. Mark A. Kellner, "50 years later, Vatican II still divides," *Washington Times*. Available at http://www.washingtontimes.com.
15. *The Lonely Man of Faith* (New York: Doubleday & Company, 1965); *Halakhic Man* (Philadelphia: The Jewish Publication Society, 1983).

THE HOLOCAUST AND *NOSTRA AETATE*: TOWARD A GREATER UNDERSTANDING

16. Boston College's Center for Christian-Jewish Learning has made available online its November 23, 2003 journal issue entitled "Rabbi Joseph Solveitchik on Interreligious Dialogue: Forty Years Later," with papers by both Jewish and Christian scholars (Eugene Korn, David Berger, Aryeh Klapper, Philip A. Cunningham, Edward Breuer, Alan Brill, Erica Brown, Shalom Carmy, Joseph H. Ehrenkranz, Reuven Kimelman, David Rosen, Jonathan Sachs, Marc B. Shapiro, Deborah Wasserman, and Michael Wyschogrod).
17. George E. Johnson (2013), "We Have Found the Enemy, and the Enemy is Us." Available at http://www.jewishideas.org.
18. www.icjs.org/resources/dabru-emet.
19. One highly critical response to this document, however, was that of Harvard scholar Jon D. Levenson to what was apparently an advance copy and which appeared in *Commentary Magazine* (December 2001, 112(5); pp. 31-37), entitled "How Not to Conduct Jewish-Christian Dialogue."
20. For further information about the Christian Scholars Group on Christian-Jewish Relations, see http://www.ccjr.us/members/christian-scholars-group.
21. Those Christian scholars were Norman Beck, Mary C. Boys, Rosann Catalano, Philip A. Cunningham, Celia Deutsch, Alice L. Eckardt, Eugene J. Fisher, Eva Fleischner, Deirdre Good, Walter Harrelson, Michael McGarry, John C. Merkle, John T. Pawlikowski, Peter A. Pettit, Peter C. Phan, Jean-Pierre Ruiz, Franklin Sherman, Joann Spillman, John T. Townsend, Joseph Tyson, and Clark M. Williamson.
22. http://www.jcrelations.net/A_Sacred_Obligation__Rethinking_Christian_-Faith_in_Relation_to_Judaism_and_the.2372.0.html.
23. "Can There Be Jewish-Christian Dialogue After 'The Passion'?" in *Re-Viewing the Passion: Mel Gibson and His Critics*, ed. S. Brent Plate (New York: Palgrave Macmillan, 2005), pp. 43-54; "Jewish 'Officialdom' and *The Passion of the Christ*: Who Said What and What Did They Say?" *Shofar: An Interdisciplinary Journal of Jewish Studies*, 23(3), 2005, pp. 114-123.
24. Abraham Joshua Heschel," No Religion is an Island," *Union Theological Seminary Review*, 2(1), 1966, and reprinted in Harold Kasimow and Byron L. Sherwin (Eds.), *Abraham Joshua Heschel and Interreligious Dialogue* (Maryknoll: Orbis Books, 1991), p. 6.
25. *Pirke Avot*/Sayings of the Fathers, 2:16. My own commitment to Jewish-Christian dialogue —and by extension, Jewish-Christian-Muslim trialogue — has most recently been addressed in "Two Takes on Christianity: Furthering the Dialogue," *Journal of Ecumenical Studies*, 47(4), 2012, pp. 508-524.

Dare We Hope?

Mary C. Boys, S.N.J.M.

Recipient of the 2015 National Catholic Center for Holocaust Education Nostra Aetate Award; Dean of Academic Affairs and Skinner and McAlpin Professor of Practical Theology, Union Theological Seminary, New York, NY

I take my title from a conversation between two elderly men on a June day in 1960 in Rome. One man was French, a distinguished historian, 83 years old, and, by his own admission, very deaf: Jules Isaac. The other, a mere 78, was Pope John XXIII, who had spent many years as an apostolic nuncio in Turkey and Bulgaria (1925-1937), Greece (1938-1944), and France (1945-1953). Isaac, whose wife, daughter, and son-in-law had been deported to Auschwitz and murdered, had spent many years researching the Church's teaching about Jews and Judaism. Encouraged by his prominent Catholic friends in France, Isaac had petitioned for the audience in the hopes of convincing the Pope to place the question of the Church's relationship with Jews on the agenda of Vatican II, which was still in its planning stages.[1] Isaac suggested at the end of their conversation that the Pope set up a commission to study the "The Jewish Question." "Dare I hope?" he asked the pontiff. "I thought of that from the beginning of our meeting," John XXIII replied, adding with a smile, "You are right in having more than hope … I am the head, but I must also consult … Here is not an absolute monarchy."[2] On June 15, 1960, just two days after his meeting with John XXIII, Isaac met with Augustin Cardinal Bea, to whom John XXIII had entrusted major responsibility for establishing the Council's agenda. In turn, Bea appointed a sub-commission for studying the question regarding the Church's relations with Jews.[3]

When the Second Vatican Council promulgated the declaration *Nostra Aetate* (*NA*) – the "Declaration on the Relation of the Church to Non-Christian Religions" – five years later on October 28, 1965, neither Jules Isaac (d. September 5, 1963) nor Pope John XXIII (d. June 3, 1963) was alive.[4] Yet, despite five drafts and a contentious debate at the Council before the document emerged on October 28, 1965, their meeting proved decisive. What Isaac had dared to hope for was in large measure fulfilled. The process of formulating and disseminating *NA* launched a movement of reconciliation fundamental to the Church's moral integrity, a catalyst for other Christian traditions to examine their relationship with the Jewish people, and a sign of hope that enmity could be turned into amity.

So it is fitting that as we celebrate the 50th anniversary of *NA*, we recall this 1960 meeting of Isaac and (St.) John XXIII. The declaration that emerged five years after their encounter provided a foundational, if flawed, text that subsequent statements have nuanced and developed. We have now an entire documentary library that builds upon and supersedes *NA* – and not only in the Catholic Church, but in Protestant churches as well.[5] In commemorating the anniversary of *NA*, we should emphasize both what Vatican II initiated and particularly what subsequent documentation has advanced.

To that end, I propose to highlight what I believe is the key paragraph of section 4 of *NA*:

> Even though the Jewish authorities and those who followed their lead pressed for the death of Christ (see Jn 19:6), neither all Jews indiscriminately at that time, nor Jews today, can be charged with the crimes committed during his passion. It is true that the church is the new people of God, yet the Jews should not be spoken of as rejected or accursed as if this followed from holy scripture. Consequently, all must take care, lest in catechizing or in preaching the word of God, they teach anything which is not in accord with the truth of the Gospel message or the spirit of Christ.[6]

My original intention was then to suggest a rewrite of this paragraph in view of successor documents of *NA* and contemporary biblical scholarship. In the process of composing such a paragraph, however, I realized I was formulating a second edition, as it were, of the entirety of *NA*, no. 4, which is the longest of the five sections of the Declaration and deals with the relationship with the Jewish people.

I realize that my approach may appear to be a monumental act of Catholic *chutzpah*. After all, a team of learned priests worked for several years over the five drafts of *NA*, and the world's bishops and heads of male religious orders tested those drafts in intense and often disputatious debates at the Council itself. Nevertheless, we have now had many years of discussion and commentary, as well as many new documents in the *NA* trajectory. In this sense, I believe I've simply joined an international team of drafters, as integral to my formulation is the documentary tradition that has developed around *NA*. In celebrating *NA*, we must take note of the full stock of ecclesial resources.

Moreover, this 50th anniversary has provided a teachable moment to educate about the entirety of theological advances in Catholic-Jewish relations, not simply about *NA* itself. When I gave the lecture at Seton Hill University on October 26, 2015 that forms the basis of this essay, there was no indication of the issuance of another document in celebration of the anniversary. Thus, I thought I might start a conversation rather than bemoaning a lost "teachable moment." Six weeks after that lecture, however, and just a week before this essay was due, the Vatican's Commission on Religious Relations with Jews issued a lengthy statement on December 10, 2015, *The Gifts and the Calling of God Are Irrevocable*.[7] It is a complex document that invites further study; given the limitations of time, I have drawn only a few excerpts from it. I intend my own "anniversary edition" of *NA*, no. 4, to contribute to the conversation. It certainly does not purport to be the last word, but I do hope it will provoke further conversation and study.

NA, no. 4, and Interpretation of the Bible

A long and painful history is the requisite context for grasping the significance of the paragraph cited above from *NA*, no. 4, since in fact the Church had for nearly two millennia placed responsibility for the death of Jesus on Jews – a charge that constituted the theological heart of its hostility to Judaism. The passion narratives of the canonical Gospels, as well as Luke's second account, the Acts of the Apostles, certainly attribute responsibility for the death of Jesus to Jews, whether to the scribes, priests, and elders of the people, or, in the Fourth Gospel, to "the Jews." Moreover, lurking just below the surface of this paragraph is a note of triumphalism, as if God were not sufficiently capacious to have more than one people. Oddly, just two paragraphs before the one cited here, the Council had said, "Nevertheless, God holds the Jews most dear for the sake of their Fathers; He does not repent of the gifts He makes or of the calls He issues – such is the witness of the Apostle [Rom 11:28]." *NA* is not without its weaknesses.

Read at the distance of 50 years, we see that this section of no. 4 is based on outmoded biblical scholarship. The U.S. bishops provided a more adequate formulation in a 1988 monograph:

> The Gospels are the outcome of long and complicated editorial work. ... Hence, it cannot be ruled out that some references hostile or less than favorable to the Jews have their historical context in conflicts between

the nascent Church and the Jewish community. Certain controversies reflect Christian-Jewish relations long after the time of Jesus. To establish this is of capital importance if we wish to bring out the meaning of certain Gospel texts for the Christians of today. All this should be taken into account when preparing catechesis and homilies for the last weeks of Lent and Holy Week (*Guidelines*, II, *Sussidi per l'ecumenismo nella diocesi di Roma*, 1982, 144b).[8]

Foundational to modern biblical interpretation is to approach the Gospels as the "outcome of a long and complicated editorial work" rather than as historically reliable documentaries. The importance of this principle for understanding the New Testament's depiction of Jews (including subgroups such as the Pharisees) cannot be sufficiently emphasized. In the citation above, *Notes* argues that controversies in the authors' (and/or editors') communities played a significant role in shaping the NT depiction of Jews, particularly with regard to the crucifixion of Jesus. This is evident as well in the Pontifical Biblical Commission's lengthy 2001 monograph, *The Jewish People and their Sacred Scriptures in the Christian Bible* (*JPSSCB*). For example, regarding the Gospel of Mark:

> Any interpretation of Mark's Gospel that attempts to pin responsibility for Jesus' death on the Jewish people is erroneous. Such an interpretation, which has had disastrous consequences throughout history, does not correspond at all to the evangelist's perspective, which, as we have said, repeatedly opposes the attitude of the people or the crowd to that of the authorities hostile to Jesus. Furthermore, it is forgotten that the disciples were also part of the Jewish people. It is a question, then, of an improper transfer of responsibility, of the sort that is often encountered in human history.[9]

In explaining the generally hostile depiction of "the Jews" in the Fourth Gospel, the *JPSSCB* suggests that the Johannine community's expulsion from the synagogue was the principal cause:

> At times in the Gospel the separation of Jesus' disciples from "the Jews" is evident in the expulsion from the synagogue imposed on Jews who believed in Jesus [John 9:22; 12:42; 16:2]. It is possible that the Jews in the Johannine communities experienced this treatment, since they would be considered unfaithful to Jewish monotheistic faith (which, in fact, was not at all the case, since Jesus said: "I and the Father are one": 10:30). The result was that it became almost standard to use "the Jews"

to designate those who kept this name for themselves alone, in their opposition to the Christian faith.[10]

In addition to offering some bedrock concepts about the nature of the Gospels, the post-*NA* documentary tradition also provides some principles of interpretation. I offer the following list as a summary:

1. Interpretations of biblical texts should be consonant with "evangelical justice and charity." Thus, interpretations that can be used as a "justification for racial segregation, antisemitism, or sexism must be rejected."[11]
2. Actualizations of certain texts of the New Testament that could provoke or reinforce unfavorable attitudes to the Jewish people should be "absolutely" avoided.[12]
3. Sacred texts should be situated in their context as artifacts of human culture; the human reality underlying the texts should not be bypassed in a search for spiritual meaning.[13]
4. Because biblical texts bear the limitations and wounds of human finitude – Sacred Scripture is the "word of God expressed in human language" – they should be interpreted in a discerning manner.[14]
5. The NT's depiction of Jews should be understood as a rhetorical strategy of the Greco-Roman world that no longer carries authority for our time.[15]
6. The process of interpreting biblical texts should involve inquiry into what the text has been used to inspire or rationalize or justify. Interpreters should consider the consequences interpretation of texts has had on specific people.[16]
7. Make use of disciplines, such as the social sciences, that illumine the wider context of texts.[17]

If relatively few in the Catholic Church have a clear grasp of *NA*, even fewer are aware of the existence of more expansive and nuanced statements from Vatican offices, national conferences of bishops, and offices of ecumenical and interreligious affairs. It is my hope that a second edition of the declaration might draw attention to the important work that is the fruit of 50 years of scholarship and dialogue.

Thus, I offer a new edition of *NA*, no. 4; the many notes indicate my reliance on documents issued since 1965 that constitute the "*Nostra Aetate* Trajectory."[18]

Nostra Aetate, no. 4: A 50th Anniversary Revised Edition
Fifty years ago, the Second Vatican Council gave impetus to dialogue with Jews

through its declaration, *Nostra Aetate*. In the years since, the Catholic Church has reassessed its relationship with the Jewish people, seeking a greater knowledge of Judaism and learning how Jews themselves understand their tradition in its complexity and diversity.[19] Among the fruits of this dialogue has been a new appreciation for the continuing covenant between God and the Jewish people.[20]

From its origins to the present, Christianity and Judaism have been intertwined vines growing out of biblical Israel. Competing claims about whether Torah or Jesus offered the truer path to God characterized this relationship in its early years. In later centuries, however, rivalry degenerated into hostility. The Church developed ways of teaching about Christianity that disparaged Judaism and portrayed Jews as responsible for the death of Jesus and thus as unfaithful to God.[21]

The new bonds developed with Jews have challenged the Church to grapple with its responsibility in contributing to its "tormented history" with Jews and "theological antagonism" toward Judaism.[22] Over the course of centuries, the Church has often disparaged Judaism and contributed to the rise of violence against Jews, including the painful and difficult realization that Church teachings provided a fertile seedbed for the Nazi genocide.[23] To remember the *Shoah* "is to become fully conscious of the salutary waning it entails: the spoiled seeds of anti-Judaism and antisemitism must never again be allowed to take root in any human heart."[24]

Mindful that the Spirit continues to inspire, the Church embraces ways of interpreting Scripture that provide a deeper understanding of both Old and New Testaments, as well as the complex manner in which the New Testament draws upon the Old. Although different religious perspectives shape how Jews and Christians interpret the sacred texts they share, both readings epitomize their respective tradition and provide rich resources for more profound dialogue.

Developments in the study of the New Testament shed new light on the crucifixion of Jesus, the Pharisees, and the Apostle Paul. While the Gospels appear in varying ways to place principal responsibility for the death of Jesus on Jews, the passion narratives are theological reflections on the crucifixion, not eyewitness accounts or documentaries.[25] Biblical scholarship in our time situates the Gospel narratives in the historical context of the Roman Empire. The power of the Empire's authorities (e.g., Pontius Pilate) superseded that of Jewish authorities (e.g., the high priest). While some Jewish authorities may have perceived Jesus as a rival or as a threat, his inclusive preaching of God's Reign was a far greater threat to the cult of the emperor and to Rome's imperial order in which an elite minority ruled over the masses. Ultimate responsibility for the death of Jesus thus falls not to "the Jews," as it might seem in the Gospel of John, but to the Roman governor, Pontius Pilate, in alliance with the power class.[26] Since for centuries many Christians blamed Jews for the death of Jesus, Christian reflection on the passion and death of Jesus "should lead to a deep sense of the need for reconciliation with the Jewish community today."[27]

In the Gospels of Matthew, Mark, and Luke, the Pharisees seem to be the most prominent antagonists of Jesus. Yet a close reading of these texts in context reveals that many of the conflicts between Jesus and his Jewish interlocutors – particularly the Pharisees – reflect clashes from a later period between the followers of Jesus and other Jews.[28] These later conflicts shaped the depiction of the Pharisees, with whom Jesus had many affinities.[29] Thus, Christians today should interpret the evangelists' accounts of the Pharisees not as historically accurate portraits of this Jewish movement but as symbols of religiosity run awry – a phenomenon to which every religious tradition is vulnerable.

This scholarship also resituates Paul, the Apostle to the Gentiles, as a Jew whose mystical encounter with Christ was a call to preach the Way of Jesus to non-Jews (Gentiles), whom he saw as wild shoots grafted onto the olive tree of Israel. To Paul, following the Way of Jesus reoriented rather than rejected his connection to Judaism.

These recent insights into our sacred texts offer new lenses for understanding Jesus, "the living Torah of God," and the Jewish matrix of the early church.[30] If over the centuries, contentiousness and disputation too often characterized the relationship between Christians and Jews, today differences provide opportunity for study and dialogue.[31]

On this 50th anniversary of *Nostra Aetate*, we rejoice that as a consequence of what this declaration initiated, many Christians have developed deep bonds of friendship and solidarity with Jews. We hope that these ties of kinship in the One God will deepen and broaden and that they will serve as a witness to the world that those who were once enemies can reconcile.

Questions for Discussion

1. *In what ways is the interpretation of the Bible central to developing more just relations with the Jewish people?*

2. *What seem to you to be the principal advances in theological understanding of the Catholic Church's relationship with Judaism since the promulgation of Nostra Aetate, no. 4, in 1965?*

3. *How might the insights initiated by Nostra Aetate be deepened in the life of the Church and society?*

Further Reading

Baum, Gregory. *Amazing Church: A Catholic Theologian Remembers a Half Century of Change* (Toronto: Novalis, 2005).

Boys, Mary C. *Redeeming Our Sacred Story: The Death of Jesus and Relations between Jews and Christians*. (New York: Stimulus/Paulist, 2013).

---------"The *Nostra Aetate* Trajectory: Holding our Theological Bow Differently," *Never Revoked:* Nostra Aetate *as Ongoing Challenge for Jewish-Christian Dialogue/ Louvain Theological and Pastoral Monographs 40*. Eds. Maryanne Moyaert and Didier Pollefeyt (Leuven, Belgium: Peeters Publishers, 2000), pp. 133-157.

Fisher, Eugene J. and Leon Klenicki (Eds.). *Pope John Paul II: Spiritual Pilgrimage/ Texts on Jews and Judaism* (New York: Crossroad, 1995).

Isaac, Jules. *Jesus and Israel*. Trans. Sally Gran (New York: Hart, Rinehart, & Winston, 1971). French original 1948.

---------*The Teaching of Contempt: Christian Roots of Anti-Semitism*. Trans. Helen Weaver (New York: Hart, Rinehart, & Winston, 1964). French original 1962.

Levine, Amy Jill and Marc Zvi Brettler (Eds.). *The Jewish Annotated New Testament* (New York: Oxford University Press, 2011).

Sherman, Franklin (Ed.). *Bridges: Documents of the Christian-Jewish Dialogue/Vol. 2, Building New Relations (1986-2013)* (New York: Paulist, 2014).

---------*Bridges: Documents of the Christian-Jewish Dialogue/Vol. 1, The Road to Reconciliation* (1945-1985) (New York: Paulist, 2011).

Tobias, Norman C. "Jules Isaac and the Roman Catholic Church: Advocate for Scriptural Truth," Ph.D. dissertation, University of Toronto, 2015.

Film and Video Resources

I Am Joseph Your Brother (59 mins). Produced by Tal El Productions. Available at http://jewishfilm.org/Catalogue/films/Joe.htm.

Jews and Christians: A Journey of Faith (120 mins). Produced by Auteur Productions. Available at Amazon.com.

Three Faiths, One God: Judaism (120 mins). Produced by Auteur Productions. Available at http://www.interfaithfilms.com/ (also available at Amazon.com).

Walking God's Paths: Christians and Jews in Candid Conversation (6-part film series, 15 mins each). Produced by Center for Christian-Jewish Learning at Boston College. Available at http://www.ccjr.us/dialogika-resources/educational-and-liturgical-materials/curricula/958-wgp-1.

Notes

1. Jules Isaac, "Notes on a Week in Rome," *SIDIC* (1968/3), 11; see http://www.notredamedesion.org/en/dialogue_docs.php?a=3b&id=690. The Council opened on October 11, 1962.
2. See André Kaspi, "Jules Isaac and His Role in Jewish-Christian Relations," in *Jews, Catholics, and the Burdens of History*, ed. Eli Lederhendler (New York: Oxford University Press, 2006), pp. 12-20. See also Norman C. Tobias, "Jules Isaac and the Roman Catholic Church: Advocate for Scriptural Truth," Ph.D. dissertation, University of Toronto, 2015.
3. All members of the sub-commission were priests: Barnabas Ahern, Gregory Baum, Pierre Benoit, Bruno Hussar, John Oesterreicher, Nicolaus Persich, Leo Rudloff, Antonius Ramselaar, and Thomas Stransky. See Gregory Baum, *Amazing Church: A Catholic Theologian Remembers a Half Century of Change* (Toronto: Novalis, 2005); John Hammond, *A Benedictine Legacy of Peace: The Life of Abbot Leo A. Rudloff* (Weston, VT: Weston Priory, 2005). See also Thomas F. Stransky, "The Foundation of the Secretariat for Promoting Christian Unity," in ed. Alberic Stacpoole, *Vatican II: By Those Who Were There* (London: Geoffrey Chapman, 1986), pp. 2-73.
4. The Conciliar texts, authored in Latin, are generally known by their first two words. In the rest of this essay, I abbreviate the title as NA. For an English translation, see *The Basic Sixteen Documents [of] Vatican Council II: Constitutions, Decrees, Declarations. A Completely Revised Translation in Inclusive Language*, general editor Austin Flannery (Collegeville: Liturgical Press, 2014).
5. See the two-volume anthology *Bridges: Documents of the Christian-Jewish Dialogue, Vol. 1, The Road to Reconciliation (1945-1985)*, ed. Franklin Sherman (New York: Paulist, 2011); *Bridges: Documents of the Christian-Jewish Dialogue/Vol. 2, Building New Relations (1986-2013)*, ed. Franklin Sherman (New York: Paulist, 2014). Volume 1 includes an essay entitled "A Protestant Perspective" by Alice Eckardt (pp. 1-12). I have chosen to document the statements from these volumes rather than clutter up the notes with lengthy URLs. Virtually all the documents cited in this essay are also available online, especially through the website of the Council of Centers on Jewish-Christian Relations: http://www.ccjr.us/dialogika-resources/documents-and-statements.
6. Translation from *The Basic Sixteen Documents*, p. 573.
7. The authors note that their document is neither a magisterial document nor a doctrinal teaching, but rather a "reflection." For the text, see http://www.ccjr.us/dialogika-resources/documents-and-statements/roman-catholic/vatican-curia/1357-crrj-2015dec10.
8. The section indicated by the ellipsis is as follows: "The dogmatic constitution *Dei Verbum*, following the Pontifical Biblical Commission's Instruction *Sancta Mater Ecclesia*, distinguished three stages: The sacred authors wrote the four Gospels, selecting some things from the many which had been handed on by word of mouth or in writing, reducing some of them to a synthesis, explicating some things in view of the situation of their churches, and preserving the form of proclamation, but always in such fashion that they told us the honest truth about Jesus" (no. 19). *Dei Verbum* is one of the major texts of Vatican II; see http://www.vatican.va/archive/hist_councils/ii_vatican_council/documents/vat-ii_const_19651118_dei-verbum_en.html The reference to *Sancta Mater Ecclesia* is to the *Instruction on the Historical Truth of the Gospels*, issued by the Pontifical Biblical Commission in April 1964; see www.ccjr.us/dialogika-resources/documents-and-statements/roman-catholic/vatican-curia/289-pbc-1964.
9. This excerpt may be found in section 72; see http://www.ccjr.us/dialogika-resources/documents-and-statements/roman-catholic/vatican-curia/282-pbc-2001.
10. Ibid, section 77.
11. Pontifical Biblical Commission, *Interpretation of the Bible in the Church*, IV.A.3; http://www.ccjr.us/dialogika-resources/documents-and-statements/roman-catholic/vatican-curia/287-pbc-1993.
12. Ibid.
13. See Peter S. Williamson, *Catholic Principles for Interpreting Scripture: A Study of the Pontifical Biblical Commission's "The Interpretation of the Bible in the Church"/ Subsidia Biblica 22* (Roma: Editrice Pontificio Istituto Biblico, 2001), p. 143.
14. *Interpretation of the Bible in the Church*, I.A.
15. See Clark Williamson, *A Guest in the House of Israel* (Louisville: Westminster/John Knox, 1993), p. 143.
16. *Interpretation*: "At the same time, history also illustrates the prevalence from time to time of interpretations that are tendentious and false, baneful in their effect – such as, for example, those that have promoted anti-Semitism or other forms of racial discrimination or, yet again, various kinds of millenarian delusions" (I.C.3).

17. Ibid. I.D.1-3.
18. See Mary C. Boys, "The *Nostra Aetate* Trajectory: Holding our Theological Bow Differently," in *Never Revoked:* Nostra Aetate *as Ongoing Challenge for Jewish-Christian Dialogue*, Louvain Theological and Pastoral Monographs 40, eds. Maryanne Moyaert and Didier Pollefeyt. (Leuven, Belgium: Peeters Publishers, 2000), pp.133-157.
19. "On the practical level in particular, Christians must therefore strive to acquire a better knowledge of the basic components of the religious tradition of Judaism; they must strive to learn by what essential traits Jews define themselves in the light of their own religious experience." See the "Preamble" to the 1974 *Guidelines and Suggestions for Implementing the Conciliar Declaration Nostra Aetate, No. 4*, in *Bridges*, Vol. 1, pp. 195-196.
20. [St.] Pope John Paul, in a speech in 1980, referred to Jews as "the people of God of the Old Covenant, never revoked by God, the present-day people of the covenant concluded with Moses." Similarly, in 1987 he spoke of Jews as "partners in a covenant of eternal love which was never revoked." Full texts in Pope *John Paul II: Spiritual Pilgrimage/ Texts on Jews and Judaism*, eds. Eugene J. Fisher and Leon Klenicki. (New York: Crossroad, 1995), pp. 13-16 and 105-109.
21. See Jules Isaac, *The Teaching of Contempt*, trans. Helen Weaver (New York: Hart, Rinehart, and Winston, 1964); see also his earlier *Jesus and Israel*, trans. Sally Gran (New York: Hart, Rinehart, and Winston, 1971). The original French editions were published in 1962 and 1948, respectively.
22. "The history of relations between Jews and Christians is a tormented one." See Commission on Religious Relations with the Jews, *We Remember: A Reflection on the Shoah* (1988), in *Bridges*, Vol. 2, pp. 250-259. "Arising from the same soil, Judaism and Christianity in the centuries after their separation became involved in a theological antagonism which was only to be defused at the Second Vatican Council." See Commission on Religious Relations with the Jews, *The Gifts and the Calling of God Are Irrevocable* (2015), #17; http://www.ccjr.us/dialogika-resources/documents-and-statements/roman-catholic/vatican-curia/1357-crrj-2015dec10.
23. "In the judgment of historians, it is a well-proven fact that for centuries, up until Vatican Council II, an anti-Jewish tradition stamped its mark in differing ways on Christian doctrine and teaching, in theology, apologetics, preaching and in the liturgy. It was on such ground that the venomous plant of hatred for the Jews was able to flourish. Hence, the heavy inheritance we still bear in our century, with all its consequences which are so difficult to wipe out. Hence our still open wounds." Catholic Bishops of France, "Declaration of Repentance" (1997) in *Bridges*, Vol. 2, pp. 355-360.
24. *We Remember: A Reflection on the Shoah*. See also Pontifical Commission on Justice and Peace, *The Church and Racism: Toward a More Fraternal Society* (1988): "Among the manifestations of systematic racial distrust, specific mention must once again be made of antisemitism" (#15); http://www.ccjr.us/dialogika-resources/documents-and-statements/roman-catholic/vatican-curia/291-pjpc-1988.
25. See *God's Mercy Endures Forever* (1988): "It is necessary to remember that the passion narratives do not offer eyewitness accounts or a modern transcript of historical events" (#23), in *Bridges*, Vol. 2, pp. 294-308. See also the U.S. Bishops' Committee for Ecumenical and Interreligious Affairs, *The Bible, the Jews, and the Death of Jesus: A Collection of Catholic Documents* (Washington, D.C.: United States Conference of Catholic Bishops, 2004). Also, "The Gospels are the outcome of long and complicated editorial work," in Commission on Religious Relations with the Jews, *Notes on the Correct Way to Present Jews and Judaism in Preaching and Catechesis of the Catholic Church* (1985), #21A in *Bridges*, Vol. 1, pp. 202-215.
26. See John 19: 16-17. Gerard Sloyan argues that the term "power class" more properly describes the opponents of Jesus in the passion; the term points to the alliance between the high priestly families and the representatives of the Roman Empire. See Gerard Sloyan, *The Crucifixion of Jesus: History, Myth, Faith* (Minneapolis: Fortress, 1995), p. 43.
27. *God's Mercy*, #25.
28. The separation between what became Christianity and Judaism happened over several centuries. The earliest disciples of Jesus were all Jews, though gradually in the second century C.E., more of his followers were Gentiles.
29. See *Notes*, #27.
30. Commission for Religious Relations with the Jews, *The Gifts and the Calling of God Are Irrevocable* (2015), #26.
31. Jorge Mario Bergoglio, "Dialogue entails a warm reception and not a preemptive condemnation. To dialogue, one must know how to lower the defenses, open the doors of one's home, and to offer warmth," in *On Heaven and Earth*, trans. Alejandro Bermudez and Howard Goodman (New York: Image, 2013), p. xiv.

PART 4: BEYOND THE HOLOCAUST & *NOSTRA AETATE*

The Authority of Those Who Suffer

Mary Jo Leddy

Senior Fellow, Massey College, University of Toronto; Adjunct Professor, Theology, Regis College, University of Toronto; Director, Romeo House for Refugees, Toronto, Canada

In the spring of 2015, I went on a pilgrimage to El Salvador with a group from Romero House in Toronto. We make this trip every five years to commemorate the anniversary of the death of Archbishop Oscar Romero, the patron of our little community that welcomes refugees. It is an amazing experience to gather with thousands of people from all over the world and to draw strength from the witness of the martyrs of El Salvador. During this time in March, there is usually an International Colloquium on Liberation Theology. It is an opportunity to hear about the ongoing developments in the theology that has originated in El Salvador and elsewhere throughout Latin America.

    This year one of the main speakers was Marta Zechmeister, C.J., an Austrian nun who is now replacing Jon Sobrino, S.J., as the chair of the theology department at the Jesuit University of Central America. Her main point was that suffering cannot be defined in an abstract way. It is too singular, so particular, shaped by circumstances that are always unique. However, she said, it can and must be described. She did so by describing in detail the particular suffering of one family afflicted by poverty, insecurity, and death. In the course of the talk, she used the phrase "the authority of those who suffer." The phrase captured my imagination, rang true and deep. I thought it was a very significant statement, although I did not know what it meant. I still don't know what it means. So consider this essay as the reflection of someone who is still seeking, who is naming what I do not yet fully understand or know.[1]

However partial these reflections may be, I think the effort might be significant in discussing the relationship between theologies of the Holocaust and the theologies of social justice that have developed in the Catholic Church since the time of Vatican II. It seems to me that in different ways these theologies are being guided by the authority of those who suffer.

My initial research suggests that Marta Zechmeister borrowed this phrase from one of her professors, the German Jesuit theologian Johann Baptist Metz. Considered one of the founders of political theology in Europe, he has grounded his theological reflections in the reality of suffering, particularly the suffering of the Holocaust. He evokes the "dangerous memory" of suffering as an antidote to the apathy of modernity. Metz uses the phrase "the authority of those who suffer" in different places throughout his work but, like Zechmeister, he neither develops nor defines it further. Metz himself may have been influenced by the insights of the German Lutheran martyr Dietrich Bonhoeffer, who claimed, "Only a suffering God can save us now."[2]

So I have taken up the challenge of reflecting further on what "the authority of those who suffer" might mean. I am paying attention to the authority of those who suffered at Auschwitz, to the authority of the Jewish people who continue to suffer, to the authority of the poor I met in the barrio of Chakra in San Salvador, and to the authority of the refugees I live with at Romero House. I believe the authority of each of these diverse suffering groups of people must be acknowledged and obeyed.

If a theologian is to be more than a professional guided only by the standards of academia, he or she must acknowledge this other point of reference. If a theologian is to be guided only or mainly by the authority of those in positions of authority in the church, then he or she must ask if this authority is sufficient. Such considerations became significant as the whole Church unfolded after Vatican II.

Vatican II and the Turn to Various Worlds

As we mark the 50th anniversary of *Nostra Aetate*, it is worth noting that it was a document written in the shadow of the *Shoah*. However, this deep background was not acknowledged in the document, even though it was in the foreground of the consciousness of many at that time. Just prior to the opening of Vatican II, the world was gripped by the televised trial of Adolf Eichmann in Jerusalem. The pictures and testimonies given during the trial provoked wide public discussion and a renewed sense of shock. How could this have happened in the heart of modern Christian Europe? The silence of Vatican II on this question was deafening.

However, *Nostra Aetate* was not written in isolation from the other Conciliar documents. This Declaration was developed in tandem with the Constitution on Revelation (*Dei Verbum*), which gave a new emphasis to the realities of human history, and with the Constitution on the Church in the Modern World (*Gaudium et Spes*): "The joys and hopes, the griefs and the anxieties of the people of this age, especially those who are poor or in any way afflicted … these are the joys and hopes, the griefs and anxieties of the followers of Christ" (Preface #1).

Gregory Baum, who was one of the theological experts at that time, has situated the documents of Vatican II in the context of concerns among the middle class in Europe. This was a class increasingly open to modern scientific invention, exploration, and human development, and at the same time wary of war and unsure of some of the more problematic aspects of modernity. I leave it to historians to trace the ambivalence about modernity evident in the council documents. Suffice it to say that the Church was making peace with modernity just as the secular world was beginning to call it into question. The concern for theologians in Europe at that time was the challenge to faith in a secular culture. How do we speak of God in an unbelieving world?

The Council documents, which took shape through the concerns of the European Church, were received readily in North America, in a culture shaped by the modern secular values of freedom and democracy.

In the years that followed Vatican II, different theological concerns began to emerge in other contexts. The turn to the world became the turn to many worlds. Latin America, for example, was a deeply religious culture and the question of faith was not as insistent as it was in Europe. Questions of justice, however, emerged with a new sense of urgency. In Latin America, there was an awakening to the violent gap between the rich and the poor and criticism of the Church's defense of the status quo. The animating question for many Latin American theologians was, "How do we speak of a God of Love to the poor?"[3]

It was not that Latin American theologians were rejecting answers that had been part of the Church's tradition in Europe. They were simply asking other questions as they began to face the fact that poverty kills, that the poor die a premature and unnecessary death, that there are situations in which the gap between the rich and poor is so extreme that the Church must take a side.

During the late 1970s, I was working as the editor of a small alternative Catholic newspaper called *Catholic New Times*. I remember the day a missionary rushed into our office just after he had returned from Central America. He had a tape of one of the homilies Archbishop Romero had given in the Cathedral of San Salvador. "You must listen to this! He speaks with such authority," he said. And we did listen. Thousands listened in San Salvador and many more throughout the world listened. I remember meeting with the Jesuits at the university in San Salvador in 1989, a week before they were killed because some of them had stepped forward to serve as negotiators for peace. I also reported on the Vatican's suspicion of liberation theology, the accusations of Marxist influences, the deep divisions in the Church of Latin America arising from the growing awareness of the poor and powerless that challenged the authority of the rich and powerful.

In this first phase of the development of liberation theology, there were many oversimplifications. Someone like Gustavo Guttierez, for example, noted that the reality of popular piety had not been taken seriously enough. In other places, theologians tried to articulate a liberation theology for "America" or "Canada." It did not work. It was an artificial construct trying to paste together the insights from a Latin American context with a socioeconomic analysis of a different context. In the second phase, theologians outside Latin America realized they had to take more account of the different contexts of theology and that a variety of contextual theologies was needed. What this means for the Roman Catholic Church is still being worked out. It surely involves an effort to understand "Catholic" as being universal without being uniform.

As we look back on the historic event of Vatican II, we can say that it marked the decisive turning to the world that became a turning towards many worlds, many contexts shaped by different questions. In the process, the location of authority has shifted.

The Location of Authority

It is instructive to reconsider the meaning of authority in two major worldviews: the classical/medieval and the modern. The genius of the Romans was to develop a form of authority that did not rely only on the power of persuasion (as in the debates of citizens in the Greek city-state) or only on the power of coercion and violence (as with the barbarians). The Romans understood authority as linked to a position. It was the position that focused the relationship of command and obedience. For thinkers like Max Weber or Hannah Arendt, the notion of "authority" represented a specific source of power. It represented power vested in persons by virtue of their offices or their "authoritativeness" where relevant information and knowledge was concerned. Authority did not arise simply from the attributes of an individual. Its exercise depended on a willingness on the part of others to grant respect and legitimacy rather than on one's personal ability to persuade or coerce. This notion of authority became the foundation of political and ecclesiastical power during the medieval period in Europe.[4]

Modernity challenged this notion of authority and tradition. In the modern western worldview, authority shifted to the subject, the person, the individual. If there was a source of authority, it was human reason, the power of knowledge. This worldview is still with us, although it has been critiqued by philosophers and, more importantly, by those who have witnessed the catastrophes of the 20th century (Auschwitz, Hiroshima, climate change). Voices from the global south have grown louder in their objections to the claims that western rationality gives birth to universal wisdom.

This is the context for Johann Baptist Metz's remark about the authority of those who suffer.[5] He is saying that authority comes not from those in higher positions (in society or the Church) but from those in the lowest position. He is saying that there is one authority which cannot be critiqued by the "experts" or the professional classes of modernity, and that is the authority of those who suffer.

Metz is arguing that the authority of those who suffer must challenge those in positions of power in the political world and in the Church; it must challenge the experts, the bureaucrats. If theology must be guided by some form of authority, if it is to be more than a form of self-expression, then it must be guided by the authority of those who suffer. According to Metz, the victims of the Holocaust must become an authoritative point of reference and this authority must at least form the basis for theological reflection on the Holocaust. It is the memory of these suffering victims that can and should make us attentive to the authority of those who are suffering now. To take this authority seriously is to listen to the suffering ones, the waiting ones, the long dead, and those slowly dying from poverty. It is to begin with another set of questions. It is to imagine the world and one's place in it differently.

The Authority of Suffering in Holocaust Studies and Liberation Theologies

I am aware that the relationship between Holocaust Studies and liberation theology is not always comfortable. Tensions can arise, for example, when advocates of liberation theology take the categories of oppressor and oppressed and apply them simplistically to the present State of Israel and the situation of the Palestinians. Discussions reach a dead end when someone asks, "Who has suffered more? Why should the memory of the suffering of the past take precedence over the suffering of the present?"

Nevertheless, these different experiences of suffering also suggest a way of solidarity. Theologies of the Holocaust and social injustice are shaped by memories of suffering that are deep and real. They share a criticism of the machinery and economics of modernity that would reduce human beings to expendable things. They share a suspicion of a Church that has all too often sided with the powerful. They have a common hope in a Church more shaped by the story of the Good Samaritan.

In discussions, reflections, and sermons on the Holocaust, there is often reference to the lessons learned from the Holocaust, lessons of great import in other situations of injustice today, such as the morally questionable role of the bystander, the moral vacuum created by bureaucracies, the importance of acting "in time," the challenge of "reading the signs of the times." I would say that some of the most significant theologies in the Church today recognize the authority of those who suffer, an authority at least equal to any authority in positions of political and ecclesial power or authority based on knowledge and expertise. But what does this really mean?

What "The Authority of Those Who Suffer" Does NOT Mean

I tend to agree with Marta Zechmeister that it is difficult to define what "the authority of those who suffer" means. However, I think it is possible, perhaps even necessary, to say what it does *not* mean. Otherwise, the phrase "the authority of those who suffer" could become an easy and empty maxim.

First, it is important to acknowledge that all people suffer and that each person suffers in a particular way. There are illnesses and limitations that are physical and psychological. Death is inevitable. This is the human condition. However, some people suffer unnecessarily; their death is premature or preventable. There is suffering that must be accepted and suffering that is unjust and unacceptable. However, we cannot and must not attempt to compare sufferings (i.e., that there is more or less suffering, better or worse suffering). Body-count politics, the comparison of genocides and injustices, diminishes the victims even further. It is grotesque to make any such mathematical comparisons and is fundamentally dehumanizing for all concerned.

Secondly, it is important to avoid romanticizing suffering as if it somehow ennobles, giving wisdom, insight, and a certain moral authority. After 25 years of living and working with refugees, I would say that this may be true for some, but for many, suffering is a diminishing experience. It can be soul-destroying. I think of a young woman from Guatemala who began to pack her bags after she had been with us for three months. When I asked her why she was packing, she said, "I have never lived anywhere for more than three months, so I thought it was time to go." When I asked her to stay, she began to cry and said, "No one ever asked me to stay before." Insecurity had become part of her very being. I think of a man who wore a heavy zippered jacket even in the middle of the summer; he said that if he opened the zipper, his insides would fall out. Suffering does not necessarily yield wisdom or insight. The suffering ones can perpetuate their suffering on and through others. Suffering does not automatically confer authority.

Thirdly, suffering should never be used as the basis for claiming rights. I always think it is risky to claim rights on the basis of having been wronged. What happens to those rights when a person or group stops being wronged? Sometimes the wrong has to keep being perpetuated in order to justify the rights, and so the wrongs, real or imagined, continue. People and groups have rights because they are human beings, because they are created by God. This is the only basis for claiming rights in a way that will ensure the rights of others. I offer this caution on the basis of having worked for a long time to ensure the human rights of various groups. If we make suffering the basis of claims to justice, then the suffering will in some way have to continue. If we make suffering a moral basis for justice, then those who have been victimized will have to constantly prove that they are good or morally superior. This is a terrible burden. We do not have to suffer and be good or morally better in order to have rights. We have simply to be human.

Finally, we need to be careful not to identify a person or group only with their suffering. How often we refer to whole groups of people in terms of what they lack or in terms of a problem: the poor, the unemployed, the disabled, the addicted, the refugee, the abused. It reduces the person to a problem, defines him or her in terms of suffering and struggles. This leaves little room to remind us all that there is nonetheless dignity and resilience, the capacity for joy and creativity even in the most limited circumstances, the possibility of resistance in even minimal ways. Such affirmations leave room to remember that no person or group can or should be completely defined by suffering or problems. To forget this final space of freedom is to lose sight of the core of what it means to be human. I recall a conversation with a student who had been horribly abused. She said that the important turning point in her life came when she stopped identifying herself as a victim of abuse and began to see herself as "a person who has met evil." The evil was real but it no longer defined her completely.

As we face the reality of suffering, we are faced with the mystery that even though a person sometimes seems to be nothing but suffering, at other times we know that she/he is more than their suffering. It summons us to a deeper understanding of the correlation between our image of the human person and our image of God. On the one hand, when our spirituality is shaped by an experience of human suffering and weakness, we can imagine God as merciful and compassionate. So, too, when we have an image of God as the Compassionate One, we can more easily embrace the suffering of the human person. On the other hand, when we experience the possibility and imperative of human strength, we can imagine God as just, as holding us to account for our power. So, too, when we have an image of God as just, we can more easily admit the burden of human responsibility. As God is both merciful and just, we human beings are both weak and strong.

What Kind of Authority is Exercised by the Suffering

Why then do the suffering ones have authority, an authority that exceeds that of those in positions of authority, those with the authority of knowledge, those in the know? Someone like Metz or Bonhoeffer, indeed, many liberation theologians seem to suggest that the authority comes from their position in the world – at the bottom, on the edge. It is here that the world is revealed as it is – the worst and the best stand revealed.

I think this is best expressed by Dietrich Bonhoeffer in a short reflection he wrote just before he was arrested. In his essay, "Are We Still of Use?" (1943), he reflects on the soul-destroying years under Hitler, the deceit, brutality, atrocities, the contempt of humanity. He acknowledges that those involved in the church struggle have lost their simplicity and passion: "We have learned the arts of equivocation and pretense; experience has made us suspicious of others and kept us from being truthful and open; intolerable conflicts have worn us down and even made us cynical." Nevertheless, he writes,

> There remains an experience of incomparable value. We have ... learned to see the events of world history from below, from the perspective of the outcast, the suspects, the maltreated, the powerless, the oppressed, the reviled – in short, from the perspective of those who suffer. The important thing is that ... we should have come to look with new eyes at ... strength and weakness, that our perception of generosity, humanity, justice and mercy should have become clearer, freer, less corruptible.[6]

Bonhoeffer's change in perspective is echoed in the writings of many liberation theologians who write movingly of how their view of the world, of their cultures and societies, their view of the Church and themselves has been radically transformed because of their involvement with the poor. It is nothing less than a religious experience, a new experience of God, a grace and a call that they have followed and obeyed, sometimes to the point of death. However, the authority of those who suffer comes not only from their position in the world, not only from WHERE they are but WHO they are and who we become as we meet their suffering.

The authority of those who suffer does not come from their moral superiority, from the depth or breadth of their suffering. In the eyes of many, they simply do not exist; they are of no account. The world had vague intimations of the suffering of the Jews in Europe, but their suffering carried no weight or power to command in the usual ways. They had little organizational power, few financial resources left; they mattered little in the political scheme of things. So, too, today the poor and destitute are often of no account; they are not entered into the ledger of the commercial calculations of nations and businesses because they are neither producers nor consumers.

Such as these have authority because this is all they have. They have nothing but authority. In wordless pleas or in cries of pain they say only, "WE EXIST. WE ARE HERE." There is no political or economic reason why anyone should care about their suffering, no reason at all. And it is precisely this lack of reasons to care, the lack of anything to compel us to care, that becomes the most powerful awakening of authority. Those who have nothing but suffering call us. And we who have no reason to respond answer. It is the beginning of mercy, compassion, hope, and justice. We say, "I AM. I AM HERE. I AM HERE WITH YOU. I AM HERE FOR YOU." We authorize each other.

I cannot explain why this is so. I only know that this is so and I can bear witness to this reality.[7] It happens this way:

> *There is a knock at the door*
> *Of the place that structures*
> *Everything that is familiar and safe.*

It is only the sound
Of one hand knocking.
You can choose not to answer.
For reasons unclear even to yourself
You open the door slightly
And see
THE EYES and then
The blur of a face as it looks down
And then up again.
It is the face of a stranger,
the face of a woman.
You do not know who she is,
You do not know who you are.
You could close the door.
Perhaps she senses this.
The face of a woman with a voice says,
"Please help me."
You could say No.
I am too busy.
I am too tired.
It is too late.
There are other places to go.
I do not know what to do.
You used to know before
You learned how the system can file
People away . . . forever.
But you know that you are, here and now
The one, the one who must respond.
You know, after Auschwitz,
What happens when you close the door
What happens when churches
And countries close the door.
This YOU must do. There is no other.
This WE must do. Now and not later.
You have been faced.
The stranger moves forward
and fills the frame of your mind
and slowly comes into focus.
And you become focused.
Your life becomes weighty, consequential, significant.

In the depths of meaningless, useless, unnecessary suffering, all that is left is the voice of God. It becomes, as Emmanuel Levinas has described, a summons, a call, a commandment.[8] The Voice of the Voiceless commands. It is the ultimate and last and only authority.

I have described how this authority is activated between two people, when a person answers the door and experiences the authority of the stranger who is suffering. However, this encounter can also take place between groups of people, when a group comes to a church community and asks for sanctuary. We know examples of what can happen. The Church community can say they are too busy, or the Church community can feel summoned to offer welcome and protection. In the process, the Church discovers what it means to be a Church and its life "becomes weighty, consequential, significant."

Granting Authority to Those Who Suffer

It is a grace to recognize the authority of those who suffer, even though we cannot completely understand its weight, consequence, and significance. We can grant the power of the suffering ones to summon us so far beyond ourselves that we become who we are meant to become. It is possible, for example, for the memory of the suffering of the Holocaust victims to summon the Church to become a truly Christian community. Irving Greenberg, in his now classic 1977 address, emphasized the new point of reference for doing theology after the Holocaust: never say anything that you could not repeat in the face of children being thrown into the fire.[9] The children in the fire become the test of the adequacy of our theology, spirituality, and Church life.

The great theologian Thomas Aquinas placed great weight on the adequacy of the intellect to the reality it knows. *Adaequatio intellectus et rei*. How inadequate our thinking when we try to think about the Holocaust or about the many forms of suffering in the world today.

Thus, after the Holocaust we cannot speak easily about the authority of those who suffer, but neither can we deny their authority. We must face the suffering ones, we must acknowledge their existence and refer to them often, always. We must refer to them as we judge the adequacy of our statements, the adequacy of our spirituality and our theology, the adequacy of our actions and our lives.

We must ask whether *Nostra Aetate* can survive the gaze of the children being thrown into the fire. We must ask whether our ecclesial statements on justice can be read while looking at children desperately trying to swim in the waters of the Mediterranean. We must refer to them as the first and final authority.

Conclusion

After I had finished the first draft of this essay, I showed it to my friend and colleague, Marina Nemat. She is the author of *Prisoner of Tehran* (New York: Free Press, 2007), an account of her time in Evin prison as a teenager. There she was raped and tortured. There she suffered and here and now she still suffers. And I think she has the authority of one who has suffered. Like me, she struggles to explain why and how this is so. This was her comment on this article:

> I humbly believe that suffering and its effects are a mystery really. But in practical terms and when it comes to the very strange kind of authority that suffering can give us, I think there needs to be a willingness. The word "willingness" can be misinterpreted. By it, I don't mean that when I say someone accepted their torture with willingness that they approved of the act of torture, they enjoyed it, or even that they didn't break or try to escape as pain engulfed them. No, not at all. I mean that despite the hate and the anger that suffering can bring, the moment MIGHT come, sooner or later, when the sufferer can rise above the experience and almost swallow it whole with their soul. This doesn't make the pain go away, but it gives us authority over it, the kind of authority that feels otherworldly, the kind of authority that overcomes abominable, absolute, monstrous darkness with just a spark of light. Maybe that authority is born the moment we realize that because of what happened we don't have to submit to the evil that caused it, that we can stand up to it, look it in the eye, and say, "I see and acknowledge you, but you have not destroyed me or made me your own." I find the freedom and light of that moment absolutely spectacular and better than anything else. No joy comes even close to it. ... The pain is mortal when the joy lives on forever and is so brilliant and beautiful despite the ugliness that attacked it.

Questions for Discussion

1. *What are some examples of suffering? How do they challenge you to think? To act?*

2. *What is the difference between suffering that is part of the human condition and suffering that is unnecessary?*

3. *How would you describe the particular authority of those who suffer?*

4. *Have you been summoned by the suffering of others? How and when?*

Further Reading

Arendt, Hannah. "What Is 'Authority'?" in *Between Past and Future: Eight Exercises in Political Thought* (New York: Penguin Classics, 1993).

Greenberg, Irving. "Cloud of Smoke, Pillar of Fire: Judaism, Christianity, and Modernity after the Holocaust," in *Auschwitz: Beginning of a New Era? Reflections on the Holocaust*, Ed. Eva Fleishner (New York: Ktav Publishing, 1977).

Leddy, Mary Jo. *The Other Face of God: When the Stranger Calls Us Home* (Maryknoll, NY: Orbis Books, 2011).

Metz, Johann Baptist. *Faith in History and Society* (New York: Seabury Press, 1980).

Nemat, Marina. *Prisoner of Tehran* (New York: Free Press, 2007).

Sobrino, Jon. *The Principle of Mercy* (Maryknoll, NY: Orbis Books, 1994).

Zeichmeister, Marta. "The Martyred People Today and the Hope They Bring Us." (2015). Available at http://www.congregatiojesu.org.

--------- "Theology and Biography: A Woman Political Theologian in El Salvador" (2009). Available at http://www.congregatiojesu.org.

Film and Video Resources

A Short Interview with P. Jon Sobrino (11:42 mins). Recorded by Beth Doherty. Available at https://www.youtube.com/watch?v=qg2FVrmZVNw.

Elie Wiesel: Nobel Prize Acceptance Speech (18 mins). Produced by Nobel Prize. Available at http://www.nobelprize.org/mediaplayer/?id=2028.

Radical Gratitude (35 mins). Produced by Faith Connections: Theology on Tap. Available at https://www.youtube.com/watch?v=XccLln5OCIw.

Notes

1. The English version of this talk can be found on the website of her religious congregation, www.congregatiojesu.org, as "The Martyred People Today and the Hope They Bring Us."
2. Dietrich Bonhoeffer, *Letters and Papers from Prison* (New York: Macmillan Company, 1954), p. 219-220.
3. Cf. Gustavo Guttierez, *On Job: God-Talk and the Suffering of the Innocent* (Maryknoll, New York, 1987).
4. Cf. Hannah Arendt, "What is Authority?" in *Between Past and Future: Eight Exercises in Political Thought* (New York: The Viking Press, 1968), pp. 91-143.
5. Cf. Johann Baptist Metz, *Faith in History and Society* (New York: The Seabury Press, 1980).
6. Bonhoeffer, "Are We Still of Use?" in *Letters and Papers*.
7. Cf. Mary Jo Leddy, *The Other Face of God: When the Stranger Calls Us Home* (Maryknoll, New York: Orbis Books, 2011), p. 34. A slight variation was written for this essay.
8. Cf. Sean Hand (Ed.), *The Levinas Reader* (Oxford: Blackwell, 1989).
9. Irving Greenberg, "Cloud of Smoke, Pillar of Fire: Judaism, Christianity, and Modernity after the Holocaust," in *Auschwitz: Beginning of A New Era?*, ed. Eva Fleishner (New York: KTAV, 1977), pp. 7-55.

Reconciliation: A Commitment to Unsettling Empathy

Björn Krondorfer

Director, Martin-Springer Institute; Endowed Professor of Religious Studies, Department of Comparative Cultural Studies, Northern Arizona University, Flagstaff, AZ

In August 2014, when the Israeli Defense Forces (IDF) and Hamas in the Gaza Strip fought a lethal 51-day war, I met with Israelis, Palestinians, and Germans in a location in the West Bank, close enough to the border to be within relatively safe reach for Jewish Israeli citizens. We met to continue the challenging conversations among people in conflict with people who have been hurt, injured, traumatized, fearful, and distrustful, in the belief that continuous human contact prepares us for better times, even when everything around us seems to fall apart. Besides the actual dead and injured, this war had pushed each national group even further apart, demanding and enforcing group loyalty. Internally, each group ostracized and punished individuals who dared to stay in touch with people from the other side. And yet, this group met for four days, revealing to each other their fears and opening their hearts. Then, unexpectedly, the Palestinian Authority called the retreat center, saying that we had no permission to meet and that we had to leave. One of our participants, a young Israeli psychologist and grandchild of Holocaust survivors, got so frightened that his whole body began to shake. He asked why the Palestinian Authority even knew that we were meeting here and whether it was safe to stay. His fear spread like wildfire through the group. Fear is contagious. It took us several hours to contain it, with the result that the young man decided not to leave but to stay with us for the remainder of the seminar.[1]

In the summer of 2015, we met again in the same location, yet with different Palestinian, Israeli, and German participants, a group of about 20 ranging in age from their late 20s to mid-70s. The memory of the previous year's violent confrontation was still alive, but it had receded enough for people to join together in this interpersonal setting to explore the effects and meaning of "borders" in our lives. For Palestinians, the pressure to abide by the "anti-normalization" campaign had been strong: no Palestinian is supposed to meet with Israelis unless such meetings lead to political-structural changes regarding the occupation. Hence, for Palestinians it requires courage to even attend such seminars because it goes against their community's consensus. For Israelis, it is similarly tough to attend, coming from a society marked by a siege mentality, though it is less of a personal risk.

To Palestinians, a regular dialogue meeting would have been unacceptable and judged as "normalization." I suggested that starting an "anti-fear" campaign would be much more helpful than an "anti-normalization" campaign to get both sides out of the quagmire. I also said that we needed a commitment from each other in this group to make our four-day seminar "real" and to commit to the hard work of reconciliation. This set into motion a more honest but also more demanding process. On the last day of our workshop, the issue of "trust" and "mistrust" forcefully emerged. I will return to this moment later. But let us understand first what I mean by "reconciliation" in such processes.

Nostra Aetate and Reconciliation

Let me begin by referencing *Nostra Aetate*. Proclaimed by Pope Paul VI on October 28, 1965, 50 years ago almost to the day, *Nostra Aetate* affirmed constructive relations between the Church and other world religions, especially among the Abrahamic traditions. Even though the term "reconciliation" does not appear in the Declaration itself, the document has often been referred to as a gesture of reconciliation. In September 2005, for example, when addressing rabbis in Israel, Pope Benedict XVI stated, "*Nostra Aetate* has proven to be a milestone on the road towards reconciliation of Christians and the Jewish people."[2]

When Benedict XVI used the term reconciliation in this context, he did not, of course, refer to the sacramental language of "reconciliation with God and the Church," as in the rite of penance. Rather, he used it in the common sense of repairing or restoring broken relations. *Nostra Aetate* prepared the way for such reconciliatory processes. Regarding followers of the world religions, *Nostra Aetate* admonishes Christians to engage "through dialogue and collaboration with the followers of other religions." With regard to Islam, the document affirms the "esteem" with which it regards Muslims, and it urges Christians to "forget the past [of quarrels and hostilities] and to work sincerely for mutual understanding." Regarding Judaism, *Nostra Aetate* affirms that the great "spiritual patrimony common to Christians and Jews" compels the fostering of "mutual understanding and respect."

When I speak of reconciliation, I embrace *Nostra Aetate*'s key terms – dialogue, collaboration, respect, and mutual understanding – while remaining cognizant of painful and difficult pasts. Unlike *Nostra Aetate*, I do not address primarily interreligious relations but will speak about interpersonal encounters between groups in conflict. I deliberately speak here of "encounters" rather than "dialogue," if by dialogue we refer to a more traditional model of largely rational and friendly conversations. The processes I have in mind require participants to learn honest and direct communication, unearth the residues of mistrust, explore the sore points in their relationships (rather than avoiding them), and render themselves vulnerable.

Relational Quality of Reconciliation

In my reconciliatory work I guide people toward greater respect, honesty, and trust through interpersonal encounters. This kind of reconciliation differs significantly from top-down structural reconciliation. Structural reconciliation focuses on fixing political, economic, cultural, and security problems in order to establish cooperation and coexistence between the affected parties. In contrast, I am engaged in bottom-up social reconciliation in which relational qualities are prioritized. Social reconciliation emphasizes the restoring of broken relationships and the forging of new relationships. Broadly speaking, it follows what scholars of restorative justice and reconciliation have variously called the restoring of "right relations,"[3] the "coming together again, in restored relationship, after a rift from actual or perceived wrongdoing,"[4] and the overcoming of "distrust and animosity."[5]

Concretely, what is it that I am doing? Since the 1980s, I have been engaged in facilitating and guiding a variety of meetings, seminars, and workshops in which people are marked by broken relationships due to historical injustices like the Holocaust or divided due to continuing simmering conflicts (like ethnic, racial, and religious tensions) and ongoing open conflicts (like between Israelis and Palestinians). Because I was born in Germany and belong to the so-called postwar generation, with parents and grandparents who lived through the Nazi regime and were involved in it to varying degrees, it was the Holocaust that first got my full attention. In my 20s, I worked with Jewish American and non-Jewish German performance artists on our relations in the shadows of Auschwitz; in my 30s, I organized and led one-month-long educational summer programs for Jewish and German university students; in my 40s, I worked with specific groups, like theological workshops for German Christian clergy and American rabbis in Weimar and Buchenwald, intergenerational workshops on German family history, or on generational conflicts within the Jewish community in Melbourne, Australia. Now in my 50s, I have expanded my reach and also work with Israelis and Palestinians or, to name the last example, I occasionally offer multi-day racial reconciliation retreats for American university students.

In all of these encounters – I call them "reconciliatory processes" – we address cognitively and emotionally the psychosocial and psychopolitical dimensions that underlie and feed specific conflicts.[6] When we emphasize the relational quality of reconciliation over policies geared toward structural changes, we do not disregard the political and historical settings. Rather, when facilitating groups in conflict, it is very clear that the specific contours of interpersonal encounters manifest themselves in political history and that the dynamics unfolding in such processes are embedded in the deep structures of social identity. In such reconciliation work we continuously negotiate the right balance between fostering personal transformation and social change, between individual healing and communal justice.

2015 (West Bank): Trauma and Trust

To return to the seminar in the West Bank during the summer of 2015, you may recall the moment on the last day when the issue of trust was put on the table. To provide a little more context, we need to go back two days, when this trilateral group of Israelis, Palestinians, and Germans reached a consensus to explore, under the guidance of my facilitation team, the issue of "collective trauma." We had separated each national group and asked them to write on a card what they perceived as their own collective trauma and on two separate cards what they perceived to be the traumas of the other two groups. The German group, for example, named their own trauma as "Collective Guilt"; for the Israelis, they identified "antisemitism"; and for the Palestinians, the "Naqba," the 1948 expulsion of Palestinians from their homes and villages. The Palestinians also named their own trauma the "Naqba"; for the Germans, they said "Holocaust and Guilt"; and for the Israelis, "Holocaust & Victimization." Finally, the Israelis, named their own trauma "Holocaust and Hostile Environment"; for the Germans, they identified "Third-Generation Conflicts"; and for Palestinians, they named "Naqba & Life under Occupation." As we can see, there was a lot of overlap in these perceptions, but also a few nuances.

We then worked with each group in more depth, but I will focus here only on the Israeli group. We asked the Israelis to place themselves into a space with the German Holocaust trauma on one side, the Palestinian Naqba trauma on the other side, and they themselves as Jewish Israelis caught in the middle. Despite the fact that three of the five Israelis had family histories going back to the Holocaust in Europe (they were children and grandchildren of survivors), they all turned their attention to the Palestinian group while turning their backs to the German group. In a feedback session, the Israelis said that they felt somewhat connected to the European past and even somewhat supported by the German group willing to face the Holocaust themselves, but they nevertheless felt compelled by the urgency of the Palestinian plight. The Palestinian group, however, was skeptical about the attention it got from the Israelis. They remained somewhat unmoved and reticent. This, in turn, left the

Israelis unhappy with themselves; they felt they had not delved deeply enough into issues of their own social identification, but they did not know what was missing.

All of this happened on the day that Jewish religious extremists firebombed a Palestinian home in Duba, West Bank, killing the toddler Ali Dawabsheh (Ali's father and mother later died of their severe burns). Tension was high in Israel and the West Bank and everyone was on alert. The tension was also felt in our group, and for a moment we thought the third Intifada might break out.

In the evening, however – and against any of my expectations – some of the Jewish Israelis joined a young Palestinian participant at his nearby home to walk his dogs, crossing into Area A. Entry into West Bank's Area A is forbidden to all Israelis. They went anyway and they saw the wall from the other side.

The next morning – and this was on our last day – we returned to the constellation of the Israeli group in our meeting space. The facilitator team re-engaged the Israelis with some tough questions, until one of the Israelis asked the Palestinians whether it was true that they still distrusted them. This led to several remarkable exchanges; I will mention here two. First, one of the Israeli women, who had joined the small group the previous night to venture into Area A, admitted to the Palestinian participant that she got really scared and frightened when, during their nightly walk, he made several phone calls in Arabic. She told him directly, "I was afraid you made calls to arrange for some kidnapping or do some other harm to us." Surprisingly, the young Palestinian man did not get upset, but for the first time in our four-day seminar, he relaxed. He thanked her for her honesty – because he had expected all along such fear and mistrust – and was able finally to relate to her differently.

The second exchange that I want to mention is a scene where another Israeli woman and a Palestinian were spatially placed in such a way that they were facing each other. They exchanged words with each other but averted eye contact. "Is it true," the Israeli woman asked, "that you do not trust us, although I am different from many other Israelis because I am committed to working for peace with the Palestinians?" "Yes, this is true," the Palestinian answered. "I still see in front of me a Jewish Israeli." When asked how she felt when hearing his response, she said, "I feel like shit."

A few moments later, when challenged by others, the Palestinian clarified in so many words that he did not trust Israelis unless they agreed with his political views and demands. Here, the facilitator team intervened, challenging him to rethink his position. "You can't have the Israelis according to your wishes," we said. "You can't make Israelis into people the way you like them. They cannot become Palestinian like you. But here, in front of you, is a real person who is committed to some change. You need to relate to and work with real people."

Unsettling Empathy

Moments such as these are deeply unsettling to people. And we may ask, why go through such challenging interpersonal encounters? In my experience, it is in those moments of unsettling empathy that transformation in reconciliatory processes happens.

What, then, is unsettling empathy? I am calling unsettling empathy a *posture* to indicate that it is more than just a pedagogical tool or a didactic element of dialogue; it is also more than just a skill or a method. Unsettling empathy is a posture insofar as it is a kind of practiced awareness and a relational commitment to caring responsiveness.

For interpersonal reconciliation to be effective, we must be willing to go beyond a discourse of politeness and, at times, even beyond a discourse of civility, as long as safety for and respect of each participant is guaranteed. Compassionate listening alone, however, is not sufficient. When people talk about compassionate listening, they often refer to a method in which each group in turn can air their grievances while the other group listens attentively without interrupting the narrated experience. Compassion by itself can too easily be mistaken as the kind of civil discourse that uses polite forms of rhetoric to mask underlying tensions. The Palestinians in our seminar might have said that "compassionate listening" was just another form of "normalization," which they disavowed.

Compassion too often presents all sides as victims of circumstances they cannot control. It tends to erase real social and political differences in the name of a common humanity, thus glossing over too quickly the ethical difference between harm inflicted and harm endured. Unsettling empathy, in contrast, calls us into the presence of objective ethical differences without negating the vitality of human interaction. It signals that our reconciliatory and dialogical engagement may cost us something. A posture of unsettling empathy requires the risk of vulnerability, of courage, of being shaken in one's foundation and assumptions about the world and the Other. It allows for the inclusion of both a critical perspective on power asymmetries as well as compassion with the Other despite historical injustices and contentious memories. This is the balance we need.[7]

Put into academic language, the posture of unsettling empathy is a deliberate ethical stance which, ideally and over time, might become something akin to habitus – an acquired disposition and sensibility that eventually informs, guides, and structures our attitude toward life.

Put differently, empathy that unsettles requires us to care for the other while we are respecting the differences between us. Reconciliation demands our willingness to engage with the other as she or he is, not as we wish them to be. Hence, unsettling empathy is "costly" because it compels us to question our assumptions about the other and about ourselves.

2011 (Germany): Ghosts of History
In the fall of 2011, a group of German and Jewish Israeli educators, therapists, and community organizers asked me to conduct a three-day seminar in Germany on the

effects of the Holocaust and the Second World War. This intergenerational group had already worked together for some time on peace-related activities. But the repercussions of traumatic memories kept obstructing their present-day relations. They hoped this seminar would allow each side to explore the complexity of memory's abyss.

I brought a simple cardboard container to this meeting, painted black inside and outside. This black box accompanied our work. Placed in the middle of our circle, the black box initiated and guided discussions and interactive exercises. It was our memory box, and, as memory goes, it contained as much of what was remembered as of what was forgotten. It functioned as advocate for the forgotten, retainer of familial remembrances, and a black hole into which memory disappeared.

Because the German and Israeli participants showed an extraordinary ability to take personal risks, they were ready to confront directly the ghosts of the past. In previous sessions, some of the German participants who were born at the end of the Second World War and in the immediate postwar years talked about their conflicting emotions toward their fathers and about their wish that these fathers should be present in this mixed Israeli-German encounter today. There was a sense of anger about their parents' generation not confronting the past sufficiently. They bemoaned their fathers' lack of courage to expose themselves to the presence of Jews, which I interpreted as a subtle wish to redeem their fathers. But it was also a wish to break through the unyielding silence that has encased so many postwar German families whose fathers were implicated in National Socialism. The stepfather of one of the participants, for example, remained until his death in the 1960s an unrepentant Nazi. Abusive toward his stepchildren and an accused war criminal, he kept sheltering Nazis on the run for many years after the war but escaped the clutches of justice. These fathers remained invisible figures in the midst of our Israeli-German encounter. Without flesh and blood, without name and identity, they were absent and present at the same time.

On the last evening of our seminar, I suggested we invite one of these German fathers into our midst. We unfurled a blanket next to the black box and asked for a German volunteer to step forward. A woman in her mid-70s who had experienced the war as a child in the Eastern German provinces volunteered. When she was comfortably resting on the blanket, we dimmed the lights and opened the black box, symbolically representing the opening of buried memories and of a grave. The woman was slowly guided into imaginatively embodying the persona that she felt might emerge from the black box.

She closed her eyes. Her body began to squirm and twist. She seemed to resist a presence that was taking over her being. When she finally opened her eyes, she appeared to be – for lack of a better term – possessed: a ghostly presence had taken hold of her. The woman had become a German soldier returning from the grave.

The ghostly soldier-father stared into space and asked, "What do you want from me? Why did you call me?"

The specific questions and answers that followed do not really matter here. What matters is the eerie presence of a resurrected soldier-father who put everyone under his spell. Questions were asked, but the ghost reluctantly offered only fragmented bits of information. He had returned from the grave with his silence intact. This frustrated and infuriated the group. Hypnotized by the ghost's unsettling aggressiveness, we were in the presence of a dead man teasing and threatening us by hinting at a secret, violent past.

When the ghost-father unexpectedly led us to an execution site, we almost preferred his previous silence rather than having to imagine the scene of slaughter. In a matter-of-fact style, almost catatonically, the soldier-father told of "things" that just needed to get done. He showed no emotional remorse. The group prodded but failed to elicit any small gesture of sorrow or any recognition of culpability. Now that a door had opened to a scene at the killing fields, how could any meaning emerge from this?

As is always the case when reporting about the dynamics of such group sessions, words cannot adequately describe what transpired during that evening. Time stood still (we were in the presence of the ghost for more than an hour). It seemed the group had been transposed to a historical trauma that felt so real that it took on an aura of reality. We came close to what religious language knows as spirit possession.

Let me share, then, with you just a few observations:

First, the German group was split in half regarding its attitude toward the ghost. One half was angry at his refusal to speak and his unrepentant attitude; the other half was supportive, gently prodding the ghost to show signs of regret. Both sides, it seemed, acted on two primary impulses that descendants of perpetrators have at their disposal when responding to culpable wrongdoing: on the one hand, you take a firm and angry stance toward your forefathers' past deeds, or on the other hand, you adopt a soft and sympathizing stance toward their shameful silence and reticence. That evening, however, the ghostly father remained as deaf to his "children's" angry rejections as to their tenuously therapeutic gesture of inclusion, which made his appearance so hypnotically powerful and threatening that evening.

Second, the Jewish Israeli group remained mostly silent throughout the whole séance. A few dared to ask questions but largely left the inquiry to the Germans. The Israelis felt the need to put distance to the ghost, reducing their engagement with him to a minimum, and skeptically observing the German participants. The longer the German interaction with the ghost lasted, the more anxious and threatened they became. For them, it was time to bring the session to an end.

But how do you return a ghost? This leads to my third observation: Unexpectedly, the father-soldier ghost refused to go back into the black box. His resistance was strengthened by those in the German group who did not want him to leave yet because they were still trying to reach out to him. My repeated suggestions to relieve the German woman from her ghostly possession were simply ignored. Some of the Germans protested my attempt to end the session: they felt I was interrupting their psycho-political efforts to understand the mentality and soul of a Nazi perpetrator.

The ghost himself, now that he was among us, had begun to enjoy himself. He seemed to get a certain pleasure from the fact that he was emotionally attended to without having to change. He yielded power as a bearer of terrifying secrets. I eventually had to recapture physically the space that the ghost inhabited, assertively requesting a moratorium on further questions. I put my hands on the ghost's shoulders, gently but firmly making the woman impersonating him lie down on the blanket. Slowly, the woman's body relaxed. She sighed. Finally, we were able to close the lid of the black box.

Fourth, the issue about putting the ghost back into the box remained contentious in subsequent discussions. Those among the Germans who wanted to extend the session voiced frustration because they felt that we had missed out on a chance to understand Germany's legacy without the usual confrontational attitude. The other Germans, however, felt it made no sense to keep investing so much energy into a ghost, who was as irredeemable as the history he represented. It was time to stop the ghost from spreading his poison.

The Jewish Israelis had yet another response. For them, the ghostly presence of the German soldier-father had become unbearable. Had the situation continued any longer, they later confessed, they would have left the room. What was threatening was not only the appearance of the ghost itself, but also the seemingly tireless efforts of Germans to engage him. As Jews they began to understand how difficult it is for a perpetrator society to work through the past. But they also wondered whether some of the Germans began to err on the side of sympathetic identification with the ghostly father-soldier rather than use their historical and moral judgment. They felt like uninvited guests witnessing a family feud, eavesdropping on an intense moment of cultural intimacy. Those Germans who had reproached the ghostly German father with anger quickly grasped how threatened the Israelis felt. But those frustrated about the too-early disappearance of the ghost did not notice the emotional upheaval of their Jewish friends. They were surprised to later hear how frightened the Israelis had been. Yes, it had frightened the Israelis, but they were also grateful for being a witness to what their German friends went through.

Clearly, the ghost had managed to unsettle just about everyone that evening. For some, the emphatic engagement with the ghost unsettled them because they tried but failed to understand the perpetrator's mentality; for others, it was the secondary witnessing of a re-enacted scene of severe violence that was deeply disturbing; for yet others, they felt unsettled yet rewarded by being allowed to witness the display of an intimate cultural secret.

I am not advocating for inviting ghosts on a regular basis. In fact, I would rather caution about such an approach since it comes close to trying to redeem or rehabilitate the memory of former perpetrators. But let us keep in mind that returning to troubled times is not meant to re-inscribe what is already known historically but to change and transform contemporary relations. "Ghosts are about a possibility of justice," a legal scholar once wrote. "They are reminders of a need for justice and can point to the impossibility of justice within the constraints of the law."[8] When it works well, it compels us to reconsider our assumptions and it renders us vulnerable in the presence of the Other. Revealing an internal tension in the social body of one's own community in the presence of those with whom one lives in conflict is part of the posture of unsettling empathy. It requires risk-taking. It unsettles what we perceive as reality. Unsettling empathy leaves people shaken up in their assumptions about themselves and others, and this is precisely what is needed for transformation to occur.

Outlook

There are no magic bullets in this line of work. Evidence of transformative change does not lie in miracles. I talked about two exceptionally intense moments in encounters of interpersonal reconciliation: fear and trust in the Palestinian-Israeli case, and a haunting past in the German-Jewish case. Each revealed layers of what I call unsettling empathy.

More often, however, it is in smaller gestures that we see the emergence of transformative changes, because evidence does not lie in miracles but in small signs, such as the exchange of a brief gesture between a Palestinian young man from Ramallah and an Orthodox young woman from the suburbs of Tel Aviv. I witnessed this at another Israeli-Palestinian workshop. The young man from Ramallah had never met an Israeli without wearing an army uniform. He was angry and spouted politicized phrases for much of the time. The young woman from Tel Aviv had never before met a Palestinian on a personal level. As both of these young people were standing in line for lunch, they exchanged a friendly poke with their elbows and smiled at each other. If success were measured by standards of grand political solutions, such an encounter would be disappointing. No peace agreement descended upon this troubled territory after this gesture. The little poke with the elbow (with no further words exchanged) was all that these two people were able to muster at the time. Amidst cultivated mistrust and political hatred, it signaled the possibility of a different symbolic order.

We need to seek out opportunities where we can cultivate different symbolic orders and practice caring responsiveness. Unsettling empathy is part of our responsiveness toward each other. It is mutual responsiveness that leads to transformation.

Discussion Questions

1. What is the value of moving beyond reconciliation between individuals to reconciliation between groups in conflict?

2. Krondorfer's essay argues that trust and empathy are essential components of reconciliation. Do you agree or disagree? Explain why you feel as you do.

3. What are differences between reconciliation and forgiveness?

4. Can you think of groups in conflict in your community that would benefit from reconciliatory processes? What are they? How would they benefit?

Further Reading

Bar-On, Dan. *Legacy of Silence: Encounters with Children of the Third Reich* (Cambridge: Harvard University Press, 1989).

Chaitin, Julia. *Peace-Building in Israel and Palestine: Social Psychology and Grassroots Initiatives* (New York: Palgrave Macmillan, 2011).

Grob, Leonard, and John K. Roth (Eds.). *Anguished Hope: Holocaust Scholars Confront the Palestinian-Israeli Conflict* (Grand Rapids, MI & Cambridge, UK: William B. Eerdmans, 2008).

Krondorfer, Björn. *Remembrance and Reconciliation: Encounters Between Young Jews and Germans* (New Haven: Yale University Press, 1995).

Philpott, Daniel. *Just and Unjust Peace: An Ethic of Political Reconciliation* (New York: Oxford University Press, 2012).

Film and Video Resources

The Flat (85 mins). Directed by Arnon Goldfinger.
    Available at https://www.youtube.com/watch?v=tmeY6CEmC04.
Hitler's Children (59 mins). Directed by Chanoch Ze'evi.
    Available at http://www.hitlerschildren.com/.
Little Town of Bethlehem (77 mins). Directed by Jim Hanon.
    Available at http://littletownofbethlehem.org/.

Notes

1. The organization *Friendship Across Borders* (FAB) has conducted these seminars for many years and is often invited to facilitate them (www.fab-friendshipacrossborders.net/index.php/en/). See also Björn Krondorfer, "Notes from a Field of Conflict: Trilateral Dialogical Engagement in Israel/ Palestine," *Journal of Ecumenical Studies*, 50(1), Winter 2015, pp. 153-158.
2. The statement of Pope Benedict XVI in an audience with the Chief Rabbis of Israel on September 15, 2005 has been widely quoted, and also made it into House Resolution 260, recognizing the 40th anniversary of *Nostra Aetate* in the 1st session of the 109th US Congress (available at www.pewforum.org/2005/10/06/publicationpage-aspxid712/). On October 26, 2005, the Pope also expressed gratitude to those who have "worked courageously to foster reconciliation and improved understanding between Christians and Jews" in a letter at the occasion of the 40th anniversary of *Nostra Aetate* (available at http://w2.vatican.va/content/benedict-xvi/en/letters/2005/documents/hf_ben-xvi_let_20051026_nostra-aetate.html).
3. Jennifer Llewellyn and Daniel Philpott, "Restorative Justice and Reconciliation: Twin Frameworks for Peacebuilding," in *Restorative Justice, Reconciliation, and Peacebuilding*, eds. Jennifer Llewellyn and Daniel Philpott (New York: Oxford University Press, 2014), p. 23.
4. Trudy Govier, *Forgiveness and Revenge* (New York: Routledge, 2002), p. 141.
5. Björn Krondorfer, *Remembrance and Reconciliation: Encounters Between Young Jews and Germans* (New Haven: Yale University Press, 1995), p. 71.
6. For the psycho-political dimension of group conflicts, see Vamik Volkan, *Enemies on the Couch: A Psycho-political Journey through War and Peace* (Durham, NC: Pitchstone, 2013).
7. Concepts similar to my suggestion of "unsettling empathy" have been discussed, for example, by Bashir Bashir and Amos Goldberg, who speak of "disruptive empathy" in the Palestinian-Israeli conflict, and by Dominick LaCapra, who speaks of "empathic unsettlement" in the context of Holocaust trauma. See Bashir Bashir and Amos Goldberg, "Deliberating the Holocaust and the Nakba: Disruptive Empathy and Binationalism in Israel/Palestine," *Journal of Genocide Research*, 16(1), 2014, pp.77-99; Dominick LaCapra, *Writing History, Writing Trauma* (Baltimore: Johns Hopkins University Press, 2001).
8. Christiane Wilke, "Enter Ghost: Haunted Courts and Haunting Judgments in Transitional Justice," *Law Critique*, 21, 2010, p. 77.

PART 5: AFTERWORDS

Ethel LeFrak

Gemma Del Duca, S.C.

Co-Founder and Co-Director Emerita, National Catholic Center for Holocaust Education, Seton Hill University, Greensburg, PA

In 2008, Ethel LeFrak endowed the triennial Holocaust Conference of Seton Hill University's National Catholic Center for Holocaust Education. Henceforth, this conference would be known as *The Ethel LeFrak Holocaust Education Conference*.

In October 2009, Ethel LeFrak conveyed a message to those who were participating in the Holocaust conference, expressing her hopes for them and for the world:

> Simply to think of the Holocaust and all genocides sends shivers down one's spine. It is inconceivable that during the twentieth century these horrors occurred. Nevertheless, it is now up to us to continue the fight against bigotry and ignorance by inspiring worldwide understanding and tolerance, by educating the educators to probe and dissect, to publish and disseminate the reasons behind the Holocaust and all genocide, so that abominations like that will never happen again, at any time, to anyone.

When World War II broke out, devastating and destroying the lives of so many, Ethel LeFrak was a young student at Barnard College in New York City. The memory of those years stayed with her. It was during this time that she met and later married Samuel J. LeFrak, the founder of one of the largest private building firms in the world. Ethel LeFrak, loving wife and devoted mother of four, became, along with her husband, a distinguished philanthropist, dedicating her time and resources to cultural, educational, and medical institutions. She served as a trustee of the Cardozo Law School and of the Albert Einstein Medical College, as well as a member of the Council of the Salk Institute, vice-president of the Little Orchestra Society, and patron of the Asia Society. A member of the Metropolitan Opera's "Golden Horseshoe" and "Opera Club," Ethel LeFrak was also a patron of Lincoln Center in New York City.

In her efforts to reach out to as many fellow New Yorkers as possible, she became a conservator of the New York Public Library. Her interest in international affairs moved her to become a member of the Board of the United Nations International Hospitality Committee. Ethel LeFrak's good works through this Committee were acknowledged in 1994 when she and her husband received the United Nations "Distinguished Citizens of the World" Award. The LeFraks co-edited and published two books on their family art collection: *Masters of the Modern Tradition* (New York: LeFrak Organization, 1988; catalogue by Diane Kelder) and *A Passion for Art* (New York: Rizzoli, 1994; text by Diane Kelder). In 1996, Ethel LeFrak was awarded a Doctor of Humane Letters, *honoris causa*, by Seton Hill University.

A well-deserved tribute and award came to Ethel LeFrak in October 2009. Seton Hill University and the National Catholic Center for Holocaust Education presented her with the Saint Elizabeth Ann Seton Woman of Courage Award acknowledging her commitment to the work of the University's Holocaust Center and her noble efforts to foster friendship, peace, and reconciliation among people of different backgrounds. Nobel Prize Laureate Elie Wiesel, commenting on Ethel LeFrak's life's work, said, "You have done so much for so many people of different faiths that all of us, your friends, rejoice in this very much merited recognition."

In May 2013, Francine LeFrak sent a personal e-mail to then Seton Hill University President, Dr. JoAnne Boyle, to let her know about "my mother, Ethel LeFrak's passing" on May 14, 2013. Those who knew Ethel LeFrak were filled with sadness, even as they recalled with gratitude all the good she had done during her life. She touched the lives of many people. May her memory continue to be a blessing.

What could one add to Ethel LeFrak's commitment, to her accomplishments, to her generosity? Perhaps only the poetic words of the Book of Proverbs:

> An accomplished woman, who can find her? Her value is beyond pearls,
> She is like the merchant ships; she brings her bread from afar.
> She extends her hands to the poor, and reaches out her hand to the needy.
> She opens her mouth in wisdom and the lesson of kindness is on her tongue. (*Proverbs* 31: 10, 14, 20, 26).

Seton Hill University and the National Catholic Center for Holocaust Education continue to celebrate the life of Dr. Ethel LeFrak and to acknowledge with deep gratitude her commitment to preparing educators to mend the world through understanding and dialogue, learning and teaching in the present for the sake of the future.

Ethel LeFrak
Photo by Gregory Partanio © ManhattanSociety.com

ACKNOWLEDGEMENTS

Having edited two other volumes resulting from Seton Hill University Holocaust education conferences, we are well aware of the help and cooperation it takes to produce a coherent and useful book.

First, we thank Seton Hill University and its president, Dr. Mary C. Finger for her support and encouragement. We also want to thank the late Mrs. Ethel Lefrak who so generously endowed the triennial Holocaust Conference of Seton Hill University's National Catholic Center for Holocaust Education (NCCHE). Without her generosity it would be far more difficult to invite major Holocaust scholars to participate in SHU's conference. May Ethel Lefrak's memory continue to be a blessing.

We also thank Dr. Tim Crain, director of the NCCHE and his associate director, Ms. Wilda Kaylor who so ably organized the 2015 Ethel LeFrak Holocaust Education Conference. Their on-going leadership of The National Catholic Center for Holocaust Education makes scholarship on the Holocaust and other acts of genocide accessible to educators at every level. We also want to acknowledge the wonderful support and spirit of Sisters of Charity, Drs. Gemma Del Duca and Mary Noël Kernan whose spirit permeates all that the NCCHE does.

Thanks also to the volunteers – especially, Dr. Marilyn Sullivan-Cosetti, Sarah Harmotta, Brandon McNeill, Megan Warman, and Jamarius Richardson – who spent hours transcribing some of the presentations given at the conference, especially Father Patrick Desbois's very fine presentation. It made our work very much easier.

Without the cooperation of all the scholars who prepared presentations, revised them so they would read clearly, submitted discussion questions, and other resources so teachers, clergy, and students could make thoughtful and practical use of their essays in their educational efforts, there would not be a conference volume. We thank them for all their work – and for meeting our deadlines.

ACKNOWLEDGEMENTS

Irvin Ungar, the foremost scholar and expert on the art of Arthur Szyk, deserves our grateful thanks for his generosity in giving the NCCHE permission to use the art of Arthur Szyk throughout **The Holocaust and Nostra Aetate: *Toward a Greater Understanding***. A part of *De profundis. Cain, where is Abel thy brother?* is used on the divider pages for each section of the book. Arthur Szyk's art is reproduced with the cooperation of The Arthur Szyk Society, Burlingame, California, www.szyk.org. They also deserve our thanks.

Finally, we thank Glen Powell for his great work in designing **The Holocaust and Nostra Aetate: *Toward a Greater Understanding***. His commitment to excellence is evident throughout the book. To all those at Seton Hill University and The National Catholic Center for Holocaust Education who support and encourage all of us in so many ways to continue teaching and learning about the Holocaust and *Nostra Aetate* so that we can move toward more respectful understanding of our rich Jewish and Christian traditions, we offer grateful thanks.

Carol Rittner, R.S.M.
Editor

Tara Ronda
Managing Editor

Index

Abortion, 46, 47
Abraham, 104
Abrahamic traditions, 206
Acts of the Apostles, 89, 182
Adam, Karl (Dr.), 88
Address to the Churches, see Ten Points of Seelisberg
Ahl Kiddush haShem, 76
Ahmadinejad, Mahmoud (President), 174
Alijah bet, 56, 60
Aliyah, 76
Ambrose of Milan, 103
America, see United States
American Gathering of Holocaust Survivors and Their Descendants, 125
American Jewish Committee, 3, 131, 162
American Joint Distribution Committee, 55, 57, 61
American League for a Free Palestine, 76
American military, 55, 58, 72
Amici Israel, see Friends of Israel
Anguish of the Jews (The), 142
Anschluss, 70
Anti-Christianism, 36, 85, 87-88, 109, 120-21, 144

Anti-Defamation League, 125, 132, 164, 172
Anti-Judaism, 1, 2, 16, 18-20, 80-91, 159, 162, 168, 185; Christian, 80-91, 104-05, 108-10, 155-56, 159, 161, 163; condemnation of, 103, 108-09, 111
Anti-normalization, 206
Antisemitism, 1, 3, 4, 132, 159, 168; American, 73; Christian, 80-91, 108, 111, 132, 141-44, 156, 158; condemnation of, 38, 68, 73, 81, 156, 161, 163, 184-85; economic, 81, 85, 87; education about, 164; European, 4, 36, 80-81, 109, 132, 144; German, 84-87, 87, 90-91; Islamic, 132; Latvian, 53; Middle Eastern, 36, 132; modern, 36, 38, 132, 208; North African, 132; Palestinian, 132; patristic, 108-09, 142; Polish, 58; racial, 16-17, 81, 82, 84, 85, 86, 88-89, 123, 155, 163; textbooks and, 83-84
"Apostolate of Prayer for the Conversion of Israel," 83
Aquinas, Thomas, 202
Arab-Israeli conflict, see Israeli-Palestinian conflict

227

INDEX

Arendt, Hannah, 196
Arsenal of Democracy, 72
Art, Anti-Nazi, 67-77
Aryan race, 18, 44, 46-48, 88
Augustine (St.), 18, 103, 109
Auschwitz-Birkenau, museum at, 20-22
Auschwitz, 1, 14, 15, 20, 36, 132, 133, 180, 194, 196, 207; Catholic survivors of, 20; see also Auschwitz-Birkenau
Authority, 193-196

Baeck, Leo (Rabbi), 155, 156
Baerwald, Leo (Rabbi), 85
Ballad of the Doomed Jews of Europe, 75, 96
Banki, Judith, 161-62, 164
Baum, Gregory, 144, 154, 195
Bea, Augustin (Cardinal), 143, 144, 160, 164, 180
Benedict XVI (Pope), 106-07, 111, 125-26, 128, 133, 154, 206
Bergen, Doris, 2, 4
Bergen-Belsen, 58, 61
Bergson, Peter, 74-76
Berlin, 54-55, 57, 59-60, 84-85, 90, 91, 155, 156
Bernardin, Joseph (Cardinal), 144
Bible (Christian), 17, 104, 106, 172, 174-75; history of, 84, 122; interpretation of, 109, 122, 182-83; Jewish context of, 109-10
Birkenau, 1, 21, 133; see also Auschwitz-Birkenau
Bishop, Claire Huchet, 154, 157-60, 164-65
Blood libel, 101-02
Bolsheviks, 68; Revolution of, 82
Bonhoeffer, Dietrich, 194, 199-200

Boyarin, Daniel, 147-48
Boycott, divestment, and sanctions (BDS), 111, 130-31; Presbyterian Church USA and, 111, 129-32
Boys, Mary, 3, 82, 144, 163
Brando, Marlon, 74
Braverman, Mark, 131-32
Britain, 69, 71, 77; Jewish life in, 56; criticisms of, 75-76; refugees in, 53-54, 56-57, 61, 155
British Mandate, 69, 76
British Relief Unit, 55
Brownmiller, Susan, 44
Bugnini, Annibale, 103
Bull, John, 71, 76
Bundesarchiv, 32
Cain, 2, 73, 109
Catechetics and Prejudice, 142
Catholic Church, 12, 81, 82, 83, 86, 102-03, 104, 107-09, 110-11, 120, 121, 128, 155, 157-58, 171, 174, 180, 193-95; anti-Judaism in, 1, 16, 18-20, 80-91, 104, 108-09, 111, 155-56, 159, 161, 163, 185; antisemitism in, 80-91, 108, 111, 132, 141-44, 156, 158; education in, 11-12, 83-84, 88, 142-43, 157-58, 160-62, 171; Fathers of, 109; French, 29, 157, 158, 159, 180; German, 80, 83, 84; interreligious dialogue and, 9-10, 12-13, 16-17, 86, 102-03, 110-11, 144; liturgy of, 101-12; women of the, 153-65
Catholic-Jewish relations, 3, 4, 5, 9, 20-21, 80-91, 103, 107, 108-12, 121, 124, 125, 127-28, 141-50, 156, 160, 163-65, 172, 182
Catholic-Protestant relations, 80, 111
Catholicism and the Jewish Question, 86
Catholic Theological Society, 144

228

Central Association of German Citizens of Jewish Faith, 85
Chelmno, 1, 74
Chenu, Marie-Dominique, 154
Chicago Sun, 72, 73
Children's homes, Jewish, 53, 55-56
Christ, see Jesus
Christ Event, 145
Christian Church, American, 129, 133-34; anti-Judaism in, 1, 16, 18-19, 20, 80-82, 103-05, 108-11, 122, 155, 156, 159, 161, 168, 185; antisemitism and, 1, 4, 16-19, 38, 80-91, 103, 108, 111, 132, 142-44, 156, 159, 161, 165-66, 184; apostles of, 89, 104, 170, 182; bride of Christ, 103-04; denominations of, 13, 129, 168-69; Christian-Jewish relations, 3, 4, 5, 14-21, 80-91, 101-12, 122-24, 128, 132-34, 143-47, 156, 158, 164, 168-76, 183; Christian-Muslim relations, 12, 120-21, 122, 144, 150, 170, 206; evangelical, 169; French, 157-59; Holocaust and, 122-25, 130-33; Iraqi, 143; Jewish converts to, 2, 16, 84, 86, 142; Jewish origins of, 3, 17, 89, 91, 125, 127, 145; martyrs of, 170, 193; medieval, 88, 101, 196; Orthodox, 2, 4; Palestinian, 129, 131; Pentecostal, 14; Protestant, 2, 4, 10-11, 13, 15, 80, 86, 111, 123, 146, 156, 159, 162-63, 172, 181; Quaker, 86, 155; resistance in, 109, 128, 141, 155, 199; Salvation Army, 86; social justice in, 142, 173; Syrian, 110, 143
Christian Textbook Commission, 73
Christians United for Israel, 129

Christology, 14, 144-48
Chrysostom, John, 18
Church Fathers, 109
Climate change, 148-50, 196
Collective trauma, 208
College of Cardinals, 124
Commission for Religious Relations with the Jews, 121, 126
Committee for a Jewish Army of Stateless and Palestinian Jews, 74
Committee on Ecumenical and Interreligious Affairs (Bishops'), 102, 110-11, 143, 171, 184
Concentration camp, 1, 155; sexual violence in, 44, 45, 47, 48; Ravensbruck, 156; Riga, 60
Congar, Yves, 154
Connelly, John, 16-17, 122, 142
Contra Faustum, 109
Convention on the Prevention and Punishment of the Crime of Genocide, 120
Conversion, Jewish, 83-86, 103, 126, 148, 172, 175
Council of Trent, 107
Covenant, Christian (New), 2, 104, 127, 147, 161; Jewish (Old), 2, 4, 17, 81, 104, 126-27, 145-47, 161, 175, 185
Creational responsibility, 148-50
Cushing, Richard (Cardinal), 124
Cyril of Jerusalem, 104

Dabru Emet (A Sacred Obligation), 111, 174-75
De Profundis, 65, 73
Death camps, 1, 141, 163, 172
Dedication to King George (The Haggadah), 69
Dehumanization, 45, 47, 69, 198

229

INDEX

Deicide charge, 2, 3, 4, 18-19, 80, 84, 104, 109, 124-25, 144, 161, 162, 170-72, 181
Dei Verbum (Constitution on Revelation), 194
Democracy, 68, 71, 72, 195; art and, 68, 77
Desbois, Patrick (Father), 29-40
Destruction of the Jews of Latvia (The), 60
Deuteronomy (Book of), 77
Dialogue, Catholic-Orthodox, 110-11; Catholic-Protestant, 103, 111; Christian-Jewish, 5, 9, 10, 13, 14, 16-17, 21-22, 102, 107, 110, 111, 112, 122, 124, 125, 126, 127, 131, 134, 144, 156, 160, 169, 173, 174, 176, 184-86, 206-07; Christian-Muslim, 206; evangelization and, 13, 126; German-Jewish, 205-14; intergenerational, 207; interreligious, 9, 10, 110, 122, 126, 170, 206, 210; Israeli-Palestinian, 170, 205-14
Dialogue in Truth and Charity, 126
Dignitatis Humanae (Declaration on Religious Liberty), 12, 14, 171
Displaced persons (DP) camp, 52, 53, 55, 58, 60, 61, 76
Divino Afflante Spiritu, 109
Donne, John, 176
Duderstadt Gymnasium, 88
Dungs, Karl, 90

Early Church and Judaism (The), 91
Easter Season, 110
Eastern Orthodox Church, 2, 4, 15, 105, 110, 145; anti-Judaism in, 102, 105, 110-11, 163; Rites of, 105, 110
Ecclesiology, 18, 102-04, 111, 144-45, 196

Ecumenism, 3, 14, 21, 102, 103, 110-11, 143, 154, 171, 183, 184
Eichmann, Adolf, 194
Einsatzgruppen, 31, 37
Eisenach Institute, 88, 90
El Salvador, 193-94
Elijah (prophet), 146
Emden, Jacob (Rabbi), 176
Emergency Committee to Save the Jewish People of Europe, 75
Emigration, 69, 76
England, see Britain
Esquire, 72
Ethics, 119-34
Ethnic cleansing, 131-32
Eucharist, 84, 107, 164
Eugenics, 46-47
Europe, Christian, 1, 4, 81, 148, 158, 160, 163, 170, 194-96; German occupation of, 1, 46-47, 121, 158, 163; Judaism in, 1-2, 4, 61-62, 68-69, 71, 74-76, 109, 121, 125, 131-32, 143, 148, 159, 163, 170, 200, 208; mass graves in, 29-36; World War II in, 46-47, 52, 70, 121, 155
Eusebius, 18
Evangelii Gaudium, 108, 146
Exceptionalism, Jewish, 131-32
Exegesis, 90, 108-09
Extraordinary Form, see Roman Rite

Fatal Embrace, 131
Father, Do Not Forgive Them, For They Know What They Do, 70
FDR's "Soldier in Art," 72
Final Solution, 44, 45, 90
First Thessalonians, 147
First World War, see World War I
Fisher, Eugene, 144

Flannery, Edward (Father), 4, 142, 144
Foxman, Abraham, 125, 172
Francis (Pope), 10, 108, 110, 111, 124, 125, 126, 128, 133, 134, 146-47, 150
Francis of Assisi (St.), 164
Freiburg, 156; University of, 91, 155
Friedländer, Saul, 83
Friends of Israel, 81, 85
From Enemy to Brother, 16
Fulfilled in Your Hearing, 108
Fulfillment theology, 106, 127

Garber, Zev, 147
Gaudium et Spes (Constitution on the Church in the Modern World), 14, 194
Gaza, 129-30, 132, 205
General Roman Calendar, see Roman Calendar
Genesis (Book of), 73
Genocide, 2, 36, 38, 47, 119, 120, 130-31, 198, 221; Christian contributions to, 123, 159; definition of, 38, 120; education about, 162; Nazi, 122, 185; responses to, 74; sexual violence and, 39, 43-48; women and, 43-48
Gentiles, 127; Jewish mission to, 145-46, 186
George VI (King), 69
German Catholic Caritas, 155-56
German Catholic Peace Movement, 155
German military, 39, 51, 59, 90
Germany, *Bundesarchiv* in, 32; Christian life in, 80, 83, 88, 155-56, 194; Jewish life in, 1, 38, 54-55, 70, 80-82, 87, 91, 155-58, 162-63; Ministry of Propaganda in, 59, 90; Nazi, 1, 32, 34, 36, 46-47, 68, 90, 122, 125, 149, 154-56, 162, 172, 210-12; Poles in, 89; post-war, 51-62, 76
Gestapo, 39, 156
Ghetto, Jewish, 31, 73-74, 82, 89; Lodz, 73; Polish, 89; sexual violence in, 33, 44-45; Warsaw, 73-74
Gifts and the Calling of God Are Irrevocable (The), 5, 121-22, 126-28, 182
Glasnost (open government), 163
Glory of the Lord (The), 103
God, 123; Christian views of, 1-2, 3, 5, 12, 15, 31, 38, 45, 81, 84, 86, 104, 106, 108, 122, 123-25, 126, 127-28, 131, 144-47, 148, 149, 150, 161, 162-63, 165, 170-71, 175, 181, 182, 184-86, 194, 195, 198-99, 200, 202, 206; covenant with, 2, 4, 17, 81, 127, 131, 134, 146-47, 161, 175, 185; Jewish views of, 2, 3, 45, 76, 81, 83, 122, 125, 174, 185; revelations of, 12, 106, 170;
Goebbels, Josef, 90
Goldenberg, Myrna, 45-46
Golden Rule, 157, 164
Goldhagen, Daniel, 163
Good Friday, 81, 103, 107
Good Samaritan, 86, 197
Gospel (of Jesus), 12, 86, 105, 108, 120, 181
Gospels (New Testament), 86, 90, 110, 159, 161, 182-86
Gottardi, Alessandro Maria (Archbishop), 101
Grace, doctrine of, 12, 84, 89, 103, 200
Gravissimum Educationis, 171
Great Britain, see Britain

INDEX

Great Commission, 86, 168
Great War, see World War I
Greenberg, Irving (Rabbi), 77, 147, 148-49, 202
Gröber, Conrad (Archbishop), 156
Guidelines and Suggestions for Implementing the Conciliar Declaration Nostra Aetate (no. 4), 5, 121, 182-83
Gypsies, see Roma and Sinti

Hadassah, 76
Hagee, John, 129
Haggadah, 68-70, 77
Halakhic Man, 172
Hamas-Israel War, 129, 130, 132, 205
Hasidism, see Judaism (Hasidic)
Hasidism Incarnate, 147-48
Hebrew culture, see Jewish culture
Hecht, Ben, 74, 77
Herrenrasse (master race), 46-47
Heschel, Abraham Joshua, 175-76
Himmler, Heinrich, 39, 44, 46, 53
Hiroshima, 196
Hitler as Pharaoh, 68
Hitler, Adolf, 36, 44, 48, 59, 62, 68-69, 71, 72, 73, 85, 87, 88, 91, 122, 143, 149, 155, 199
Holocaust by Bullets (The), 29, 32
Holocaust, accountability for, 72-73, 121, 124, 131; art of the, 67-76; bystanders of, 20, 35-38, 75-76, 109, 163; Christian Church and, 2-5, 13, 14, 17, 20-21, 80-91, 109, 111, 120-24, 128-29, 131-34, 156, 158, 162, 163, 171, 174, 194, 197, 202; denial of, 161, 174; education about, 4-5, 9-22, 36, 38-39, 123, 148, 162-63, 197, 221-23; remembrance of, 36-38; rescuers of, 38, 44, 133, 141, 154-65; resistance during, 128, 154-65, 161; sexual assault during, 43-48; significance of, 2-3, 20, 120-21, 123-24, 129, 133, 141, 148-50, 154, 194, 202, 207, 211; survivors of, 20-21, 31, 32-33, 35, 40, 45, 51-62, 76, 111, 125, 133-34, 155, 156, 163, 170-72, 205; victims of, 159, 194, 197, 202, 208; witnesses of, 30-36, 38-40
Holocaust fatigue, 124
Holy Land, 56, 131, 168
Holy See, 81, 85-86; Commission on Relations with the Jews, 164
Holy Week, 104, 110, 161, 183
Hosea (Book of), 9
How Catholics Look at Jews, 157

Immaculate Conception, 89
Immigration, Jewish, 56, 60, 69
Imperative of Moral Responsibility (The), 149
Infanticide, 34, 47
Ink and Blood, 77
Institute for Christian & Jewish Studies, 131
Institute for Jewish Policy Planning & Research, 173
Institute for the Study and Eradication of Jewish Influence on German Church Life, see Eisenach Institute
International Council of Christians and Jews, 158, 170
International Jewish Committee for Interreligious Consultations, 164
Iraq, 36-37, 143
Isaac, Jules, 3, 17, 124, 141, 159
Islam, 36, 38, 132, 143, 170, 176, 206

INDEX

Islamic State of Iraq and the Levant (ISIL/ISIS), 36-37, 133, 143
Islamophobia, 143
Israel, biblical, 68-69, 81, 83, 84, 104, 126-27, 131, 144, 159, 170, 185-86; Christians in, 143-44; immigration to, 60 (see also alijah bet); modern, 205-14; Muslims in, 143-44; statehood of, 69, 76, 111, 129-34, 146, 165, 168-69, 174, 196; support for, 81, 111, 120-21, 124, 126, 163-65, 174-75
Israel Bonds, 76
Israel/Palestine Mission Network (IPMN), 131
Israeli Defense Forces, 205
Israeli-Palestinian relations, 111, 120-21, 129-33, 214
Israeli Red Cross, see Magen David Adom

Japan, 71, 196
Jerusalem, biblical, 69, 103; modern, 130, 164, 194
Jewish arts and culture, 55-56, 67-78, 73, 77
Jewish Christians, 84, 89
Jewish history, 55-56, 77
Jewish-Christian relations, see Christian-Jewish relations
Jesuits, 81, 194, 195
Jesus, 39, 73, 171; ancestry of, 88-89; birth of, 104; death of, 1, 2, 3, 4, 18-19, 80-81, 84, 104, 109, 124, 125, 145, 162-63, 170-71, 175, 182-83, 185; Jewish view of, 2, 80-81, 106, 125, 127, 142, 145, 159, 163, 169, 171, 185, 186; messiahship of, 2, 80, 84, 103, 125-27, 142, 163, 175; religion of, 14-15, 17, 21-22, 73, 83, 88-90, 102-05, 108, 110, 123, 144-46, 158-59, 170, 175, 183, 186
Jesus and Israel, 159
Jesus of Nazareth, 125
Jewish Brigade, 56
Jewish-British relations, 56
Jewish-Roman War, 145
Jewish People and Their Sacred Scriptures in the Christian Bible (The), 106
Jewish Question, 86-87, 90, 180
Jewish Scriptures, 105-06
Jews, American, 74, 131, 173; Austrian, 70, 76, 158, 163; baptism of, 89, 141; chosen status of, 81, 83, 122, 125, 131, 144, 161; conversion of, 2, 16, 83-86, 89, 103, 121-22, 126, 142, 148, 163, 165, 172, 175; depictions of, 108, 183, 184, 186; deportation of, 1, 4, 8, 44, 82, 155-57, 163, 180; destruction of, 2, 45, 47, 60, 83, 125, 141, 150; discrimination against, 1, 81, 82, 158, 163; exclusion of, 87, 89, 127, 145; extermination of, 34, 76, 77, 82, 87, 121, 163; French, 3, 36, 40, 124, 134, 141, 157, 158, 159, 162, 172, 180; ghettoization of, 33, 44-45, 73-74, 82, 89; God's covenant with, 2, 4, 17, 81, 104, 122, 126-27, 145-47, 161, 175, 185; God's rejection of, 2-4, 104, 124, 145, 157, 161-63, 171, 181; Latvian, 53-54, 58, 60; mass executions of, 29-37, 73, 77, 121, 212-14; Orthodox, 83-84, 172-73; persecution of, 1, 3, 4, 18, 45, 76, 80-91, 109, 120-21, 124-25, 155, 158, 162-63; Polish, 20, 52, 58, 60, 67-77, 89, 158; secular, 81-84,

233

INDEX

149, 172; Soviet, 29-36, 38, 163; Spanish, 173
John (Gospel of), 161, 185
John Paul II (Pope), 20, 38, 108-12, 121, 124, 133, 146-47
John XXIII (Pope), 3, 124, 141, 153, 154, 159-60, 171-72, 180-81
Judaism, Christian teachings about, 1-6, 9, 14-15-22, 80-82, 87-88, 90, 101-12, 120-34, 142-47, 154-55, 161-62, 171, 172, 175-76, 180, 181, 185-86, 206; Conservative, 172; First Temple, 17; Hasidic, 147-48; Orthodox, 83-84, 172; Rabbinic, 168; Reconstructionist, 172; Reform, 145, 172; Second Temple, 17, 19, 144, 148; Sephardic, 173
Judenrein, 144
Just One Step Backwards Please, 76

Kaddish, 21
Kairos Palestine, 131
Kaller, Maximilian (Monsignor), 83-84
Kasper, Walter (Cardinal), 103, 107, 144
Kibbutz, 56
Kleine, Richard (Father), 88-90
Kolodziej, Marian, 20
Krebs, Engelbert (Father), 91
Kristallnacht, 70

Latin America, 193, 195-96
Latvia, 53, 58, 60
Laudato Si, 150
Lebensborn (fount of life), 44, 46-48
LeFrak, Ethel, 221-23
Lent, 111, 161, 183
Levebvrist movement, 102
Lerman, Miles, 61-62

Liberation, 52; British Army and, 55-56; Soviet Army and, 57
Liberation theology, 193-203
Lodz, 57, 85; ghetto in, 73, 85
Lonely Man of Faith (The), 172
Luckner, Gertrude, 16, 153-57
Luke (Gospel of), 86
Lullaby for Dying Children, 76
Lumen Gentium (Dogmatic Constitution on the Church), 12, 14, 103
Lustiger, Jean-Marie (Cardinal), 31
Luther, Martin, 18

Maccabean martyrs, 105
Madman's Dream (A), 71
Magen David Adom, 76
Maimonides, Moses, 176
Marans, Noam (Rabbi), 131
Marcion, 18
Mariology, 111
Mark (Gospel of), 183
Maronite Church, 110
Martyr, Justin, 109
Marxism, 195
Mary (mother of Jesus), 88, 89, 103, 104-05;
Mass, 84; additions to, 107; Lectionary for, 105-06
Matins, 104
Matthew (Gospel of), 161
Mauthausen, 1
Mein Kampf, 87
Melito of Sardis, 104
Messiah, Christian, 2, 18, 125, 127, 161, 163, 168, 175; Jewish, 142, 168
Metz, Johannes, 144, 147, 147, 194, 196-97, 199
Middle Ages, 175-76

INDEX

Middle East, 36-38, 123, 129-133, 170, 174
Miracle at Moreaux, 157
Missale Romanum, 103, 107
Moldova, 35
Moltmann, Jurgen, 144
Montini, Giovanni Baptista, see Paul VI (Pope)
Munich, 84, 85, 86; Jews in, 91

"Naqba," 208
National Catholic Center for Holocaust Education, 148, 221-23
National Socialism, see Nazi Party
National Socialist German Workers' Party, 86
National Socialist Priests' Group, 88
Nazi Party, 1, 2, 4, 17, 18, 32, 34, 36, 39, 44-48, 55, 68-76, 82, 84, 87, 88, 109, 121-23, 125, 141-43, 149-50, 154-59, 162-63, 172, 174, 185, 207, 211, 213
Neturei Karta, 174
New Covenant (Christian), 2, 127
New Order (The), 71
New Jersey Commission on Holocaust Education, 162
New Testament, 18, 19, 105-06, 109, 141, 145, 159, 168, 170, 183-85
New York Post, 72
New York Times, 74, 75, 158, 163
"No Man is an Island," 176
"No Religion is an Island," 176
Nostra Aetate (In Our Time), 1-3, 10-22, 13-16, 21, 101-12, 120-21, 124-25, 141, 170-72, 206-07; anniversary of, 5, 9, 107, 111, 120, 121, 123, 128, 134, 181-82, 184-86, 193, 194; education and, 4, 5, 11-22; effects of, 3, 9-10, 17-18, 20-21, 184; influences on, 1, 2-4, 141-42, 156-57, 160, 162, 170-71, 194; rejection of, 102
NSDAP, see National Socialist German Workers' Party

O'Malley, John, 15-16, 153
Oesterreicher, John, 16, 142
Office for Religious War Relief, 156
Old Covenant (Jewish), 2, 127
Old Testament, 91, 105-06, 141, 168, 174
On Heaven and Earth, 124
Optatam Totius, 171
Orationes sollemnes, 103
Ordinary Form, see Roman Rite
Origen, 103
Osservatore Romano, 85
Our Lay Apostolate, 83

Palestine, 33, 56, 58, 60-61, 69, 76, 86, 130-31; British Mandate in, 76; Christians in, 131; Christian response to, 132; emigration to, 56, 58, 76; ethnic cleansing in, 132; Israeli conflicts with, 111, 131, 208; Jesus in, 145; Jews in, 74-75
Palestinian Authority, 205
Papacy, 124, 128
Palestinian-Israeli conflict, see Israeli-Palestinian conflict
Parting of the Ways scholarship, 145-47
Passion (of Jesus), 19, 81, 158, 161, 162, 171, 174, 175, 181, 182, 185
Passover, 68, 69, 73, 101
Paul (Apostle), 145, 186
Paul VI (Pope), 101-02, 103-04, 107, 110, 120, 124, 153, 206
Pawlikowski, John, 82
Pearl Harbor, 71

INDEX

Perfectae Caritatis (Decree on Religious Life), 171
Pharisees, 183, 185, 186
Pilgrims, 76
Pius V (Pope), 102-03
Pius X (Pope), 102
Pius XI (Pope), 81
Pius XII (Pope), 109, 128-29, 153, 159
Pogrom, 82, 159
Poison Mushroom (The), 18
Poland, 2, 20-21, 30, 31, 34, 57-58, 68, 70-71; Arthur Szyk in, 67-70; Jewish life in, 20, 58, 89, 155, 158; Lodz, 57, 67-68, 85; Oświęcim, 14; Rawa Ruska, 29-30
Pontifical Biblical Commission, 106, 183
Pontifical Council for Interreligious Dialogue, 126
Pontius Pilate, 185
Preaching the Mystery of Faith, 108
Pregnancy, forced, 43, 47
Presbyterian Church, 111, 129-32, 169
Priestly Society of St. Pius X, 102
Principle of harmony, 105-06
Pro Conversione Iudaeorum (For the Conversion of the Jews), 103
Propaganda, 87; Allied, 68, 72; antisemitic, 83-84; German Ministry of, 59, 90
Prostitution, concentration camps and, 43, 47-48; post-war, 54, 57
Protestant Church, 2, 4, 10-11, 13, 15, 73, 80, 86, 110-11, 123, 146, 156, 159, 162-63, 172, 181
Protocols of the Elders of Zion, 81
Proverbs (Book of), 222

Quaker Church, 86, 155
Qumran sect, 146

Ratzinger, Joseph (Cardinal), see Benedict XVI (Pope)
Ravensbruck, 156
Rassenschande (race defilement), 44
Reconciliation, 205-14; Christian-Jewish, 13-14, 156, 181, 185
Red Light District, 54, 57
Redemptive antisemitism, 83
Reductionism, 106
Reeperbahn, 57
Refugees, Jewish, 61, 76, 149, 157; modern, 193-94, 198-99
Refugee camps, sexual violence in, 44
Refusniks, 163
Reich Union of Jews in Germany, 156
Rejectionism, 104
Religious education, 10-11, 84, 88, 161
Religious pluralism, 14, 124, 125, 128, 133
Repentance, 111, 132, 163
Reproductive abuse, 46-48
Repulsed Attack, 74
Rescuers, 22, 38, 44, 51-52, 133
Resistance, 30, 38, 109, 119, 128, 141, 155, 199
Restorative justice, 206-07
Riga, 60
Righteous among the nations, 157
Roma and Sinti, 2, 29, 34-35, 46, 59, 143
Roman Rite, 102-07, 111, 206; Extraordinary Form of, 102, 106-07; liturgy of, 3, 14, 101, 103-07, 153, 159, 171; Ordinary Form of, 102
Romans (Book of), 121, 146-47
Romania, 35
Romero, Oscar (Archbishop), 193
Roncalli, Angelo Cardinal, see Pope John XXIII

INDEX

Roosevelt, Eleanor, 72
Roosevelt, Franklin D., 68, 70-71
Roots of Anti-Judaism in the Catholic Church (The), 108
Rosa, Enrico (Father), 81
Rosen, David (Rabbi), 3, 122
Roth, John K., 3
Roth, Josef (Father), 86
Russia, mass graves in, 32-34; postwar, 53; World War II and, 2, 30-34, 70
Rwanda, 36, 38

Sabbath, 56
Sacks, Jonathan (Rabbi), 1
Sacred Obligation (A), 175
Sacrosanctum Concilium (Constitution on the Sacred Liturgy), 14, 105
Saldarini, Anthony, 145
Salvation, 11, 19; Christian view of, 12-13, 14, 81, 83-84, 111, 126-28, 175; Judaism and, 108, 111, 127
Samson in the Ghetto, 73
San Salvador, 194, 195
Save Human Lives, 75
Schreiber, Christian (Bishop), 85
Schulweis, Harold (Rabbi), 168
Scriptures, Jewish, 105-06, 110, 123, 147; Christian, 104-05, 108-09, 123, 153, 159, 174, 181, 184, 185
Second Testament, see New Testament
Second Vatican Council, see Vatican II
Second World War, see World War II
Secretariat for Ecumenical and Interreligious Affairs, 144, 171
Sermon on the Mount, 90
Shoah, see Holocaust
Signer, Michael, 174
Simon of Trent, 101-02
Singer, Robert, 31

Sister Rose's Passion, 164
Sixtus V (Pope), 101
Skorka, Abraham (Rabbi), 124
Sobibor, 1
Soloveitchik, Joseph (Rabbi), 112, 172-73
Sonnenschein, Carl (Father), 86
Southern Baptist Convention, 111
Soviet Extraordinary State Commission, 32
Soviet Union, see Russia
Spellman, Francis (Cardinal), 124
St. Peter's Basilica, 3, 111, 160
Stalingrad, battle of, 90
Star of David, 34, 73, 76
Sturzo, Luigi (Father), 155
Südhannoversche Volkszeitung, 88
Suffering, authority of, 193-202; Jewish, 45, 70, 73, 75, 162, 171
Summorum Pontificum, 106, 107
Supercessionism, 2, 12, 104, 125, 126-28, 131, 144
Survivors, 20, 21, 33, 35, 40, 46, 47, 50-62, 76, 111, 124, 125, 133, 134, 163, 172, 204, 208
Swastika, 69, 71, 73, 87
Swit, Loretta, 157
Syria, 36-37, 110, 143
Szyk, Arthur, 8, 65-77

Tanakh, 17, 174
Tanenbaum, Marc (Rabbi), 143
Teaching of contempt, 3, 4, 15, 16-20, 83-84, 106, 124, 142, 159, 161-62, 172, 175, 199
Teaching of respect, 15, 20-22
Teaching the Historical Jesus, 147
Tears of Rage, 8, 74
Ten Points of Seelisberg (The), 11, 13, 21-22, 142

INDEX

Theology, Christian, 4, 5, 11, 12, 14, 16, 18, 88-89, 101-04, 144-48, 153, 159, 193-203; exclusivist, 12-14, 16; Jewish, 91, 147-48; Muslim, 12
Theresienstadt, 156
Thering, Rose (Sister), 154, 160-64
Third Reich, 48, 71, 73, 85, 87, 90, 143
Thomas Jefferson's Oath, 67
To Be Shot as Dangerous Enemies of the Third Reich, 73, 140
Tolerance, 10, 36, 73, 161, 164, 176, 221
Torah, 172, 174, 185, 186
Tsaddik, 148
Tshuvah, 111-12
Transit camp, 61
Treblinka, 1
Trent, Archbishop of, 101; Simon of, 101-02
Twenty and Ten, 157

Ubermenschen, 52, 59
Ukraine, 29, 30-32, 34, 37, 40
Unitatis Redintegratio (Decree on Ecumenism), 14, 171
United Jewish Appeal, 76
United Nations, 44, 47, 120, 130
United States, arts and culture in, 67-77; Christian-Jewish relations in, 123, 129, 133-34, 141, 142, 160, 170; Holocaust education in, 123-24, 164; immigration to, 57-62; international affairs of, 37, 164; Jewish life in, 173, 175
United States Council of Catholic Bishops (USCCB), 108, 111, 144
United States Holocaust Memorial Council, 154
United States Holocaust Memorial Museum, 61, 77, 123

Universal Declaration of Human Rights, 120
Universe of moral obligation, 4, 159
Unsettling empathy, 209-10
Untermenschen (inferior race), 46, 71

Vatican, 1, 5, 15, 91, 108, 124, 128, 141, 142, 144, 153-54, 174, 182, 184, 194
Vatican II, 3, 5, 13-16, 102-07, 110, 120, 153, 157, 159, 160, 163, 164, 165, 170, 171, 175, 180, 181, 193, 194, 196
Victims, 21, 40, 73, 143, 150, 197, 198, 202, 210; black, 46; children, 32-34, 46-47; communist, 34; disabled, 2, 34, 143; homosexual, 2, 46, 143; Jewish, 2, 34, 208; non-Jewish, 2, 29, 34-35, 46, 154; Polish, 52, 144; prisoners of war, 2, 29-31; Roma and Sinti, 2, 29, 34-35, 46, 143; women, 45-48, 199
Völkisch, 84, 85, 86, 88
Völkischer Beobachter, 86
Von Faulhaber, Michael (Cardinal), 85-86, 91
Von Hildebrand, Dietrich, 16
Von Paulus, Friedrich (Field Marshal), 90

War and Genocide, 2
War and "Kultur" in Poland, 70
Washington and His Times, 68
Warsaw Ghetto Uprising, 73-74
Washington Post, 74
We Have Found the Enemy and the Enemy is Us, 173
We Remember, 5, 121, 174
Weimar Republic, 84, 85, 86, 207

West Bank, 129-30, 132, 205, 208-09
Westboro Baptist Church, 173
What Happened at Vatican II, 153
Wiesel, Elie, 134, 154, 222
World Jewish Congress, 31
World Union for Progressive Judaism, 130
World War I, 85, 86, 155
World War II, 1, 2, 4, 16, 29-36, 40, 44, 52, 62, 68, 70, 76, 120, 124, 128-29, 141, 154-59, 171

Yad Vashem, 111-12, 157
Yahad In-Unum, 29, 31-34, 37, 40
Yamamoto (Admiral), 71
Yom Hashoah, 123

Zachor, 76
Zionism, 56, 60, 129, 131-32